Recollecting Dante's *Divine Comedy* in the Novels of Mark Helprin

Recollecting Dante's *Divine Comedy* in the Novels of Mark Helprin

The Love That Moves the Sun and

the Other Stars

Barry Craig and Sara MacDonald

LEXINGTON BOOKS
Lanham • Boulder • New York • London

Published by Lexington Books
An imprint of The Rowman & Littlefield Publishing Group, Inc.
4501 Forbes Boulevard, Suite 200, Lanham, Maryland 20706
www.rowman.com

Unit A, Whitacre Mews, 26-34 Stannary Street, London SE11 4AB

British Library Cataloguing in Publication Information Available

Library of Congress Cataloging-in-Publication Data

Craig, Barry, 1960-
Recollecting Dante's Divine Comedy in the novels of Mark Helprin : the love that moves the sun and
the other stars / Barry Craig and Sara MacDonald.
p. cm.
Includes bibliographical references and index.
ISBN 978-0-7391-8196-6 (cloth : alk. paper) – ISBN 978-0-7391-8197-3 (ebook)
1. Helprin, Mark–Criticism and interpretation. 2. Dante Alighieri, 1265-1321–Influence. I. MacDonald, Sara (Sara Jane) II. Title.
PS3558.E4775Z57 2015
813'.54–dc23
2014033071

Printed in the United States of America

For Robert Crouse and Patrick Malcolmson

* * *

Tu m'hai con disiderio il cor disposto
Sì al venir con le parole tue,
Ch'i' son tornado nel primo proposto.
Inf. II, 136–38.

Contents

Preface

This book arose out of two personal literary interests, one of long standing, the other more recent. Our love of Dante's *Divine Comedy* goes back, for one of us, almost four decades, having encountered it as an undergraduate student listening to the masterful lectures of Fr. Robert Crouse at the University of King's College in Halifax, Nova Scotia. In his hands the *Comedy* was an encyclopedia of ideas, containing the summation of medieval philosophy, theology, political theory, and literature. These areas led to his deeper ruminations on ancient philosophy and culture, both pagan and Christian. When, twenty years later, the opportunity came to teach the *Comedy*, it was every year a privilege, always hearing Fr. Crouse's voice in the background.

Mark Helprin's work was something we came to, almost by accident, our eyes having been caught by *Freddy and Fredericka* on a bookstore shelf. We were stunned by the combination of broad comedy and profound reflection on the comparative virtues of the American and British regimes contained in a contemporary best seller. We eagerly sought out every other Helprin book we could find and our enjoyment deepened, transforming into a growing sense that this body of work could be fertile ground for scholarship. We were then somewhat surprised to discover that relatively little scholarly attention had been paid to what we believed was a major and unique modern voice.

It so happened, again, as if by chance, that one of our close friends, a former teacher and now a colleague, Dr. Patrick Malcolmson, hearing us talk about Helprin, mentioned that one of his friends was a friend of Helprin's. His friend, Keith Morgan, responded to Sara's inquiries and then generously connected us directly with Mark Helprin. The spirit of generosity continued as Mr. Helprin became a correspondent with Sara, sharing ideas, funny observations, and encouragement with us.

From our first reading of *Freddy and Fredericka* to the discovery of *A Soldier of the Great War*, *Winter's Tale* and most recently, *In Sunlight and in Shadow* (along with Helprin's other novels, short stories, and commentary pieces) we were immediately struck by the frequent references to, and even deeper intellectual connection with, Dante. Our correspondence with Mr. Helprin, and our reading of many interviews he had given over the years, verified that this influence was conscious and the references deliberate. Needless to say, finding a contemporary popular writer, an author of serious literary fiction, who deliberately represented the thought of the *Divine Comedy*, taking seriously the ideas of not only Dante, but Dante's own literary, religious, and philosophical sources, was indeed to have discovered a *rara avis*. That these novels were immensely enjoyable and able to be accessed by a contemporary audience only deepened our admiration and interest. When you read a book that is filled with Plato, Augustine, Dante, the Bible, and countless other classical references and allusions that is also of sufficient accessibility to be made into a Hollywood movie starring Russell Crowe, you know that you have discovered something quite remarkable. Put another way, Helprin has found a way to speak about ancient truths that both resonates to a contemporary audience and also connects those truths to modernity.

This unity, one might say, between ancient thought and contemporary reality, is ultimately what we find so attractive in Helprin's work. Particularly in *Freddy and Fredericka*, there is a robust defense of modern virtues. The vindication of the genius of the American regime that is revealed in the last third of the novel is genuine and profound. We believe it goes a step beyond Tocqueville and is more reflective of the recognition of modernity's virtues found in Hegel. On the other hand, *Winter's Tale* is a moving expression of a metaphysical perspective that predates modernity by many centuries. If Helprin were simply aping the *Divine Comedy*, writing romantic fantasies, either for mere amusement or antiquarian quirkiness, we would not have spent much time on his work. If his celebrated conservativism was merely a cranky reactionary rejection of the modern spirit and contemporary society, again, we would have been quickly bored.

Instead, what Mark Helprin has done is to mount a stout defense of the ancient virtues, both intellectual and moral. The love of beauty and the quest for truth are combined with portrayals of courage and self-sacrifice. These are presented not with wooden didacticism, but in the moving struggles and, particularly, genuine loves, of his characters. However, what elevates his novels in our eyes is the seriousness with which he takes the virtues of modernity, particularly freedom. In his books, justice and beauty are not alternatives to freedom and even equality. Rather, freedom is a necessary precondition to a just life and a just society. In this way, the account of modern society, and its core principle of subjective freedom, as described in

Hegel's *Philosophy of Right*, is linked through the poetry of Helprin's novels to those objective principles that formed the core of ancient good.

We have written in more detail about the philosophic character of the position described above in a recent book that explored the relation of Leo Strauss to the thought of Hegel. In reflecting on Helprin's writings we have been afforded the opportunity to explore these ideas as they have been expressed in literary form. That we are able to reflect on the *Divine Comedy*, as a lens through which to understand Helprin better, provides even greater satisfaction. We believe that Dante's work provides both illumination of Helprin's central ideas, but also, by contrast, demonstrates those ideas that make Helprin's work so distinctively modern and, we think, valuable to a contemporary audience.

More than anything, what Helprin's novels and the *Comedy* share in common is the idea of mediation. For both Dante and Helprin, there is clearly an objective good. There is also free human choice and the possibility of human knowing and willing the objective good. However, for Dante and Helprin, while each would (and do) acknowledge the possibility of immediate and mystical apprehension of the divine, the ordinary path is one of ascending intermediaries. Friendship, art, and nature are used by both authors as mediating agents between human beings and the absolute. But, for both authors, the pre-eminent means by which human beings come to know the divine is through love, specifically romantic love. For Dante, this movement is expressed through a re-working of the medieval courtly love tradition, where love is purged from baser metals, including lust. Helprin takes a different position, while acknowledging the virtues contained within that older tradition. His mediating love is able to accommodate erotic and physical love and the relationships within families. Rather than being rivals to the one true love that ought to animate us, they are forms of love that are integral to full humanity.

Anyone who writes anything on Dante must always know that, however much one writes, the outcome can only be a pale slice of the light from that great master. In Canto IV of *Inferno*, Dante finds himself in Limbo, surrounded by the shades of the great ones of antiquity. Moving over to the circle of the poets, Dante the author, eschewing false modesty, has Dante the pilgrim welcomed as a peer by the select group that includes Homer and Virgil. In the seven centuries that have passed since the writing of that scene, no one can seriously challenge the appropriateness of his inclusion.

One of the great benefits that we have received from this study is that Helprin's novels have opened to us new avenues of interpretation of Dante's work. The corollary to this is that, in reflecting on the *Divine Comedy* once again, we have gained an even deeper appreciation for Helprin's work. Teaching in a Great Books program, we have assigned the *Divine Comedy* to our students for the past fifteen years. Recently, we have added *Freddy and*

Fredericka and *Winter's Tale* to the reading list and have been pleased to see them be enthusiastically embraced by our undergraduate students.

This has been a thoroughly enjoyable project, notwithstanding the countless moments of confusion and doubt that accompany the writing of any book. The kindness of Keith Morgan and especially Mark Helprin must be acknowledged. We also wish to thank Lindsey Porambo at Lexington Books for her encouragement, assistance, and, above all, efficiency. Several of our students assisted at various points, including Hillary Ball and Kate Cameron. Our girls, Catherine and Mary, also pitched in, helping with proofreading, and acting as sounding boards for our ideas. In the *Apology*, Socrates says that there is no greater life than to be able to go about the city discussing ideas every day. Surely a close second is the privilege to read great works and then be able to write about them.

Introduction

Casual readers of Dante, and certainly most students first encountering his greatest work, often wonder why it is called a comedy. There is a simple answer, of course, that refers to a particular literary genre; in this sense a comedy is a work of literature in which one or more of the main characters avert destruction or experience restoration of their fortunes, thus distinguishing it from tragedy. There is a more profound answer that goes to the heart of Dante's enterprise. That is, the *Divine Comedy* is a drama of redemption, in which the protagonist, finding himself lost, must experience the torments of the damned, remake his soul, and ultimately achieve a beatific vision, in which there is a reconciliation of seemingly incongruous elements. By means of love, the particular, while yet individualized and even finite, is shown to be sufficient to be united to the universal and infinite.[1] The pilgrim Dante recognizes that his proper end lies in his unity with the divine and he hopes that, despite his deficiencies, this end will be possible for him. In the *Epistle to Cangrande*, Dante clarifies, "And hence it is evident that the title of the present work is '*the Comedy*.' For if we have respect to its content, at the beginning it is horrible and fetid, for it is hell; and in the end it is prosperous, desirable, and gracious, for it is Paradise."[2] We are given to understand that a corresponding comedy is the potential good end of all human beings.

In three of the most significant novels of the American writer Mark Helprin, the protagonist dies at or before the end of the story. Yet, from Helprin's standpoint, his novels are comedies, in precisely the way that this is said of the *Divine Comedy*. When asked about the nature of comedy, Helprin points to the definition of comic romance as established by one of his professors at Princeton, Henry Knight Miller.[3] On the nature of comedy, Miller writes, "Festival . . . is never entirely absent even in the grimmest circumstance; for the mature and benign presence of the Narrator, like that of a providential deity, continuously assures us that we do indeed inhabit a world of festive hope."[4] In this present study, we will explore the relationship between the novels of Mark Helprin and Dante's *Divine Comedy*, with particular attention to what we regard as the main focus of Helprin's novels and the hope suggested by their "narrators"—a comic and eternal redemption of the natural order that corresponds to human freedom.

In Helprin's argument, human redemption is not easily separated from freedom. In this, he is of one mind with Dante. The entire movement of the one hundred cantos of the *Divine Comedy* has been a preparation for the final vision of "the Love which moves the sun and the other stars."[5] Fundamental to the recognition that the moving force of the entire universe is *amor*, is the reordering of one's soul so that a pilgrim's love becomes aligned with the divine. This is only possible upon the assumption that our wills can, in fact, be free—neither enslaved to lower desires nor guided by misjudgment. Everything that occurs through the first two canticles of the *Comedy* is about freeing Dante's will and making him, by the top of Purgatory, once more, "Free . . . upright and sound."[6] This is, of course, in contrast to the opposite position at the bottom of Inferno, where the souls are frozen in the ice of Cocytus, their wills utterly forfeit and their *amor* extinguished eternally. At the peak of medieval culture and on the edge of that culture's dissolution, the *Divine Comedy* offers a radically strong assertion of human freedom as both the precondition for, and essential element of, eternal redemption. The revolutions that follow, whether the protestant theology of Calvin, or that of modern science beginning with Copernicus, Bacon, and Newton, and moving through the Enlightenment, will offer challenges to the extreme latitude that Dante grants to human autonomy.

Helprin, then, is a kind of throwback. He too insists on the possibility of human freedom. Yet, his is not the existentialist freedom that would describe human beings as radically unformed and without limit as moral actors, defining themselves as they wish, in a cosmos without meaning or external definition. In a sense, this is exactly the view that Helprin is challenging in his fiction (and his non-fiction, for that matter). Set against an existentialist account, Helprin's moral universe is home to eternal and knowable principles, such as beauty, truth, and justice. Helprin's characters are called to recognize these principles and then freely act in accordance with them. Uniting their particular wills with the eternal powers that govern the universe is what redeems them. The novels that we will discuss in this book illustrate both the personal and particular dramas of the struggle to unite subjective lives with absolute powers. However, as we will also see in *Freddy and Fredericka*, Helprin has a vision of a political expression of this argument such that might be embodied in particular regimes.

Mark Helprin has been occasionally described as, among other things, "a stern Victorian" and "a neoconservative polemicist."[7] His assertion of transcendent yet knowable truths certainly sets him apart from most contemporary American writers of serious literature. Combined with his own reluctance to participate in the normal categorization of fiction writers, the controversy surrounding his political views (or perceived political views) has perhaps contributed to obscuring the remarkable depth and breadth of his literary career. His novels, notoriously lengthy, cast a wide net over allusions, references, evocations, and direct representations of various literary, artistic, and religious antecedents from diverse historical and cultural traditions. Painting, sculpture, architecture, poetry, prose, and historiography—all provide fertile resources for his work.

Among all of the sources drawn upon by Helprin in his novels, none are more important than the works of Dante Alighieri. Trained formally at Harvard and then afforded the opportunity to study in Italy and read Dante in the original medieval Italian, Helprin peppers references from the *Divine Comedy* (and *La Vita Nuova*, among other works) throughout his writing and cites Dante as one of his greatest influences.[8] However, his relationship with the great Florentine poet goes beyond quotation, allusion, and even literary influence. We argue that the structure and argument of the *Divine Comedy* thoroughly informs Helprin's major novels. In particular, we believe that *Winter's Tale*, *A Soldier of the Great War*, *In Sunlight and in Shadow*, and *Freddy and Fredericka* are all built upon the intellectual foundation of the *Divine Comedy*.

Helprin's novels are so wide-ranging and ambitious that it is challenging to even offer a précis of any one of them, let alone work out a clear structure or argument. Helprin does not simply take the blueprint of the *Divine Comedy* and use it as the template for his novels. The relationship between Helprin and Dante is far more complex and nuanced. Instead, moments of *Inferno*, *Purgatorio*, and *Paradiso* are present in all of his novels. But, in the three major works that we will focus on, one can see a particular emphasis of each on Dante's three canticles.

One challenge in making the argument that we present here is the peculiarity of what we will choose to call (for ease of reference) Helprin's theology. He is often referred to as a contemporary Jewish writer.[9] In terms of objective categories, all three descriptors are undeniable facts, but as a guide to interpreting his writing, they are not particularly reliable. Helprin's Judaism undoubtedly influences his thinking and writing. *In Sunlight and in Shadow*, and, even more directly, *Refiner's Fire* consider what it means to be a Jew in the modern world. However, this question is hardly an *idée fixe*, around which every other element turns in his writing. In fact, as we show in this book, Helprin's fundamental ideas are far more universal than those of a particular religion or cultural tradition.

Significant elements of Jewish thought are present in Helprin's novels, but they are joined by principles of Christian theology, as well as ancient

Platonism and Neoplatonism, for example.[10] The latter categories are never explicit, and may even be unconscious, yet nevertheless shape the worldview of central characters and the general arguments of all four novels under consideration. Some of this eclecticism is deliberate and explicitly part of what Helprin wants to say. He is himself a gallimaufry of influences and ideas. From his own biography to his literary output, the range and diversity of connections and influences is astonishing. His mother, Eleanor Lynn Helprin, was a Broadway star, after arriving in America as a refugee. Along with others in her circle, she was, for a time, a communist. His father, Morris Helprin, was a journalist and, with Alexander Korda at London Films, a filmmaker responsible for one of the greatest films ever made, *The Third Man*. Prior to that, however, he had been a member of the OSS in the Second World War. That organization was the forerunner to the CIA.[11]

As a consequence of his parents' professional lives, Helprin encountered figures as diverse as Laurence Olivier and the leading gangsters of New York.[12] Helprin was educated at Harvard, Princeton, and Oxford. He then served in the British merchant marine, and the Israeli army and air force.[13] Taken together, this is a somewhat more colorful background preparation for a novelist than, say, earning a degree in creative writing. Since becoming a writer, his diversity of interests and depth of knowledge has allowed him to become a noted commentator on politics and international affairs for the *Wall Street Journal* and a fellow of the Claremont Institute. He has also been a speechwriter for, among others, Robert Dole during his campaign for the presidency in 1996. It is in connection to these latter avocations that he gained the "conservative" label.

All of this suggests that one ought not to be surprised to find significant challenges in simplifying Helprin's thought. We will argue that what is present is in fact an amalgam of Jewish, Christian, and Platonic thought, fully recognizing that the forms of Jewish and Christian theology presented in these novels are often regarded by some as unorthodox in their presentation and perhaps their substance.[14] For example, several of Helprin's novels touch on eschatology, in particular *Winter's Tale*. This eschatological vision includes elements of resurrection, which owe something to Christian, but also Jewish theology. There are references to the last judgment and eternal life. And there is a suggestion of universal salvation for everyone, or more exactly, all things. This latter element perhaps owes more to Neoplatonism in terms of Western theology, but also has antecedents in some Jewish and Christian thinkers.

God is not particularly prominent in explicit or direct form in Helprin's novels. Yet, divine agency and mediated forms of the divine are recurring themes. Here we see the closest and most profound relationship to Dante's work. The *Divine Comedy* is a tale of a pilgrim, making an ascent from hell, through purgatory, finally to heaven. This ascent is externally presented through a physical journey. Yet, this is understood to be representative of a *peregrinatio animae*. This is a type of journey that is represented by, for example, Augustine's *Confessions*, but also Homer's *Odyssey*, and, in national form, by the journey of the people of Israel in *Exodus*.

For Dante, as for Augustine before him, the sources for this lie in ancient Platonism, re-presented in a Christian form. What is at the heart of this Platonic ascent is the "use" of physical elements to achieve spiritual ends. Another way of saying this is that one cannot apprehend the universal except by means of the particular. This goes all the way back to Plato's *Republic*, if not to Homer, in the Western tradition. When asked to describe the Good, Socrates responds to Glaucon and Adeimantus that he cannot, but instead can speak only of children of the good. Then, he offers three poetic images: the Sun, the Line, and, finally, the famous Allegory of the Cave. Each of these images describes the ascent of human understanding from external physical things, through an inward movement of thought, to a final vision of the Good.[15]

Augustine takes up this tradition in his *Confessions*. Itself the story of a pilgrim, the author uses his own biography as a form of philosophical and theological exposition of the Platonic meditative ascent.[16] It is through his experiences in the material world, chiefly via his relationships with other people, that Augustine moves through various intellectual and religious positions prior to his conversion. Each anecdote—of an event at school, or with his friends, with mentors and teachers, with his mother, or with religious groups with which he becomes affiliated—mark very specific moments along this journey of the soul. Ultimately, these lead, through the essential addition of his reading of the *platonicorum libri*, to his Christian conversion.[17] It is important to understand that what Augustine achieves at the point of conversion is stability in the apprehension of the good that he has achieved by means of the Platonic ascent.

In Dante's *Divine Comedy*, this tradition is taken up, re-worked and transformed yet again.[18] Unlike the *Confessions*, which at least purports to be a historically true biography, the *Divine Comedy* is a pure literary creation. However, Dante draws, famously and strikingly, upon his own lived experiences and the existence of actual human beings (albeit, for the most part, celebrities) to ground his poem in reality. The central argument is that Dante, awakening in a dark wood, cannot restore his soul, or achieve reunion with Beatrice, or union with God without a journey. He cannot, in fact, even undertake this journey without assistance. And so, a series of guides, Virgil, Beatrice, and Bernard of Clairvaux, lead Dante from the woods to a vision of the Trinity at the top of Paradiso.

These guides are mediators, in ascending importance, of the divine. Each one is a preparation for the next and all are preparations for that beatific vision which cannot be enjoyed directly or immediately. This is consistent with the Platonic tradition, where, for example, the man chained at the bottom of the cave in Socrates' allegory cannot easily apprehend the sun. He must ascend through shadows, to physical things, to images of the Sun, before finally attaining the vision of the Sun itself. Our eyes, our minds, our souls must be conditioned before we can consider the Good. This is all in accordance with Plato's epistemological account, presented in the image of the Line and everywhere represented in the dialogues, that indicates that the particular, even as the particular is inconstant and transitory, is still the only means by which the universal can be known. Insofar as there is a criticism of poetry in the *Republic* (and elsewhere in the dialogues), Plato does not repudiate poetry absolutely, but instead, proposes a reform of poetry, so that poetry might serve its true end, the apprehension of the eternal forms. In the same vein, Helprin says of images and art, "Just as I don't believe that God is in the machine, but that He is in us, I don't believe that God is in design, but that He is in art."[19]

In the *Divine Comedy*, Dante is not worthy of reunion with Beatrice, much less of seeing God at the outset of the poem. In fact, it appears that only poetry, personified by Virgil, can move him from his intellectual and moral slumber. Having incited Dante to action, Virgil directs Dante's gaze inward, encouraging him to know himself, before he can look upward. The *Inferno* records the descent into Dante's soul, whereby he comes to understand the nature of the three animals, the lonza, the lion, and the wolf, that prevent him from making any spiritual progress. Even here, the journey is imaged through the external forms manifest in the lives of others. In this way Dante the pilgrim, and through him, we the readers, see the corruption that exists with his and our souls.

Virgil remains Dante's guide through Hell and even through most of the ascent of Mount Purgatory. All along we are conscious that Virgil's home is not heaven. He is only a guide for part of the journey. He cannot mediate what he does not know. While Virgil can lead Dante to a partial knowledge of vice and virtue, via the knowledge contained in the ancient world, as described in Aristotle's *Ethics*, he must eventually pass the baton to Beatrice. Through his encounter with Beatrice, Dante is able to connect his desire, his *eros*, with his spiritual end. Up to this point, his desires are still tinged with base metals. Put differently, Virgil is able to lead Dante because Dante's desires are yet attached to the world of images as represented by the beauty of Virgil's poetry. While these images participate in and reveal something of the nature of the absolute, they are only partial. Beatrice, in her perfected state, stands more fully for the divine itself. She is thereby able to direct Dante's desire to its proper and most satisfying end.

All of Purgatory is about the *ordo amoris*, the order(ing) of love, until our desire can finally be relied upon to point in the right direction.[20] Dante represents an essential progression from the position of Augustine. In the argument of the *Divine Comedy*, the end clearly does not require the renunciation of the particular. This is, at the very least, an open question in the *Confessions*. We would not argue, as some have, that Augustine remained a dualist at heart, even after his conversion. [21] It is clear that the rejection of such dualism is crucial to the intellectual movement that makes possible his conversion to Platonism and then Christianity. However, we argue that Augustine's embrace of celibacy and monasticism as the highest forms of Christian life signifies a position that does not fully integrate human desire with divine union. [22]

For Dante, Beatrice is the particular woman he knew in Florence. His love for her, purged of lust certainly, still remains a love for her in particular. Even when she leaves his side and is replaced by the mystic, Bernard of Clairvaux, Dante's vision of the Empyrean would not be complete until he sees, among the petals of the celestial rose, Beatrice. All of this alludes to the medieval tradition of courtly love, but it also represents an intellectual and theological transformation. Unlike Augustine, Dante renounces the girdle of chastity. [23] Hence, of Dante and Beatrice's relationship, Mazzeo writes that, in Dante, one sees "the universalization of the particular, the eternalization of the temporal." [24] And Foster similarly notes, "Because reality shines with God's presence, one only has to open one's eyes to love it; and particularly of the eye of the mind; which discerns, through the sensible beauty of bodies, the rational beauty of order, the divine design." [25] Dante does not reject the particular woman he loves as he makes his way towards his divine vision, but rather he makes this journey through the vehicle of their reciprocated love. The particular is not overcome by the universal, but is the means by which the universal is known and loved.

Within two centuries of the *Divine Comedy*'s appearance Martin Luther begins the great religious revolution that ultimately destroys the medieval world and ushers in Western modernity. One of the byproducts of the Reformation is the erosion of the enormous medieval monastic enterprise and a radically new understanding of the private sphere and its relation to the state. [26] The modern West establishes a new place for private life and a new recognition of the value of the particular and natural. This is reflected in the theology, the philosophy, and the art of the Renaissance and the early modern period that follows. As we have argued elsewhere, the modern Western position is a more complete demonstration of the Christian unification of the universal and the particular than that represented by antiquity and the Middle Ages. [27] Even though Christian theology proclaims such unification, the forms of medieval society were not fully adequate to this conception. Until all human beings have the opportunity to participate freely in this civil life, society will not fully realize the principle contained in that theology.

Despite the undeniably conservative elements in his writings, and despite the shallow caricature of this thought by some critics, Mark Helprin's novels

are only possible in modernity. While he takes up the thought of antiquity in
its essential forms, as represented by Judeo-Christian theology and anthropology, he brings those thoughts to their completion within and by means of
modernity. Essential to Helprin's modern argument is the emphasis he places
on human freedom, both philosophically and practically.

Some have dismissed Helprin's novels because of their romanticism, but
we contend that it is by means of romance that Helprin's emphasis on freedom is revealed.[28] Helprin himself describes his novels as romances, saying
specifically of *Freddy and Fredericka*, "It's a romance. The oldest form of
literature is romance. There are always these elements involved—characters
originating in paradise, being expelled from paradise, going on a quest, experiencing some rite of passage and then returning to paradise having learned
important lessons."[29] By means of their travels, the loves of Helprin's characters are ordered in such a way that they achieve the freedom Dante seeks in
the *Divine Comedy*. Miller writes, "the crucial emphasis in Christian (and
many pagan) views of the soul is always upon its free will, however cor-
rupted by sin, to make moral choices in circumstances that may not at all be
of its own choosing. This is the primal fictive situation of romance: the Test
of the Soul on its pilgrimage through the world of the actual."[30] Helprin
elsewhere suggests that this is the intent, conscious or unconscious, of all
journeys, saying, "People travel not to visit museums and churches . . . but to
free themselves."[31] All travel is a quest in which the individual seeks to
achieve a form of happiness that will remain stable even when she or he
returns home. Finally, on the point that his novels might be regarded as
merely romances, Helprin writes, "What could be more substantive, serious,
and elevated than the love between man and a woman? Dante expressed this
even in the deepest theological terms when he wrote, '*Beatrice in suso, ed Io
in lei guardava*.' Beatrice looks to God, whose light shines upon her face,
and Dante, in seeing and loving Beatrice sees and loves God. It has nothing
to do with candles around a bathtub."[32] It is only by means of love that one
will be free.

We further argue that Helprin's novels are romantic in a very particular
way. What is romantic in his novels is the way in which his protagonists, all
pilgrims of a sort, refuse to surrender their attachment to the particular, even
as they reach for the universal. The loves they have for family, friends, or
lovers are the means of coming to see the Absolute certainly. But, what is
particularly modern, as compared to the resolution in Plato, Augustine, and
even Dante is that they need not renounce the particular forms of their attach-
ments when they are presented with the Good or God. When Dante is reconciled with the *perfected* Beatrice, their relationship is bathed in the sharp,
brilliant, and even blinding light of Paradiso. Helprin's characters, alternatively, know the particular pleasures of a more natural love and seek to
maintain the goodness that they thereby experience while also attaining a

supernatural grace. The finite, particular world is redeemed in all of Helprin's novels.

Herein we see the full comedic nature of Helprin's work, for what is in many ways incompatible even with Dante's account of redemption is made possible in Helprin's vision. For example, while Dante imagines Inferno as the eternal end of those who have chosen not to will the good, an alternative resolution is offered in Helprin's work. Helprin takes Dante's suggestion that God's judgment might be moved by any inclination towards the good to its logical extreme. In the most otherworldly of all of Helprin's novels, *Winter's Tale*, each character is granted the opportunity for change and redemption. Hence, Jackson Mead, who appears as the image of Lucifer, is seen as progressively making his way back towards the divine, while the villainous Pearly Soames is not sentenced to Inferno, but rather returns to the city that he, albeit imperfectly, loves. There is the chance that even Soames might eventually find redemption with the Absolute. Inasmuch as comedy represents the reconciliation of seemingly opposed positions, Helprin's novels imagine the greatest of oppositions as overcome: the finite reconciled to the infinite, the particular with the universal, and even the fallen made one with the absolute. In this, Helprin takes Neoplatonic logic to its conclusion: if something *is*, then it is good in some measure, and thus might be redeemed. All being participates in the Good.

Helprin's emphasis on the redemption of the particular indicates its integrity and value. He argues that such redemption results in a spiritual and political freedom, as foreshadowed in Dante's *Divine Comedy*. The central cantos of the *Divine Comedy* contain Dante's meditations on freedom of will. All individuals are free to choose their paths and ends. In making his journey to Paradiso, Dante seeks an even fuller freedom, one wherein his soul is wholly unified, and he is neither constrained by a false understanding of the good nor a secondary or lesser desire.

This is a poetic expression of the Augustinian *ordo amoris*. Fundamentally, it involves the assertion of an even earlier Platonic idea, that the will must serve the intellect.[33] The state furthest removed from this is where we find the souls in Inferno. There, we are told, dwell those "who have foregone the good of the intellect."[34] Their wills, detached from the light of the intellect, ultimately shrivel and die, their freedom sacrificed to directionless brute will. This is represented first in those monstrous giants that stand guard over the ice of Cocytus, but also the image of the frozen souls themselves. In Paradiso, by contrast, the appetites are directed by a will informed by intellect. This is, for Dante, as it was for Plato, the portrait of an integrated human personality no longer at war against its own good.

In addition, we discover that, for Dante, there are a variety of paths by which souls can make their way to the divine, such that even a pagan poet might be the means to one's salvation. While Virgil and Beatrice are Dante's mediators, we are given to understand that the multitude of souls in Purgatory and in Paradise have been brought there through countless ways. The variety of their occupations alone—poets, politicians, soldiers, philosophers, and prostitutes, among others—suggests as much.

Helprin's argument corresponds to Dante's. However, Helprin's insistence on the integrity of the finite order, suggests even more diverse paths by which the absolute might be recognized and attained. Hence, his theology admits elements of Judaism, Christianity, and Neoplatonism, while never insisting on a synthesis that would subsume any one to the other. All are potential paths to the good. The natural order, pieces of art, individual people, and particular religions might all be sufficient means to direct one to the good. Helprin thereby suggests that whatever one loves, with the exception of non-being, can be a means to redemption. As a result, one might be freed to love as one wills.

It is perhaps for this reason that these themes in particular are expressed in Helprin's fiction rather than his essays. The nature of poetry is such that it necessitates interpretation, and good poetry is such that no gloss is ever complete or certain. Boyle suggests that it is because of the open nature of poetry that Dante is able to complete his masterpiece the *Divine Comedy*, while Aquinas could not complete the *Summa Theologica*. She writes, "Dante exposes the limits of philosophy, which must yield to poetry in evoking wonder . . . *Paradiso* transgresses the limits of scientific discourse through the exhaustion of analytic methods in the volitional delight of the beatific vision."[35] Dante consistently reminds the reader that his images, particularly of Paradiso, fail to do justice to the truth they seek to reveal.[36] The nature of poetry is such that it frees the reader to follow her love in a way that discursive philosophy does not. Helprin himself says as much when, referring to various interpretations one might have of his novels, declaring "'Look, my job is to make the doughnuts, and your job is to eat them. I can't really tell you anything about them: that's up to you.'"[37]

While we argue that Helprin presents a strong argument in support of human freedom in respect to ethical activity, as well as political freedom, certain qualifications apply. The freedom described and celebrated in his novels is not simple abstract subjectivity, the unfettered exercise of impulse or will. Instead, the repeated message is that we are free to the extent that we release ourselves from the captivity of selfishness and direct our wills to something absolute and external. There is here some resemblance to Tocqueville's account of the American spirit.[38] However, we argue that while there are elements of Tocqueville's account present in Helprin's novels, Helprin points to a more complete reconciliation of private and public than is contained in Tocqueville's enlightened self-interest. Particularly, in *Freddy and Fredericka*, Helprin envisions a political order that more comprehensively takes up both the subjective and objective elements of human nature. Helprin thus assents to the potential goodness present in individual subjectivity such that a diversity of particular desires is incorporated into his novels and imagined cities and it is understood that these desires need not negate or impede a fuller love of the good itself. Attending to these details reveals the inherent compassion or love that is at the heart of his understanding of justice.

CHAPTER OUTLINE

Following the structure of Dante's *Divine Comedy*, we examine three of Helprin's novels, namely, *A Soldier of the Great War*, *In Sunlight and in Shadow*, and *Winter's Tale*, in relationship to Dante's *Inferno*, *Purgatorio*, and *Paradiso* respectively. In the conclusion we take up Helprin's *Freddy and Fredericka* and show how Dante's heavenly account of justice can be reconciled with the secular, modern world. In each chapter we explore the ways in which Helprin's argument corresponds to Dante's as well as the significant ways in which it differs. By demonstrating the degree that Helprin has been influenced by Dante and then pointing to places where his argument departs or differs from the *Divine Comedy*, we describe how Helprin expands the account of autonomy and freedom that, while present in Dante's argument, is only fully expressed in the modern world and its institutions.

In the first chapter we take up the image of Dante's *Inferno* as it is represented in *A Soldier of the Great War*. As we shall see, of all the novels we have chosen, *A Soldier of the Great War* most closely tracks Dante's *Divine Comedy*, specifically the movement of *Inferno*. Both Dante in the *Inferno* and Alessandro in *A Soldier of the Great War* find themselves off course. Although both are lovers of beauty, in various moments in their lives they lose themselves in its images and forget what true beauty and love entails. Both are asked to confront the state of their souls and the lack of beauty therein so that they might, upon reflection, recognize the light of beauty and know the nature of love. In particular, a question throughout *Soldier* is not whether there is a god, but rather whether there can be any reconciliation between the divine and the particular whereby the particular is not lost. Alessandro fears losing his autonomy and that of those he loves within the infinite beauty of the divine.

In *Purgatory* Dante has affirmed his faith in God and is moved to a position wherein he can recognize real beauty and not merely its reflections. His love and understanding, however, have to be trained so that they are strong enough to enable him to see the highest of beauties, the perfectly just city. In Chapter Two, we explore Helprin's *In Sunlight and in Shadow*. Like Dante who moves from Inferno to Purgatory, so in *In Sunlight and in Shadow*, Harry has just returned from the Second World War and Catherine, only twenty-three, has endured a decade of an abusive relationship with a much older man. Having experienced human depravity, Harry and Catherine reject cynicism and choose love. Yet throughout the novel, each faces a trial that requires suffering, loss, and death. Each fights in love, for justice. However, while Dante regains Beatrice in Purgatory, in Helprin's novel, Harry dies in a gunfight that he initiates against mobsters who are driving him out of business, and Catherine must live the rest of her life without him. Whatever Harry and Catherine face, they face it separately. Their autonomy is thus highlighted, but one is left with further questions about the nature of love and divine justice. Of particular interest in this novel is the theological reconciliation between Harry's Judaism and Catherine's apparent Christianity. In the argument of the book, loving each other requires that they enter into the account of the good the other holds, while still retaining their particular identity. In this one sees an image of divine love such that it takes up and retains the particular perceptions of the good of all its beloveds.

In Chapter Three, we examine the connection between Dante's *Paradiso* and Helprin's *Winter's Tale*. *Winter's Tale* is Helprin's vision of a perfected justice, wherein time and space are confounded so that the injustices of the past are redeemed in the present and in the future. In *Paradiso* we are given Dante's vision of a heavenly city wherein all of the earlier questions are resolved and love and justice fulfilled. While Dante's image of *Paradiso* is entirely otherworldly, the perfected justice of *Winter's Tale* takes place in New York. Helprin's *Winter's Tale* shows the relationship of the divine to the created order such that the nature of the infinite is knowable and present in a complete way in human communities and by means of human love.

In Chapter Four, we connect the threads of the preceding chapters and address what Helprin's work on Dante reveals both about the *Divine Comedy* and its relevance in a predominantly secular and democratic Western world. Helprin's novel *Freddy and Fredericka* suggests how political communities might embrace the account of justice that is suggested throughout Dante's travels in the afterlife and in Helprin's metaphysical, if seemingly fantastical, *Winter's Tale*. Helprin and Dante agree that no purely human effort will be sufficient to ensure the perfection of any political community; nonetheless, in *Freddy and Fredericka*, Helprin implies that a liberal democratic regime is most conducive to the virtue and love that Dante's image of *Paradiso* presents.

NOTES

1. On the comedy of Dante's *Divine Comedy* see William Franke, "Dante's Deconstruction and Reconstruction of Prophetic Voice and Vision in the Malbowge (*Inferno* XVIII–XXII)," *Philosophy and Literature* 36 (2012): 112; Robert Pogue Harrison, "Comedy and Modernity: Dante's Hell," *MLN* 102 (December 1987): 1043–61; Robert Hollander, "Tragedy in Dante's Comedy," *Sewanee Review* 91 (Spring 1983): 240–60; Peter S. Hawkins, "All Smiles: Poetry and Theology in Dante," *PMLA* 121 (March 2006): 371–87.

2. A. G. Ferrers Howell and Philip Henry Wicksteed, trans., "Epistola X" in *The Latin Works of Dante* (London: Temple Classics, 1904), 346–52.

3. Mark Helprin, e-mail to authors, March 26, 2014.

4. Henry Knight Miller, *Henry Fielding's* Tom Jones *and the Romance Tradition* (Victoria: English Literary Studies, 1976), 30.

5. All quotations from the *Divine Comedy*, unless otherwise indicated, are from the nineteenth century translation by Henry Wadsworth Longfellow. This public domain text has been accessed from the Project Gutenberg website between January 1–June 30, 2014, http://www.gutenberg.org/cache/epub/1004/pg1004.html.

6. Dante, *Purgatory*, XXVII, 140. On Dante's account of freedom see, for example: Barbara Barclay Carter, "Dante's Political Ideas," *Review of Politics* 5 (July 1943), 339–55; Christopher J. Ryan, "Free Will in Theory and Practice: *Purgatorio* XVIII and Two Characters in the *Inferno*," in *Dante Soundings: Eight Literary and Historical Essays*, ed. David Nolan (Totowa, NJ: Rowman and Littlefield, 1981), 100–112; John A. Scott, *Dante's Political Purgatory* (Philadelphia: University of Pennsylvania Press, 1996).

7. Ranen Omer-Sherman, "Mark Helprin's Politics Doesn't Get in Way of Prose," *Jewish Daily*, October 23, 2012; and David Brock, *Blinded by the Right: The Conscience of an Ex-Conservative* (New York: Random House, 2003), 328. See also, Murray Friedman, *The Neoconservative Revolution: Jewish Intellectuals and the Shaping of Public Policy* (Cambridge: Cambridge University Press, 2005), 227.

8. Helprin studied Dante in Italian, while at Harvard with Dante Della Terza. Mark Helprin, e-mail to authors, August 1, 2012. See also, "Mark Helprin Interview by Grover Gardner," accessed April 2, 2014, http://www.downpour.com/authors/spotlight/mark-helprin-interview.

9. See, for example, Mark Helprin, "The author, like Israel, takes risks—and lives in opposition to nebbishy Jewish New Yorkers," interview with Alexander Aciman, last accessed April 6, 2014, http://www.tabletmag.com/jewish-arts-and-culture/books/113658/mark-helprin-tale; Ramen Omer-Sherman, "Mark Helprin's Politics Doesn't Get in Way of Prose," *Jewish Daily*, October 23, 2012; Joel Shatzky and Michael Taub, *Contemporary Jewish-American Novelists: A Bio-Critical Sourcebook* (Westport, CT: Greenwood Press, 1996).

10. Somewhat surprisingly, the *Entertainment Weekly* review of Helprin's *Soldier of the Great War* references its Neoplatonic heritage. See L.S. Klepp, "A Soldier of the Great War (1991)," last accessed March 24, 2014, http://www.ew.com/ew/article/0,,314436,00.html.

11. For these biographical references see an interview with NPR's Scott Simon, http://www.npr.org/2012/10/06/161842861/a-love-song-to-family-new-york-in-sunlight=2012, last accessed on July 26, 2014. See also, http://harvardmagazine.com/2005/05/literary-warrior.html, last accessed on July 26, 2014.

12. Interview with WNYC, http://www.voicebase.com/voice_file/public_detail/160089/refine/protagonist.

13. See the author's own website, http://markhelprin.com/about, last accessed July 26, 2014.

14. Helprin claims to not remember reading Plato; nonetheless, we contend that his arguments correspond to several dominant themes in the tradition of Platonic thought. Helprin, e-mail to author, June 29, 2014.

15. Plato, *Republic*, trans. G.M. Grube (Indianapolis: Hackett Publishing Inc., 1992), 507d–517b. For a clear account of the spiritual ascent in the images, see Wayne Hankey, "Conversion: Ontological & Secular from Plato to *Tom Jones*," a Guest Lecture sponsored by CREOR, McGill Centre for Research on Religion / Centre de research sur la religion in partnership with 'Early Modern Conversions' Tuesday, February18, 2014, to be published in *Numero Cinq*.

16. On Augustine's Platonism, we know of no clearer account than Robert Crouse, "*Paucis Mutatis Verbis*: St. Augustine's Platonism" in *Augustine and His Critics*, ed. Robert Dodaro and George Lawless (London: Routledge, 2000), 37–50. For an account of the meditative ascent, see Robert McMahon, *Understanding the Medieval Meditative Ascent* (Washington, D.C.: Catholic University of America Press, 2006).

17. Augustine, *Confessions*, trans. Henry Chadwick (Oxford: Oxford World Classics, 2009), VII, 21.

18. On Dante's Platonism and Augustinianism, for example, see: C. M. Bowra, "Dante and Sordello," *Comparative Literature* 5 (Winter 1953): 1–15; Robert D. Crouse, "Dante as Philosopher: Christian Aristotelianism," *Dionysius* XIV (1998): 154; Kenelm Foster, *The Two Dantes* (London: Darton, Longman and Todd Ltd., 1977), 42–43; William Franke, "Dante's Inferno as Poetic Revelation of Prophetic Truth," *Philosophy and Literature* 33 (October 2009): 252–66; Peter S. Hawkins, "Divide and Conquer: Augustine in the Divine Comedy," *PMLA* 106 (May 1991): 471–83; Douglas Hedley, "Neoplatonic Metaphysics and Imagination in Dante's *Commedia*," in *Dante's Commedia: Theology as Poetry*, Vittorio Montemaggi and Matthew Treherne, ed. (Notre Dame: University of Notre Dame Press, 2010), 245–266; Roger Theodore Lafferty, "The Philosophy of Dante," *Annual Reports of the Dante Society* 30 (1911): 1–34; Joseph Mazzeo, "Dante, The Power of Love. Dante and the Phaedrus Tradition of Poetic Inspiration," *Proceedings of the American Philosophical Society* 99 (June 1955):133–145; H.R. Patch, "The Last line of the Commedia," *Speculum* 41 (January 1939): 56–65.

19. Helprin, e-mail to authors, 21 December 2011.

20. See Dante, *Purgatory*, XVII 85–139, where Virgil explains to Dante this structure.

21. For a representative of this view see: L.C. Ferrari, "Young Augustine: Both Catholic and Manichee," *Augustinian Studies* 26 (1995): 108–128.

22. To read Augustine's argument for the superiority of the celibate life, see his treatise *de Virginitate*.

23. Dante, *Inferno*, XVI, 106–8.

24. Joseph Anthony Mazzeo, "Plato's Eros and Dante's Amore," *Traditio* 12 (1956): 316.

25. Kenelm Foster, O.P., "The Mind in Love: Dante's Philosophy," in *Dante*, John Freccero, ed. (Englewood Cliffs, NJ: Prentice-Hall, Inc., 1965), 56.

26. On the practical influence of Dante's writings on the transition to political freedom, see Dennis Looney, *Freedom Readers* (Notre Dame: University of Notre Dame Press, 2011).

27. See Sara MacDonald and Barry Craig, *Recovering Hegel from the Critique of Leo Strauss: The Virtues of Modernity* (Lanham, MD: Lexington Books, 2013).

28. See, for example, *the New York Times* review of *In Sunlight and in Shadow*: "Passionate, earnest, nostalgic and romantic in multiple senses of the word (infused with love, straining with valor, prolific in fable), it resurrects with throat-catching regret and nickel-gleam luster the automats and assumptions of the America of the 1940s, both the sets and the sensibilities." Likening the novel to the cinematic works of "Curtiz and Capra," the review concludes with the tart suggestion that "To see what Harry saw, you'd need the author's romance-colored glasses." Liesl Schillinger, "Halcyon Years," *New York Times*, October 5, 2012.

29. Jeff Guinn, "Author Q&A," www.philly.com/mld/inquirer/entertainment/books/12439767.htm. Helprin describes his other novels in similar terms, for instance see Alexander Aciman, "Helprin's Tale," *Tablet: A New Read on Jewish Life*, accessed April 2, 2014, http://www.tabletmag.com/jewish-arts-and-culture/books/113658/mark-helprin-tale.

30. Henry Knight Miller, 57.

31. Helprin, e-mail to authors, December 6, 2011.

32. Helprin, e-mail to authors, December 23, 2011.

33. See Plato, *Republic*, 449a.

34. Dante, *Inferno*, III, 18.

35. Marjorie O'Rourke Boyle, "Closure in Paradise: Dante Outsings Aquinas," *MLN*, 115:1 (January 2000), 5.

36. For example, Dante, *Paradiso*, I, 7–12; XXIII, 28–32; XXX, 19–21.

37. Helprin, e-mail to authors, December 6, 2011.

38. See Sara MacDonald, "Democratic Royalty: Mark Helprin's Freddy and Fredericka," in *American Political Thought* 2 (Fall 2012): 298–318.

Chapter One

Soldiering Through Inferno

In many ways, Mark Helprin's *A Soldier of the Great War* combines the movements of Dante's *Inferno* and *Purgatorio*.[1] The bulk of the story describes the life of Alessandro Giuliani, as he remembers his past and tells his story to his young companion Nicolò. As the novel begins, Alessandro is hurrying through the streets of Rome in the early morning of August 9, 1964. A man of education and some means, he is rushing to catch a streetcar that will be the first part of a longer journey out of the city. We learn in short order that Alessandro is a veteran of the Great War and a professor of aesthetics. In an act of kindness, Alessandro forsakes riding to his destination, some seventy kilometers away, in order to walk with a young man, Nicolò, who has been denied passage on the streetcar. Nicolò is the auditor to Alessandro, who through the course of their relatively short pilgrimage will recount his experiences during and after the Great War. Much of the novel consists of Alessandro's recollections told to Nicolò, periodically interrupted by conversation between the two, whereby the reader sees transformations in both Nicolò and Alessandro.

Alessandro's recollections chiefly revolve around stories of war and love. Not a violent man by nature, Alessandro was profoundly affected by his experiences in the mountain campaign of northern Italy and his subsequent tribulations in the south. Preceding the war and interspersed through it are various romantic encounters, the culmination of which is with Alessandro's own Beatrice, a woman named Ariane. A second level of the story concerns a strange character named Orfeo, who becomes Alessandro's nemesis and the cause of his greatest spiritual decay.

While Alessandro's life is filled with love and beauty, we learn that it is also marked by loss and vice. What is most remarkable in the story that Alessandro tells is the degree to which he willingly confronts his own fail-

1

ings and flaws. His tale is a confession of a lifetime spent descending into Inferno. In this chapter we examine the exploration of vice and the correction of the will that is offered in Alessandro's reflections on his life. In retelling his story to Nicolò, Alessandro is awakened; however, the story itself shows his fall. As he tells it, Alessandro self-consciously reflects on his descent through Inferno. By the end of the novel, it is suggested that he understands his error and seeks a different end. Unlike Dante, Alessandro explicitly tells the story of how he got lost in a dark wood. As one reviewer notes, "Alessandro's desertion and long punishment . . . are the book's center of gravity; they provide the dark ordeals from which the protagonist's vision of life as heroic chiaroscuro will emerge."[2]

Dante narrates the *Divine Comedy* as a recollection of a journey. More deeply, the poem itself depicts Dante as trying to find or remember himself. His recollection is thus two-fold. By highlighting the significance of memory, recollection is presented as an essential means of understanding one's life and purpose. This intellectual approach reaches back to Augustine's *Confessions* and to the long Platonic and Neoplatonic tradition that Augustine inherits and transforms.[3] The poet Dante, informed by this tradition and further educated in the philosophy and theology of Thomas Aquinas, presents *memoria* in a powerful narrative that weaves together his own distinctive medieval synthesis.

As *Inferno* begins, Dante, we are told, has lost his way. In recollecting what he has loved, both properly and improperly, he rediscovers himself and the right road or the path to his happiness. The journey Dante describes is a meditation and journey into his own soul, an *itinerarium mentis*.[4] In each of the various ditches that he visits in Hell Dante sees reflections of himself. The external and literal story of *Inferno* is an allegorical account of Dante's confrontation with his soul and the vice that pervades Inferno reflects the vice that is present in Dante.[5] Without recognizing his corruption, Dante cannot realize that he has to orient his desire toward the good in order to achieve the end that he seeks. In other words, by finally coming to know himself, Dante is given an opportunity to make a truly free choice—he can stay in the darkness and achieve the end depicted at the bottom of *Inferno*, or he can seek the light. This movement suggests something about the nature of the soul. Turning inward and remembering his true identity, Dante grows in his understanding of the divine.

The process of redemption does not end here. Readers of the *Divine Comedy* know that Dante's recollection of his otherworldly journey is generally progressive in nature. Throughout the description of his pilgrimage, we understand that the character Dante is still mortal and will return to his earthly life after his ascent into the heavens. He is not perfected like the other souls we meet in *Paradiso*. There is the likelihood that he will sin and the possibility that he will lose his way again. Nonetheless, as witnesses to his journey, we understand that, if not perfected, Dante has nonetheless been morally strengthened. Now, whatever may happen to him, including his exile from Florence, Dante is prepared to face it with faith, hope, and love. Thus, having completed the journey, Dante then turns to the task of remembering what took place and making his recollection of the events objectively and beautifully manifest in his poetry. The *Divine Comedy*, in both its content and form, further makes Dante's knowledge of himself complete. His journey only nears its completion when he is able to objectively "see" it and thereby measure himself against what he now knows is the true path, achieving an epistemological end by writing. At the same time, his writing serves an ethical end. By his poetry, Dante habituates himself to the good that he has seen and his activity seeks to make this good manifest for others. Knowing and loving the good, Dante becomes more loving himself, willing the good for us by the beauty of the images he crafts.

Dante's task is the same work he asks of his readers, hoping that we will also embark on a recollection of our natures and ends. The beauty of Dante's poetry depends on the particularity of his images. A person's response to these images is subjective; she or he is attracted or repulsed, depending on her or his tastes. By means of the images in the *Comedy*, the reader is directed inward and shown the nature of her or his desires. At the same time, the images reflect the objective truth that Dante understands, and readers of the poem are directed from Dante's particular images and their conscious reflection on themselves to these more universal truths. Reflecting on the *Comedy*, Dante and readers are given an image of themselves through which they might better understand or recollect themselves and the divine.

As noted, Helprin's *Soldier* is similarly a recollected tale. The majority of the story is the narration by a now elderly Alessandro of his life's journey. By the end of the novel, Alessandro has come to the point where all his sins have been remembered and confessed, while his virtues and loves have been recollected and reclaimed. The novel concludes with Alessandro's final prayer and his death. Like Dante, whose poetry strengthens his understanding and serves as an act of love, Alessandro's life story is told so that he might better understand both himself and God, while, at the same time, providing the means for his young companion, Nicolò, to think about his own life and ends.

Like Dante and the Augustinian-Platonic tradition that formed his thought and poetry, there is a dialectical movement from outward to inward, and from lower to higher things in the story of Alessandro's life. These movements are not simply linear, but repeated over and over as the spiritual ascent is brought to completion. Dante experiences this journey at the midpoint of his life and will have ample opportunity to descend and, hopefully, ascend again. Although Alessandro makes this final recollection on the eve of his death, in his story, moments of vice and betrayal are counterpoised against reflections on grace and love. Throughout his life, Alessandro rises, falls, and rises again. In each downward and then upward movement, Alessandro is shown as having gained a greater awareness of the depths into which he might fall, and the infinite nature of a divine love that seeks to draw him upwards nonetheless.

Freedom of will is at the heart of *Inferno*. The souls there have chosen Hell as their destination and even which ditches they will occupy. Importantly, Dante's accounting for vice or sin does not have the same moralistic tone that a modern reader might perceive in his text, believing that the individuals committed to the ditches of Hell are being punished by God. This is not Dante's argument. Instead, Dante suggests that the logic of an individual's placement in Inferno is based on what she or he desired in life. In the end, one is not punished, as if by external judgment, but rather the essence of what is desired is made clear and one receives what was wanted.[6] Any punishment we see in Inferno is not externally imposed, but rather is the logical fulfillment of the choices an individual has made in life. No one is in hell accidentally; for Dante, one can only get there by moving with ever deepening conscious deliberation against the known good.

Ironically, the deeper one goes in Inferno, the more this freedom is eroded. It is the place where souls "have foregone the good of intellect."[7] The final depiction of the souls frozen in the ice of Cocytus illustrates the end result of directing one's will against the known good. Metaphorically, having freely turned from the light that illuminates the path forward, individuals are trapped in darkness, unable to see which way to go. Philosophically, Dante indicates that the true object of human desire is reconciliation with the divine.[8] Recognizing and willing this end is the only way to achieve what one wants and be free. While individuals are also free to reject this end, in so doing they are not thereby freed from their ends, but rather experience the consequences of having turned against themselves. In rejecting the good, people attempt to reject their nature and, insofar as they are successful, they destroy themselves. Just as an alcoholic, in drinking destroys her or his liver, making further drinking impossible or destructive, so Dante imagines that one can similarly make choices that corrupt the very nature of the soul itself. The capacities for thought, will, and desire are progressively eroded in Inferno. As all of the individuals at the bottom of Inferno are frozen in a lake of ice, Dante suggests that when vice proceeds unchecked, our wills become further and further immobilized, such that we can no longer desire nor choose anything else. We become so habituated to error that we cannot change, addicted, as it were, to our destructive behavior. Following Dante's imagery, once we have reached this state of corruption, our eyelids are frozen shut, allegorically making self-knowledge impossible.

As we shall further explain in the next chapter, *Purgatorio* describes the opposite movement. In Purgatory, the will, in the form of love, is progressively corrected by the acquisition of habit, even as the mind is illuminated. Escaping Inferno and arriving at the base of the mountain depends on having recognized and chosen the good as the proper object of desire. With the good illuminating the path, in Purgatory a person's task is to order the rest of her or his loves such that they assist in the progression to the good that she or he seeks.

The similarities in form and substance between *Inferno* and *Soldier* are many, but just as interesting are the differences, suggesting that Helprin's meditation on *Inferno* is not a merely an imitation of Dante's work, but rather one that offers additional insights into the human condition and human ends. For instance, the nature of war and its effects on the soul are clearly of interest to Helprin, a veteran of the Israeli military. In this novel, as with *In Sunlight and in Shadow*, wrath, vengeance, and even murder are considered in the context of the continuous violence that characterizes armed conflict between states.

Helprin indicates that the Great War of the title is not World War I, but rather the struggle all individuals of a finite order face; it is, he says, a struggle in the face of mortality.[9] Political communities are organized, at least in part, to overcome the difficulties that nature presents to a human life. The state offers means to a more secure physical existence. In many ways, however, this protection is illusionary, as is most clearly the case when states go to war and the individuals that the *polis* was designed to protect are placed in jeopardy for political causes.[10] Even in times of peace, the state can only offer a more comfortable existence, not an eternal one. As horrific as actual war is, Helprin suggests that the finite nature of the material order is such that all individuals are always at war and require the same virtues as his soldier. Rather than focusing on the geopolitical aspects of the Great War, Helprin personalizes the struggle, as others, such as Remarque in *All Quiet on the Western Front*, have done in the past. Unlike Remarque however, Helprin sees redemption, and not just destruction, as one of the possible outcomes of battle.

Helprin's focus recalls the perpetual political struggles of Italy and particularly of Florence that Dante describes throughout the *Divine Comedy*. In *Soldier* the parallel between the crisis of a soul and the crisis of a state is even more crisply drawn, indicating a broad difference between *Inferno* and *Soldier*. While Helprin's novels are sometimes criticized as romantic or idealized, they are actually firmly set in modernity. There is no moral institution, such as the medieval church, to provide guidance or limits to society. Individuals are adrift in their own subjectivity, and must find the ground of ethical life themselves. Moreover, as other institutional forms of mediation fall away, individuals are more immediately confronted with their mortality and the moral crisis that such a confrontation may create. This is particularly the case with *Soldier*, insofar as a collapse into barbarism threatens not only individuals, but seemingly the world itself. Finally, the protagonist in Helprin's novel is struggling to find both justice and love, not in the afterlife, but in the concrete world of earthly human beings.

In the *Comedy*, the character Dante descends through Inferno, and ascends through Purgatorio to Paradiso; he will next return to his mortal life and seek to better understand what he saw, while living in accordance with his new knowledge. Alessandro is not given these final opportunities. Instead, all that he learns on this last walk through the mountains must be sufficiently clear to him and move his heart accordingly so that at his death he is reconciled to his proper end. While Dante is granted a vision of the purpose of human activity, ending in a final meditation on the nature of the divine, Alessandro's reflection is much more limited and particular. Whatever it is that he comes to understand by the end of his journey, it has been derived from the memory of his particular life and loves.

Just as we understand that Dante's vision is one that he draws from reflection on his nature, with Alessandro, Helprin makes this explicit. Helprin thereby indicates that an individual life has such integrity that, in reflecting on it, the nature of the divine and the basis for all human happiness can be sufficiently, if not fully, revealed. Moreover, while the events of Alessandro's life are epic in scope and unlikely to be regular occurrences, Alessandro's ability and virtue are not so heroic that his example stands as that of an Achilles beyond our grasp. Alessandro's life offers a remarkably complete and realistic account of a human being who struggles with temptation and corruption. In Helprin's other novels these moments are either not extensive or are so magical in nature that it is not as obvious how they might specifically relate to a particular reader. Alessandro is a complete portrait of a finite human being whose actions in life have taken him to the very bottom of Dante's *Inferno*. As with the poet Dante, Helprin maintains sympathy for his protagonist, even as we see revealed the deficiencies in his character. Several reviewers of the novel mistake the scope of Alessandro's activities through the course of the novel as making Alessandro a kind of *übermench* for whom one can have little sympathy, because he is too perfect. These reviewers clearly missed elements of the plot, including Alessandro's obsession with killing Orfeo, his desertion from the army, and his attraction to his sister. Alessandro is no superman. Indeed, that he has the many advantages he does, both natural and circumstantial, only makes his fall that much greater.[11] Dante tells us that the story of his character is the story of everyone.[12] But the journey Dante takes often seems so extraordinary that it is easy to lose sight of this point. By contrast, Alessandro says, "'God gives gifts to all creatures. . . . Contrary to most theologians, I have always believed that even worms and weasels have souls, and that even they are capable of salvation.'"[13] Helprin suggests that what is possible when we reflect on Alessandro's life is available to us in the smaller scope of our own lives.[14] In this, Helprin's argument seems much more democratic.

As a final point of introduction, Dante's position at the beginning of *Inferno* is superior to that of Alessandro's. *Inferno* opens with Dante waking up and knowing he is lost. Read allegorically, we are to understand that Dante awakens to a crisis of conscience. His choices have led him to a place of such darkness that he cannot escape. Alessandro, alternatively, does not seem to be undergoing a comparable crisis of soul as *Soldier* begins. Instead, he knows exactly the path or trolley that will take him to his granddaughter's house and he gets to the station in plenty of time to buy gifts for his arrival. Two interconnected things indicate that things are not as straightforward as they appear. First, as Alessandro rushes to catch his trolley, he is so caught up in arriving on time, that he does not look up, and he misses the angels of light that dance on the tiles of the rooftops along his pathway. Even further, we are told that, had he been aware of these angels, he still would not have looked. For, he had seen angels before, and "it was better to get to the end of the road."[15] Angels, it seems, are common enough, and in this moment Alessandro chooses instead to rush to the bus that will take him to see his particular loved ones. Second, Alessandro closes his eyes to the angels that surround him and he closes his mind to the memories of his life. These, he claims, are "both too painful and too beautiful to remember."[16] And while the proprietor of the café at the bus stop, also a veteran of the war, agrees that these things are difficult to speak of, nonetheless he admits that when these memories resurface, they move his heart.[17]

However terrible Dante's plight is at the beginning of *Inferno*, he at least knows he is lost. Alessandro, alternatively, makes his way to the bus stop with confidence; he knows the way and he understands where the road he is on will take him. Alessandro, however, proceeds without having fully reflected on how he has gotten here, refusing to remember the particular details of his own journey and the angels that have lighted his path. He later explains to Nicolò that he has avoided going back into the mountains for "fear of encountering . . . [his] lost self."[18] Alessandro is lost, but unlike Dante, he is initially reluctant to acknowledge his state. Given that Alessandro is on the very eve of his death, while Dante meets us mid-way through his life, there is a greater degree of urgency to Alessandro's situation. Helprin indicates that any life, when reflected on, can be a means to redemption; he also suggests that the path of redemption is ever open, even when one does not realize she or he is on it. Dante wakes up and only then does he begin to recollect himself. Alessandro's recollection begins when he is still unwilling, and, nonetheless, by the novel's close, we are hopeful regarding the state of his soul.

By all of these means, highlighting and granting significance to both the finite and particular, and suggesting a diversity of paths, *Soldier* emphasizes the extent to which human beings are free. There is no singular path to the good, nor is there any set time upon which one must begin one's ascent. When one examines *Inferno*, one sees the freedom of individuals progressively restricted. However, in seeing the state of Inferno and the counterpoint moments of grace revealed between Dante and Virgil, one also realizes there is an opportunity for an ultimate freedom commensurate with the absolute. Unlike the souls who reside in Inferno, Alessandro is never so lost that his freedom cannot be regained. Readers are encouraged to recollect their own lives, confront their corruption, and realize that, despite these failings, there is always hope that one might find the freedom that Dante and Alessandro seek.

DESCENDING TO ASCEND

In the *Divine Comedy* Dante descends into Inferno in order to ascend to Paradiso, and we know that at the end of *Paradiso* he will again descend to earth. For Dante, the path to redemption is neither straightforward nor unidirectional. Alessandro's path is ever more alternatingly ascendant and descendent throughout his life. There are moments of great beauty and great love, followed by opposing moments of suffering and loss. As for Dante and Augustine before him, this intellectual and spiritual movement is accomplished in the repeated act of recollection. One moves from exterior to interior, from inferior to superior. This is the medieval meditative ascent, rooted in the Platonic tradition. This cycle continues until one is finally reconciled to the divine.[19]

The finite order of physical and inferior beings is recognized as the means by which one learns to love and will the infinite. In the images of this pattern in Western literature, the finite world initially holds one's full attention, such that one is tempted to see its limited good as absolute. Only after suffering the consequences of this position, are individuals directed from it to the divine. Hence, one must first experience the plight of the "City of Women," in Book V of Plato's *Republic*, before moving to the Divided Line in Book VI; Augustine loses himself to earthly love before his conversion in Book X of the *Confessions*; and Dante suffers the depths of Inferno before the story gives way to Mount Purgatory. In each of these images, the limitations of the good as present in the finite world act as a preparation of the intellect, desire, and will for the good.

Adam and Eve's expulsion from the Garden of Eden, a story alluded to throughout *Soldier*, further helps to explain this movement. In the biblical account, Adam and Eve eat from the Tree of Knowledge and gain understanding of good and evil. They are consequently exiled from the Garden and prevented from eating from the Tree of Life. Metaphorically, Adam and Eve represent all human beings who develop from a state of childlike innocence and lack of knowledge to a greater understanding of themselves and their natures. Part of this development is a realization of our mortality or our inability to eat from a tree of life. At the same time, individuals are capable of imagining the possibility of an infinite and eternal good. Self-conscious individuals know that it is because of its mortality that all of nature is "fallen" or other than the infinite. So, both Dante and Helprin imagine an Inferno as the core of the natural world.[20] Unlike the rest of nature, humans, understanding themselves as finite, can, at the same time, imagine an infinite end and hope that it might somehow be theirs. Insofar as human beings accept a finite end as theirs, they reject the possibility that the power of the absolute is such that it might overcome even this. In succumbing to this temptation, humans descend more fully than any other natural being. Unlike plants or animals, our descent is deliberately chosen.

Dante indicates something about the innate and natural fallenness in human beings, by imagining unbaptized infants in limbo, a point that raises the ire of many contemporary readers. Dante's point, however, is not that babies are inherently evil, but rather that innately present in human life is a fallenness that separates it from the divine; the very fact that these babies died is the cause of this separation. That the seemingly arbitrary form of baptism might have saved these babies is understood more fully if one realizes that baptism merely indicates that God's grace is the means by which this finitude is overcome. While consistent with medieval Catholic doctrine, Dante's fuller position here is elsewhere belied by illustrations of divine grace overcoming contingencies such as historical circumstance. Thus, Trajan is present in *Paradiso*.[21] While this could be explained by an appeal to an early church myth that purported to provide for the pagan emperor's conversion, no such invention is possible to explain the presence in heaven of Rhipeus, a fictional figure from the *Aeneid*, who lived at the time of the Trojan War.[22]

This same distance from God is made manifest in the character Dante. When he awakens, lost in the dark wood, he first attempts to climb the mountain that he finds in front of him. Animals, increasingly terrifying in demeanor, block his path: a lonza, a lion, and a wolf. The image of the animals is preparation for Dante's descent though hell. Dante sees a mountain and wants to climb it, seeking the light. It seems that he is prevented from making progress by external forces. However, without even allegorizing the animals, further consideration reveals that Dante is prevented from ascending the mountain by his own fear; he fears that these animals might physically harm him and so instead of seeking an infinite good, and hoping that it might sustain him, Dante descends into darkness with the aim of maintaining and fulfilling his physical, finite existence. However much Dante thinks he desires the good suggested by the light, his actions indicate a stronger desire for the finite and material.

In Canto III of *Inferno* Dante explains that all the individuals who are met in hell have "foregone the good of intellect."[23] Having turned away from the good that ought to direct their desires and wills, the souls of Inferno no longer have any reason to choose one end over another and they are left to the contingency of desire. In other words, rejecting the rational, universal, and supernatural principle to which they might direct themselves, the people in Inferno seek merely to fulfill their finite natures and, as a result, experience and participate in the full effects of the instability and deficiency of the natural order. For example, with no good or necessary grounds upon which to guide their actions towards others, the individuals we meet in the bottom of Inferno will betray anything or anyone to get the limited goods they desire. The descent through Inferno entails an ever more conscious and deliberate rejection of the known good, moving from individuals who have not reflected on the nature of the good or the vice they commit, to those who knowingly betray what they ought to love.

The story of Alessandro's life reveals a corresponding descent into Inferno. Throughout the story, Alessandro returns to his early friendship and then obsession with the strange character, Orfeo, a man who works for Alessandro's father with a seemingly fragile grasp on reality. Orfeo worships the blessed sap of the moon and is terrified of typewriters. Seemingly out of place in an otherwise realistic novel, Orfeo is a fantastic character, providing an oversized image of the corruption that is more delicately traced in Alessandro's character. Alessandro hates Orfeo and thus projects as external to himself what he should recognize as an element of his own soul. Alessandro has to recognize that what he perceives in Orfeo is also present within himself in order to come to terms with the state of his soul. Helprin indicates that Orfeo is modeled on a man by the same name, who he once knew in Italy: a "short, very dark, very old, very crazy, a gatekeeper."[24] However, he notes that we might think of this Orfeo, as Charon, the gatekeeper and thus the path by which we gain entrance to Inferno.[25] In other words, Helprin suggests that we might understand all of vice if we properly understand Orfeo's character. In light of what he judges to be "grotesque" and "mad," one of the book's reviewers rightly concludes that Orfeo works as a symbol of the arbitrary nature of war itself.[26]

Orfeo's parents died when he was just a child and, despite the obvious affection of the Giuliani's, Orfeo believes that his physical deformities are such that no one else will ever be able to love him. His physical, finite form thwarts his desire and even his capacity to love. However, rather than believing that the love he desires might be satisfied by the divine, Orfeo is without hope, and, despite the terrible limitations mortality and the finitude of his body place on him, Orfeo gives in to the temptations the natural order poses. This is prefigured in the god that he worships—the blessed sap of the moon. Rather than an image of an infinite and supernatural being, Orfeo imagines the divine in the terms of the natural world. Becoming the chief scribe for the Ministry of War, Orfeo devotes himself entirely to the sap and becomes an arbitrary force of irrational nature. Hence, in transcribing the orders of war that are given to him, Orfeo ignores the original dictates and instead orders whatever arbitrary desire governs him at that moment. The thousands of people his orders affect every day are irrelevant to him. Describing the soldiers of war as though they are animals, Orfeo says, "'The war goes brilliantly, and I don't even care . . . I'm not after anything but the sap. It doesn't make any difference. . . . It doesn't matter which way one is drawn—except for the monkeys, the effect is the same.'"[27]

When just a young man, Alessandro tells Orfeo that his pen is his most valuable possession, including his penis.[28] However, Alessandro says this before he has had much opportunity to use the latter, and we have reason to believe that an older Alessandro would not agree with his younger self. Orfeo, however, never experiences sexual pleasure; he knew even before he had desire "that it would be gnarled and knotted, black and hard, a tree that would never bear fruit."[29] With his physical desires thwarted, Orfeo's pen becomes the medium through which his desire flows. Just as there are indications through *Inferno* that the formal beauty of images might be used to vicious ends, that the form of Orfeo's script is lovely, does not dictate a corresponding beauty in its content. No rhyme or reason governs the changes he makes to the orders he is supposed to transcribe; he merely writes what he chooses.[30] And, unlike everyone else upon whom the world places limits, Orfeo's power is seemingly infinite: "'Politicians and king's suffer the agony of constraint. Not I, I need merely dip my pen in the holy blessed sap and my orders are followed to the letter, with never any consequences for my person.'" Orfeo is "lightning"; he is a "lion."[31] The root of Orfeo's corruption and, as we shall see, that of Alessandro lies in their fear of a future which they cannot control, and one in which they and those they love will die. In the image of Orfeo and that of Alessandro, Helprin suggests that the fear of mortality and a corresponding lack of hope that this mortality might be overcome are at the root of all human corruption. In response to this fear, both Orfeo and Alessandro assert their wills in the place of the divine.

The finite order, however, is not to be understood as solely a cause of one's fallenness, and, thus, a thing to be avoided and despised. Dante's *Divine Comedy* and all of Helprin's novels, describe the mediation of the universal through the finite and particular. Again this is part of a long tradition, stretching back at least to Plato. Plato's *Republic*, at its heart, is a demonstration of the capacity of poetry to mediate the universal. The intricate construction of images, from the frame that begins the dialogue at the Piraeus, through the construction of the ideal city in thought, including the ironic criticism of poetry, to the central images of the Sun, the Line, and the

Cave, all argue for the possibility, indeed the necessity of mediating the apprehension of the Good through the means of the particular.

Augustine's *Confessions* employs the same method. Through the artfully arranged recollection of events in his life, Augustine moves through his own ascent, and leads his readers along with him, from very particular, even if common occurrences, to the apprehension of God. In relating his Platonic vision in Book VII, Augustine describes his ascent in clear terms:

> And thus by degrees I was led upward from bodies to the soul . . . and from there on to the soul's inward faculty . . . and thence on up to the reasoning power. . . . And when this power of reason within me also found that it was changeable, it raised itself up to its own intellectual principle, and withdrew its thoughts from experience, abstracting itself from the contradictory throng of fantasms in order to seek for that light in which it was bathed . . . [I]t cried out that the unchangeable was better than the changeable. . . . And thus with the flash of a trembling glance, it arrived at that which is. . . . But I was not able to sustain my gaze.[32]

Dante and Helprin, like Plato and Augustine before them, suggest that the beautiful is akin to the good, and a means by which the divine reveals itself and is made known in the natural and human world. Works of beauty, natural or manmade, inanimate or full of life, capture one's attention, arouse desire, and mediate a path to the good. Both Dante and Alessandro, lacking hope, are finally moved by their love of beauty. In each instance, love of the beautiful is shown to be stronger than their fear of death and loss.

Dante is first moved by Virgil, who he describes as the poet all the other poets honor, and the writer from whom Dante "took the beautiful style that has done honour to [him]."[33] Virgil invokes Beatrice's beauty, reminding Dante of the particular woman he loves and whose beauty, when we finally meet her, increases exponentially the closer she moves towards her place in the celestial sphere. Finally, Bernard of Clairvaux, another poet moved by a still more beautiful woman, the Virgin Mary, replaces Beatrice. Each of Dante's mediators surpasses the previous in their capacity to embody the divine in their lives.

Helprin's Alessandro is a professor of aesthetics, and throughout his life, works of beauty consistently remind him of his love for the good even when he is in the depths of vice and despair.[34] Most notably, Raphael's *Portrait of Bindo Altoviti* and Giorgione's *La Tempesta* are visited and revisited in the course of the novel, each time reminding Alessandro of the good he imagines he had lost. Helprin's novels are reflections on beauty's capacity to indicate the nature of the good and draw attentive individuals to better ends. In both Dante's work and Helprin's novels, the beauty made manifest in the characters of other people is shown as the most apt means to move individuals to the good.

ALESSANDRO'S DESCENT

Adam and Eve are ejected from the Garden of Eden and their own innocence because they gain an awareness of good and evil, being and non-being. Insofar as a person embraces the finite world in whose nature they share, they travel further and further from the initial knowledge they have gained of the good itself. In the following sections, we trace the increasingly conscious descent in Alessandro's soul. Just as the structure of *Inferno* shows an increasingly conscious betrayal of the good and greater images of vice, Alessandro descends further and further into his corruption as *Soldier* progresses. Throughout the novel, he is given opportunities to gain greater awareness of the nature of the good and his proper end through images of tremendous beauty. Each time he rejects the good that he knows, only to fall further than before. In the final stages, Alessandro is brought to the very bottom of Inferno and, even there, made to realize the power and force of God's love.

Leaving the Garden

The first layers of *Inferno* catalogue a series of crimes that are striking, inasmuch as the souls Dante encounters appear to have been virtually innocent. While it is clear that these souls have committed sinful acts, they do not seem to have intended any real betrayal of the good. Instead, incontinence, as formulated by Aristotle, and then modified by Dante, is recognized in acts that can be non-deliberatively engaged in, such as when desire overcomes reason and one finds oneself taking pleasure in what better judgment suggests one should not.[35] Dante faints as he leaves Limbo, only to awaken within the circle of the lustful, and so one might seemingly slip into an illicit sexual encounter, a gluttonous meal, or an act of rage. By placing these individuals in Inferno, Dante suggests that they are nonetheless complicit in these activities insofar as they could have reflected on their choices and governed themselves more fully. For example, in Canto V of *Inferno*, Francesca presents herself as guiltless. All she did was go out to read one day with a handsome boy. The next thing she knew they were kissing and then locked in an eternal embrace in Inferno.[36] Her lust for Paolo damns him in a way that real love would not. In other words, Francesca is not concerned with Paolo's good; indeed, she does not even name him. Instead, she is concerned with how he might fulfill her desires, regardless of the consequence for either of them. While Dante swoons when he sees the pain of the incontinent in Inferno, Virgil later warns him, "'Here piety lives when pity is quite dead./ Who is more impious than one who thinks/that God shows passion in his judgment?'"[37] To pity individuals in Inferno, even those in the upper levels, is to suggest they are not culpable for their actions and God's discernment, as evidenced in the afterlife, is not just. The initial stages of Alessandro's life reflect a similar state of innocence, where Alessandro is not fully conscious of his activities or the harm that they might cause others. Nonetheless, just like those in the circles of incontinence, Alessandro's blindness to his faults is willful. His participation in the war reveals to him his culpability and the gates of the Garden of Eden are then locked behind him

In their respective roles as artist and aesthetician, it is no surprise that Dante and Alessandro love beautiful images, and are prone to a kind of romanticism that falls within the circles of incontinence. The limitations of Alessandro's understanding at this stage (and hence the degree to which he might be considered innocent) are clarified in light of Raphael's *Portrait of Bindo Altoviti*, "his portrait when he was young."[38] Alessandro chooses to go see this painting, behind enemy lines, just prior to his entrance to the war. In the painting, Alessandro sees himself reflected, for here is a young man consumed by the very earthly pleasures that Alessandro himself is consumed by. He imagines Altoviti looking out at the beauty of the world and saying, "'These are the things in which I was so helplessly caught up, the waves that took me, what I loved.'"[39] Even further, however, Alessandro sees in this painting the possibility of an eternal youth and innocence. For, although he recognizes that he will one day be "stilled," just as Altoviti is, Alessandro does not imagine the corruption, both physical and moral, that will occur prior to his death. As such, he is neither cognizant of the limitations of the world he loves nor of the degree to which he will be tempted to accept this partial world as the whole.

As Alessandro's autobiographical tale begins, he is just a young man who sees the world as a place of beauty, and who believes that in this world all his desires will be satisfied. Alessandro continues to approach the world in a childlike innocence, unaware of his participation in a fallen order. He is thus not cognizant of the negative effects his activities have on the well-being of others. This attitude is evident in the first memory that Alessandro is drawn into. Alessandro remembers when he was just a young boy of nine and his father first took him to South Tyrol. While there, Alessandro falls in love at the sight of a little girl in the entourage of an Austrian princess. Visiting her that night in her room, he is discovered. Rather than have Alessandro taken in by the Princess's guards, his father pretends to be angry with him, and, for the first and only time, Alessandro's father hits him. Reflecting on that day, the problem Alessandro knows is not the innocent trip he made to the princess's bedroom, but that in the thoughtlessness of his desire, he forced his father to an act of punishment that his father would never be able to forgive himself for even though Alessandro had long ago done so: "'it made him unhappy all out of proportion; not only at the time but for the rest of his life. He believed he had betrayed me, and I could never convince him that it wasn't so.'"[40]

Alessandro's romantic dalliance with Lia, his first true relationship, leaves her correspondingly wounded. Having initiated a relationship with Lia, Alessandro happens across Ariane and although they do not meet, he falls in love with her and she remains the woman that he loves throughout his life. That Alessandro continues his relationship with Lia, despite his known love for Ariane, is understandable. Many factors indicate that a relationship between Alessandro and Ariane is impossible: "she was too young, she was French, he didn't know her name, she had been surrounded by protective company, and their encounter had been like a dream."[41] Lia may also be a kind of forerunner, even a necessary *preparatio* to Ariane. Lia's name and her place in the story indicate that we might understand Alessandro's relationships to her and Ariane as parallel to the story of Jacob with Leah and Rachel, about whom Dante dreams in Canto XXVII of *Purgatory*.[42] Leah, who gathers flowers in Dante's dream, is representative of the active life, and would seem to be a necessary preparation for Rachel, whose bright eyes indicate the greater life of contemplation.[43] Interpreted broadly, Dante's dream of Leah and Rachel suggests that the habituation in ethical virtue that Dante achieves while climbing Purgatory is necessary to his assumption of the contemplative life found in Paradiso. In the same way, Virgil, as a representative of ancient ethical virtue, precedes the mediation of Beatrice. Helprin thereby suggests that Lia is a necessary preparation to Ariane. Alessandro's relationship with Lia and his loss of her habituates him to the nature of love, such that he is prepared when Ariane reappears.

Nonetheless, the benefits Alessandro receives from his relationship with Lia come at some cost to Lia herself. At the very beginning of their relationship, Lia arranges for Alessandro to attend a formal dinner at which she is also a guest. After a night of food, debate, and dancing, Alessandro leaves, knowing that whatever his feelings are for Lia, they are not quite love. He reflects,

> she was exquisite, and he feared that he was blinded to everything else that he was drawn to her by weakness, that his passion for her was incomplete. . . . He knew very well that love could be like the most beautiful singing, that it could make death inconsequential, that it existed in forms so pure and strong that it was capable of reordering the inverse. He knew this, and that he lacked it.[44]

Thinking that it might be more beautiful to suffer in the absence of such love, Alessandro continues to pursue a relationship with Lia. In this he has no concern as to whether she is deserving of a more complete love.

Alessandro is further careless about how his opinion of international affairs might be in conflict with those of Lia or her family. While this would not generally be problematic, Lia's brother is in the cavalry of the Italian army and Alessandro's position is that war is not necessary. When war is declared and Elio is sent to northern Italy and then to Libya, Lia and Alessandro's dispute is still manageable: "in the first round neither he nor Lia had to contend with anything unpleasant," for "the war was not yet bitter, [and] neither were they."[45] When Elio is killed in battle, everything changes. The garden gate by which Alessandro used to visit Lia is now locked and he is told that they won't see him.[46] The locked gate prevents Lia from using the garden, and the image mirrors Adam and Eve's expulsion from Eden. Now knowing death, Lia cannot return to a state of innocence. Alessandro, who was unwilling to concede any of his theories for the honor of Lia's brother and her family, is no longer welcome. His part in the unspoken bitterness that Lia must have experienced is clear, for what seemed like harmless arguments when her brother was alive, might well be remembered as enemy blows when her brother is dead.

Like Dante, we might swoon when we imagine that these crimes would be sufficient to damn Alessandro. Surely, he is thoughtless, but of course he did not intend to cause Lia harm, and he played no role in Lia's brother's death. Yet, Alessandro is no more innocent than Dante's Francesca. No one would presumably hold the young Alessandro culpable for the pain his actions caused his father, for, at the time, he was just a child. When Alessandro meets Lia, however, he is no longer a child, and his father, worried about illegitimate grandchildren, even cautions him about entering into anything rashly, thereby suggesting that Alessandro would do well to reflect on his intentions and actions. Unlike his childish self, Alessandro is given the opportunity to think about the nature of his desire and the consequences of not governing it. As such, his treatment of Lia cannot be easily passed over. He may not have intended to hurt her but he willfully ignored the potential consequences for his actions when he might very well have attended to them.

Unlike Lia, Alessandro is still literally able to enter the garden that separates their homes, for the gate on his side has not been locked. Metaphorically, however, Alessandro remains in the garden only because he refuses to recognize that he has eaten of the same tree as Adam and Eve. Alessandro is old enough to know right from wrong and is able therefore to attend to the future consequences of his activities. To do so, however, would mean taking responsibility for his actions and this is something that Alessandro is not prepared to do. Alessandro's vice at this stage is his willful ignorance of the good that should order his activities and which would provide the satisfaction of his desire. Like Adam and Eve, however, Alessandro is unable to ignore the limitations of his nature forever. Lia comes to understand the nature of mortality with the death of her brother. Alessandro is brought to the same realization by means of the war.

Imagining that he can avoid death, Alessandro joins the navy before Italy has entered the war, so as to avoid being drafted to the infantry. All of his strategizing is for naught, however, and he soon finds himself in the midst of battle, "coldly" killing, so as not to be killed.[47] With respect to the role the war has on Alessandro's descent, it is important to recognize that Helprin does not suggest that war is unnecessary and should be avoided at all costs. Some wars are necessary and even justified. This becomes clear later when Alessandro enters the circles of fraud and betrayal specifically when he deserts the army, hoping to return home unnoticed. However, that there are wars and that we participate in them is an indication of the corruption of the finite world in which we live and a sign that another end should be preferred and sought. It is neither Dante's nor Helprin's argument that faith in, and hope for, a divine end will miraculously overcome the difficulties of our particular natures and the circumstances in which we find ourselves. Many, if not most, of the individuals we meet in Dante's *Paradiso* lived a life of corruption. Their reconciliation with God is based neither on their activities nor their virtue, but rather on their acceptance of divine grace as a means of recompensing for their deficiencies. Alessandro's descent, like that of Dante, is indicative of the condition that all who live in the finite order participate in. The arbitrariness of the war, its violence, and the uncertainty and fear it causes is merely a heightened example of the outcomes of the natural world. In experiencing war, Alessandro is brought to know the consequences of a purely finite life.

Alessandro acknowledges this when he writes home and explains the nature of the war to his parents: "a nightmare is having to play by rules that make no sense, for a purpose that is entirely alien, without control of either one's fate or even one's actions . . . [T]he war is ruled inordinately by chance, to the point almost where human actions seem to have lost their meaning."[48] In so describing the war, Alessandro also describes the state of a life lived only in relation to the finite world. Helprin indicates that the war is a metaphor for mortality. Regardless of a person's plans or strategies, one day she or he will die. This "fate" is outside of her or his control. Realizing this, Alessandro does not then speak of a hope for an eternal end wherein death is overcome. Instead, he writes that should he live, he wants to buy back the garden, "take out the weeds, thicken the grass, prune the trees, and make it what it once was."[49] Now knowing death, Alessandro seeks to return to the state of his innocence, a time when death was unknown but, also a time when an infinite good was unthinkable. In this, he is like the cat that stays with the troops in the trenches. What is sad about the cat, he says, is that "'if she wanted, she could bound out . . . and she could go anywhere she wanted, away from battle. . . . But she doesn't know. She stays with us.'"[50] While Alessandro cannot avoid his death, like the cat he does not imagine the possibility of a different kind of life. Indeed, when he imagines what kind of life he might have, he hopes not for a life where death is overcome, but a life like cats enjoy, where death is inevitable but just not known.

The City of Dis

In *Inferno*, the City of Dis is home to the lower levels of hell where the violent and fraudulent are housed. It is walled and heavily guarded. The demons that guard it refuse Virgil's entreaties to let them in, and Virgil and Dante must wait for divine assistance before they are able to pass through.[51] Allegorically, the suggestion is that these latter forms of vice are more intentional in nature and ultimately worse. Premeditated violence and betrayal are conscious choices that require effort. They are states of being wherein we have ample opportunity to recognize our state of vice and change accordingly. In the first stage of his descent, Alessandro seemingly falls into corruption. In so doing, he does not fully understand the good that he is forsaking. In the midst of the war and in the face of a painting, Alessandro consciously recognizes something of the true nature of the good. He then rejects it and enters the City of Dis and the lower levels of Inferno.

Taking an unapproved leave from his base to spend a day in Venice, Alessandro finds himself at the Accademia, in front of Giorgione's painting *La Tempesta*. The experience of the war has dramatically affected how Alessandro sees the painting. It is not the dream-like pastoral, of a shepherd and a young mother, that Alessandro, as a young scholar, had taken it to be. This previous interpretation was only possible prior to Alessandro's confrontation with the limitations of the natural world. Having experienced war, Alessandro no longer views nature in purely romantic and innocent terms. To Alessandro, the shepherd is now clearly a soldier and the mother and child are his only salvation: "Unclothed and unprotected, with her baby in her arms, she defies the storm unwittingly. Entirely at risk, she shines out. . . . She is his only hope."[52] The soldier who has suffered the storm of battle and is intimately acquainted with hatred, violence, and death, might be redeemed through the love a mother has for her child and the possibility that this love extends to him. The painting suggests that the suffering of war might be redeemed by love and Alessandro reflecting on it, says, "'Though it has broken and razed everything that once stood within me, I've lost nothing. The ceiling is still there, but now blue, with stars.'"[53] In the image of a mother's love, Alessandro recognizes the possibility of more permanent and sustaining ends. The good imagined in the painting is not finite, but the infinite good manifest in the nature of love itself. The mother never stops loving the child, nor is her love ever diminished. Further, the painting of the mother and child speaks to a continuity of life, even to immortality, just as the sky and the stars speak to the possibility of something that is eternal and unchanging. The source of the baby's life and the means by which it is sustained, as imaged in *La Tempesta*, is love. Whatever the injustices of the natural order, they are not the result of the love of a mother or of a god. Hence in seeing the beauty of the painting, Alessandro remembers the beauty of nature—the blue of the sky and the light of the stars. What *is*, he knows, is good. Finally, by means of this painting, Alessandro recognizes how, in the face of such possibilities, one ought to act. The young mother bravely endures the storm for the sake of the child she loves. Assuming the storm is representative of the mutability and impermanence of the finite world, the woman does not despair, but rather, in the face of inevitable death, produces and sustains life. Despite what she knows of the storm, she courageously hopes for a good end.

In seeing the *Portrait of Bindo Altoviti*, Alessandro recognized the possibility of eternal life. However, as a young man who had never truly suffered or faced a trial, it was easy for him to believe that he might continue in this same way forever. He later reflects, "His home on the Gianicolo had been a fortress against time. Never had he returned to anything but a loving family, he had taken for granted the fraternity of the university, and the world was a garden of exquisite and invulnerable women."[54] At this stage, it was easy for Alessandro to have faith. Suffering through the war, Alessandro later admits that this early faith was challenged and even lost, but now in light of *La Tempesta*, Alessandro is moved to realize that by means of love, the suffering of the finite world might be overcome such that the infinite good he had previously thought was his own might be regained.[55]

Alessandro then discovers that his own mother has died and moves further into Inferno. Alessandro has a fuller understanding of his own nature and that of the divine. Turning from what he knows, Alessandro's descent is now much sharper and more deliberate. Like Virgil, who has to work to enter the City of Dis, descending into the lower level of Inferno requires a much more conscious betrayal of the good. From *La Tempesta*, Alessandro knows that a mother's love is eternal; however, when his mother dies, Alessandro believes that her love has died as well. Alessandro neither hopes for, nor conceives of his mother's redemption, but rather falls into despair at her loss. In this, he is like Dante after Beatrice dies, for, as she recollects,

> when I'd reached my second age, and there
> E'en on the threshold, life for life exchanged,
> Then he forsook me and made friends elsewhere.
>
> When, risen from Flesh to spirit, free I ranged,
> In beauty greater and in virtue more,
> His mind was turned from me, his heart estranged.[56]

Despite the goodness and love made manifest to Dante in Beatrice, after her death his attention is still fixed on the finite world of which she is no longer a part. Falling into despair, Alessandro now wonders if she even loved him.[57] Having recognized, if only momentarily, the strength and invincibility of love, Alessandro now doubts that such love could be extended to him, even by his own mother. Just as Orfeo is too ugly, Alessandro is too terrible a son to love; no one is sufficiently good to forgive Alessandro his faults and love him regardless. Having lost his mother, Alessandro also loses sight of the infinite love of God.

When Dante loses sight of Beatrice, he loses sight of the good that he should seek and his path forward. Alessandro loses sight of his most proximate source and consequently loses sight of himself—his true nature and end. Returning from Venice, Alessandro and the remaining members of the River Guard are assigned to a boat that has no name, are not told their destination, and are asked to forget who they are.[58] Given the task of hunting and capturing their countrymen, other Italians who have broken from the ranks and deserted the army, the River Guard must forget who they are and where they come from. This is an image of the further consciousness required to enter the City of Dis. While at war with an unknown and foreign enemy, one might be sufficiently moved by fear and anger that any conscious recognition of the other as a fellow human is readily overcome. Hunting and killing one's countrymen, potentially one's neighbors and relatives, presumably requires a more determined effort. It is premeditated aggression that, while necessary and even just, is nonetheless necessitated by participation in the finite order.

Having forgotten who he is and the path that he ought to seek, Alessandro chooses to desert the army himself, and, like those at the bottom of Inferno, he consciously betrays those for whom he has sworn to fight. Alessandro understands the logic of the River Guard's mission in Sicily—if people are allowed to desert the army without consequence, there would no longer be anyone to defend Italy from invading forces. And Alessandro believes that it is worth dying to protect Rome, "Because you'll die anyway, sooner than you think. . . . In history . . . will is only an illusion and success does not last. You can only do your best in the short time that you have."[59] Moreover, when Alessandro comes face to face with Gianfranco, the man he is hunting, he explains that, in deserting, Gianfranco has made it harder on those who have remained in the line. War, Alessandro suggests, is an inevitable facet of human life and all one can do is to find an honorable path through it, a path that takes into account not only one's desires, but also the desires of those one fights for and with.[60] By deserting, Alessandro condemns another soldier to the task of hunting his countrymen; Alessandro thus tempts another with the circles of the lion and the wolf.

When he finally reaches the shores of Italy, Alessandro finds his passage to Rome with sheep and shepherds.[61] However, rather than tending to the flocks, he leads them to their slaughter, and even these animals "knew they had been betrayed."[62] The image of Alessandro betraying sheep and lambs evokes the image of the betrayal of Christ. The act of betraying his country is representative of the same intent found in Judas, who Dante imagines in the very bottom of Inferno, now food for one of Satan's three heads.

Alessandro's betrayals extend beyond deserting the army, to deserting all of the goods that he knows and has loved. Although Alessandro leaves the army to be reunited with his family, he ultimately betrays them as well. While Alessandro is described as loving his father without measure, he does not explain how he has come to be home, letting his father believe that his leave from the army is legitimate.[63] He knows this is an act of betrayal, telling Guariglia, "I don't want them to come for me at my father's bedside. He's sick. It would kill him. I have a strange feeling that, if I tell the truth, I can keep him alive."[64] Moreover, and compounding Alessandro's desire to "tell the truth," is the news that the Germans have broken through the Italian lines. As a flood of Italian casualties fills the hospital, Alessandro regains a sense of his purpose in the war. Despite both of these facts, he does not immediately act. Instead, he hesitates, telling Fabio that he must wait until his father is first at home, ten days perhaps. Alessandro risks ten days during which it is probable that he will be arrested at his father's bedside and will allow ten more days to pass during which any number of other soldiers might fall in his stead. Alessandro's betrayal of family, friends, superiors, and country is complete. This, of course mirrors the divisions of the souls found at the very bottom of Inferno, frozen in the ice of Cocytus.[65]

When Alessandro looks at *La Tempesta,* he sees a soldier, rather than a shepherd, and knows that the only salvation for a soldier is in the love a woman has for her child. Alessandro goes to Rome, expecting to experience the love of his family and dreaming of meeting a woman. The circles of fraud, however, are circles of betrayal, in which no true love can be maintained. As a result, instead of meeting his romantic interest, we are given uncomfortable moments in which Alessandro's lust is awakened and directed at his sister.

Reawakening the Virtues

Alessandro is given yet another chance. What he previously understood only theoretically, by means of the paintings, he is now given to experience practically. In the death of his father, he realizes how one might face the battle of mortality with faith and hope in an eternal life. Meeting Ariane, he knows love as the end of all that he desires. Despite this even greater comprehension, Alessandro is not able to sustain his desire and will for the good, but is drawn back into the struggle of his natural existence.

Having deserted, Alessandro returns to Rome, only to find his father in the hospital. In the face of his dying father, Alessandro, a soldier for whom death is ever present, sees his own fears, but also the necessary response. While Alessandro's war is one that might be won by strength and will, "his father's was the great war, less a contest, than a mystery, it was gossamer, silent, and absolute. No one had been victorious in the war his father was fighting, except by faith and imagination, and of these victories no one could really be sure."[66] Despite his incapacity to "do" anything to prevent himself from dying, Mr. Guiliani faces it "almost cheerfully," his only regret being that he will have to leave the children he loves.[67] Mr. Guiliani clarifies the nature of the good and the proper object of desire. Alessandro wakes up in his childhood home and luxuriates in the things he finds there.[68] His father, however, notes that, "in memory, things, objects, and sensations merely stand in for the people you love."[69] On the verge of his death, Mr. Guiliani does not think about his previous ambitions, successes, or losses. Instead, he hopes and imagines that time and space might be overcome, so that he can hold his wife as he did when she was just a young woman, be reacquainted with his children as they were when still infants, and be a child again for his own father. Mr. Guiliani hopes for miracles that have their source and end in love.

When Alessandro is caught and taken to prison to await his execution, the lessons of his father's death sink in. When Alessandro first sees his father, his father asks him if he has faith that God will grant him all that he desires. Alessandro responds that he does not know, but then improvises, saying, if not what he believes, at least what his father wants to hear: "'I can't imagine that God, who is so adept at linking parents with children, would so cruelly separate them.'"[70] Now, having been caught, and on the verge of his own death, Alessandro affirms a faith that he had previously only mouthed. With a renewed understanding of the nature of God's love, Alessandro has faith and even hope that he might be redeemed, saying to the priest who comes to him the night before the execution is to take place, "'I don't need your job of words to propel me directly into God's hands. If God will have me, it will have to be without an introduction.'"[71]

Alessandro's faith is then providentially rewarded. His execution stayed, Alessandro falls in love, finally meeting Ariane, his Beatrice. When Alessandro views *La Tempesta* while in the midst of war, the woman he sees is a mother; he then loses his own mother. The soldier of the painting, however, does not see just any mother, or even his own mother, but presumably the woman he gazes at is his beloved and the mother of his child. Prior to meeting Ariane, the nature of God's love is mediated for Alessandro by the love of his family, particularly the love he has for his mother and his father. Helprin suggests, however, that one more properly understands the full nature of divine love in the reciprocated love of a beloved and lover. In this we are given an image of God, by whose love, the beloved is raised and made equal to the divine. Helprin further indicates the integrity with which his theology views the particular and the finite. The divine is not merely one's source, nor even one's friend, but something of a lover. In contrast, Orfeo is unable to consummate an erotic relationship and this has devastating effects on his psychology and his end.

Ariane more fully mediates the nature of the divine for Alessandro, and, in their relationship, he is given a greater opportunity to know the fullness of God's love. In the *Divine Comedy*, Beatrice replaces Virgil as Dante's guide at the top of Mount Purgatory and she accompanies him through most of Paradiso. In *La Vita Nuova* Dante writes about the few occasions he was in Beatrice's presence. He first sees her when he is nine and she is eight and, although they do not exchange any words, in this first early meeting Dante is so taken with Beatrice's beauty that his heart is moved to declare, "Behold a god more powerful than I, who, coming, will rule over me."[72] Dante sees Beatrice only a few more times, and we are not aware of any close conversation that he may have had with her before she dies. Dante then devotes his life to writing a work that is worthy of her—the *Divine Comedy*. In his love for Beatrice, as expressed in *La Vita Nuova*, Dante hews to the conventions of the courtly love tradition. Beatrice exists as the image of his ultimate love and he devotes his life to seeking to be worthy of her. That the two never "have a relationship" in the modern sense, is in part necessary for Dante's devotion to her. Seeing her only from a distance, Dante is able to idealize Beatrice and attribute to her all beauty and virtue. Dante never truly knows Beatrice as a particular and finite individual and so he never acknowledges her faults or limitations. Further, from what we know, his love is never consummated, nor even perhaps acknowledged, let alone returned.

Nonetheless, Dante also reinterprets the courtly love tradition. For, in the *Divine Comedy*, he is given occasion to meet Beatrice, albeit in her perfected state, and, we learn, that, in this realm at least, his love for her is reciprocated. Although she has to be directed by Lucy to turn her eyes to Dante's suffering, once Beatrice realizes his condition, she descends into Inferno, persuading Virgil to become his guide.[73] Finally, we understand that, unlike Virgil who leaves Dante, Beatrice will never be lost. In a scene parallel to that in which Dante turns, only to realize Virgil is gone, Dante turns to Beatrice to ask her a question, only to find that she has been replaced by St. Bernard. However, rather than crying as he had for Virgil, Dante is directed to look upward and there, despite the great distance, Beatrice can be seen in full detail.[74] Regardless of where Beatrice is in the Empyrean, Dante knows that, insofar as he becomes a citizen of that eternal city, the nature of her love is such that she will always be present for him.

While we do not accompany Alessandro after his death and so do not see his reunion with Ariane, Alessandro's initial relationship with Ariane mimics that of Dante and Beatrice. Leaving a party, presumably in his late teens, Alessandro happens across Ariane and two friends, three girls on the verge of being women. Alessandro and Ariane do not speak, although our narrator tells us that she is the most "beautiful woman Alessandro had ever seen in his life."[75] And although Alessandro is in the beginnings of his relationship with Lia, he cannot stop thinking of this young girl: "she was more familiar to him than someone he has known his entire life."[76] Finally, Alessandro must live an extended period believing that Ariane is dead and lost to him, before she is returned.

Despite these broad similarities, the relationship between Alessandro and Ariane is quite different from that of Dante and Beatrice. While we do not see much of Alessandro's life with Ariane either during the few weeks they have together during the war or after their reunion in Rome, it is clear almost immediately that their love is reciprocal as well as physical, in addition to being spiritual and intellectual. Only moments after finally meeting as adults, they become intimate; later they have a child, eventually marrying and sharing a life together. Again, Helprin's account is particularly modern and thus distinguished from Dante's. The particular and subjective elements of human life are celebrated in their fullness; they are not simply means to achieve heaven; they have inherent, even infinite, value.[77] One could suggest that Helprin's view is simply not that of the Christian Dante, for the reconciliation of the universal and the particular in Christ should not be part of Helprin's Jewish theology. This however is a superficial and ultimately an inadequate interpretation. The complete recognition of the sufficiency of individual subjectivity to the universal is a distinguishing characteristic of Helprin's novels. In Helprin's work, unlike Dante's *Comedy*, the redemption and restoration of the particular is effected in the world of nature, even if by means that are themselves supernatural.

While Dante's Beatrice is revealed in her perfected form, with Dante going so far as to imagine her as a replacement for Christ in the *Corpus Christi* pageant in Purgatory, in first meeting Alessandro, Ariane understands herself quite differently, saying "'I'm just a woman. I'm not the end of the war, or the end of your suffering, or some magical, higher being who will undo all that you have seen.'"[78] And, however much Alessandro loves her and however much virtue she inspires in him, what she says is correct. Ariane's presence in Alessandro's life does not preclude further suffering nor does it ensure his virtue and happiness.

We know that, like Dante, Alessandro is morally lost when he believes Ariane is dead, going so far as to seek revenge against the pilot who has killed her. And Alessandro regains his life when he imagines that Ariane might still be alive.[79] In their relationship we see not merely the love of a saint for a sinner or an angel for a human, although, for Alessandro, Ariane is certainly a saint and an angel, revealing the full nature of God and of love.[80] While Dante reveals how a perfected Beatrice can be an emissary of God to Dante, through Ariane, Helprin demonstrates how individuals, of finite and particular natures, can serve this role for someone who loves them and whom they love. More specifically, Helprin takes up the *via affirmativa*, the ascent to the Good through the affirmation of the created order, that marks Dante's *Divine Comedy*, and shows explicitly how the finite and particular world can be a means for infinite redemption. More completely than other members of this long tradition that we have spoken about, the romantic relationships between men and women, marriage, and family life are portrayed in Helprin's novels as vital forms of mediation for his various protagonists. This is certainly in marked contrast to the portrait of Socrates in Plato's *Phaedo*, for example, or to the Christian Neoplatonism of Augustine in the *Confessions*. Helprin's use of the *via affirmativa*, even more that that employed throughout the *Divine Comedy*, leaves nothing behind in the redemption of the natural order.

In his initial encounters of the *Portrait of Bindo Altoviti* and *La Tempesta*, Alessandro is in many ways a child, unprepared to understand the beauty of these works. Hence, when his cellmate tells him that, as a professor of aesthetics, he does nothing, Alessandro has to admit the truth. Up to this point in his life, at least, "it was all talk, lovely talk, with no power."[81] While Alessandro may have understood much of what these paintings showed, that knowledge was not then consummated in his life. Instead, he rejected what he knew in favor of lesser truths. Alessandro then experiences the truth he saw in these paintings in his practical life. He then revisits each painting and his understanding is further deepened.

Alessandro first sees *La Tempesta* prior to the death of his mother and reflects on its meaning the day before he thinks he loses Ariane. That day, Alessandro describes the meaning of the painting in its simplest terms: "It means love. It means coming home."[82] Just as his mother died, so he thinks Ariane has died. As such, the home he had believed he had found, is again lost. Alessandro spends much of his final days of the war strategizing as to how to seek revenge. In the end he is incapable of doing so for the pilot who bombed the hospital is an artist, but more importantly, a father. Perhaps reminded again of *La Tempesta*, but this time allowing that knowledge to direct his will, Alessandro recognizes the love the child has for her father and leaves without killing the pilot.[83]

Alessandro then makes his way back to the *Portrait of Bindo Altoviti*. Whereas previously, Alessandro saw the essence of eternal innocence and youth, he now sees "the burden of morality."[84] Despite this knowledge, Alessandro reflects that the young man's quiet expression comes from an understanding that "nothing and no one are lost." Moreover, Alessandro does not allow this knowledge to forestall his desire to go home. Whatever his end might be, he has to desire and will it, not merely know it. As Alessandro climbs the mountains that separate Germany from Italy, the reader is invited to imagine Rome as standing in for Paradiso: "Were he to find strength . . . the war would finally be over. . . . [H]e was overcome by a surge of affection for the golden autumn in Rome. There lay his future and his past, all that had been lost, and all that he might piece together. He looked calmly at the driven snow, and with the last his heart could offer, he climbed directly into it."[85]

Alessandro returns to Rome and becomes a gardener at his family's former estate. Alessandro now knows that the finite order requires tending if it is to remain beautiful. He is then granted a mystical experience and is convinced that contrary to both his knowledge and belief, "he had not yet lost Ariane."[86] He is led again, by some unseen providence, back to Venice and *La Tempesta*, wherein he sees a soldier and a mother, "joined and consecrated" by a bolt of lightning.[87] Whereas he had imagined that Rome might be the home he seeks, he now realizes that it is Ariane.

In his first viewing of *La Tempesta*, Alessandro explains the painting to the self-assured young scholar who is visiting it. Now, however, it is Alessandro who needs and accepts the help of the security guard who tails him, believing him to be a vandal or a thief. The unlearned guard notes that often people come to the painting and cry. Rather than pontificate on the reason for their sadness, Alessandro seizes this thin reference. Interrogating the guard further, he prompts the guard to search his memory, leading to his recollection of a young woman who had visited the painting, that Alessandro intuits with conviction to have been Ariane. By recollecting Ariane, the guard reminds Alessandro of what he has forgotten and what he should seek.

VICE CLARIFIED

Just as Dante regains Beatrice in Paradiso, so Alessandro and Ariane are reunited, and Alessandro learns that they have a son. A kind of Paradise is thus made manifest for Alessandro in his finite life. Even further, although Alessandro believes Ariane is dead, she is returned to him, resurrected in a way. Despite all of the things that should indicate to Alessandro the possibility of a loving God and a redemption that overcomes the limitations of the temporal world, Alessandro continues to fall. In this section we will explore more fully the root cause of Alessandro's vice and trace his final betrayals.

Alessandro knows that it is only by means of the contrast between the whole and the broken, the complete and the disordered, that the beautiful and the good can be recognized:

> Miracles and paradoxes could be explained by the marvelously independent courses of their elements, and perhaps real beauty could be partially understood in that it was not just a combination, but a dissolution; that after the threads are woven and tangled they are then untangled and continued on their separate ways; that the trains that pulled into the station in a riveting spectacle as clouds of steam condensed in the midnight air, then left for different destinations and disappeared; that the drama of a striking clock was impossible without the silence that was both its preface and epilogue.[88]

The beautiful is described here as a complex rather than simple substance. It is comprised of distinct elements, which, when brought together, achieve a kind of beauty that is not possible when they are apart. Recognizing the nature of beauty depends, Helprin suggests, on acknowledging the full autonomy of the elements of which the beautiful is comprised. Distinct elements come together, and they will also fall apart. The nature of the beautiful lies in the perfect congruence of distinct elements that need not be congruent at all.

Alessandro is drawn to these thoughts only after having first met Ariane and while waiting and hoping that she, his nurse, might return. Alessandro concludes his meditation on beauty, thinking, "In this metaphysics, and in these metaphysics alone, it hardly mattered if she came or not."[89] Love, as Alessandro imagines here, is akin to the nature of beauty. For love to have meaning the individuals one loves must remain distinct people, otherwise one merely loves the other insofar as she is a reflection of oneself. Moreover, when a beloved then reciprocates one's love, it is understood as having significance because it comes from another whose love is neither guaranteed nor necessary. The love that is awakened in Alessandro's recognition of Ariane's beauty is like her beauty itself; he explains that it exists in the contrast of their distinct entities. That she is separate from him, indeed that she is absent from him, is the cause of his longing, and in knowing his desire for her, he knows himself as in love.

There are two difficulties with Alessandro's early interpretation of the nature of beauty, and more importantly, of love. The first difficulty is that while Alessandro recognizes individual autonomy and even the nature of earthly finitude as necessary to beauty and love, practically speaking, he does not accept the limits this autonomy imposes on either. Hence, when it becomes clear to Alessandro that those he loves will, and do, die, he responds with anger and betrayal. As Alessandro says, it is in *metaphysics* alone that it does not matter whether Ariane comes. For of course it matters that she come and that Alessandro's love might be satisfied.

Following what he believes is Ariane's death, Alessandro's despair brings him to the verge of becoming one "who has forgone the good of intellect." He returns to his unit and engages in an almost mad dialogue with a major. In the course of this he identifies Orfeo as the cause of the entire war. If Orfeo had been killed earlier, he declares, "the world would have been preserved, and everyone I love would be alive today."[90] Alessandro blames Orfeo for all of the terrible things that have happened to him, not realizing that his inward corruption and temptation are caused by the same vice present in Orfeo. Orfeo is driven mad by the advance of the typewriter, for it means the loss of his power and agency as a scribe. Orfeo's resentment of the typewriter represents a rejection of the temporal order in which things change and people, like parents, die. Rather than seek an eternal and infinite end, Orfeo tries instead to control the finite world and somehow turn back time. While Orfeo worships the sap and hates the typewriter, at the end of his life, Alessandro similarly prefers trolleys to automobiles, saying "These *automobiles* . . . are everywhere, like pigeon shit. I haven't seen a naked piazza in ten years. They put them all over the place. . . . Someday I'll come home and find automobiles in my kitchen, in all the closets, and in the bathtub."[91]

More fully, just as Orfeo seeks to return to a time when he knew love, Alessandro is so attached to the particular people that he loves, that in the face of the loss that time necessarily brings to the finite world, he in turn loses the ability to recognize the virtues of the present, and has no hope that what was once lost can be found. As a result, like Orfeo, Alessandro seeks to replace the divine will with his own in an attempt to stop time and save the people he loves from their inevitable deaths. It is his lack of hope that is ultimately in question at the end of the novel and prior to Alessandro's death. We should keep in mind that Dante is similarly prone to this temptation, even in the moment of his entrance to the Garden of Eden. For, in seeing Beatrice, Dante's first thought is to look backwards to Virgil.[92]

Alessandro believes that objects of beauty come together and then fall apart. Similarly, the individuals he loves eventually leave and die. Alessandro, however, does not hope that there might be some full reconciliation wherein the individuality of particular elements and people are retained, and are at the same time unified as part of an eternal whole. Alessandro tells the major that his life has consisted in trying to bring back the dead. The images of the great paintings he has studied, including, he says, *La Tempesta*, are eternally alive through the act of recollection. This is in contrast to nature, where "you cannot bring back the dead."[93]

Early in the novel, we have an indication of Alessandro's commitment to the past over and against the future in his distress that his father has sold their garden. Even though the terms of sale include their continued use of the land for the next twenty years, Alessandro is incensed.[94] When Alessandro begins his relationship with Lia, whose family has purchased the garden, he imagines them marrying and his reacquiring it. At this point Alessandro is just a young man. The stakes seem rather low and are universally experienced in one fashion or another. The loss of the garden is emblematic of the loss of Alessandro's childhood. This garden, much like the Garden of Eden, is the place of his innocence and a place wherein all of his relatively simple desires have been met.[95] Alessandro's childlike desire for things to remain the same is an indication of his desire for an eternal satisfaction; it is an indication of his desire for the good. The finite order can never offer Alessandro what he seeks, and the loss of the garden and then Lia are merely forerunners of all the things that Alessandro has loved that he will ultimately lose.

In response to Alessandro's anger that the garden has been sold, his father explains, "I was much the same as you, but everything changed, and everything changes, even if you don't know it yet."[96] What looks like just an obsession with the past in Orfeo, is clarified in Alessandro. It is not the past *per se* that he seeks to hold onto. Instead, it is the necessity of change and the nature of time that Alessandro rejects. The events of Alessandro's life indicate the impermanence of all finite things. Alessandro's life, like all lives, is marked by loss. The effect of this on Alessandro is complex. The fragility of the finite order heightens Alessandro's attachment to it, such that at times he seems to prefer it to the absolute itself. However, the people that Alessandro loves die, leading to a sense of despair and a rejection of the goodness still present and offered to him.

When her building is bombed, Alessandro has no proof that Ariane has died. Indeed, we find out that it is because of an error in his perception of time that he believes she is still inside.[97] Leaving the town, Alessandro had looked at the hospital and caught sight of Ariane in the window. Seeing her, Alessandro willed time to slow, and, as such, believes she must have still been standing there when the bombs struck. Seeking always to slow time down, to return to the moment past, Alessandro rejects the possibility that time might bring good things, and that with sufficient time the woman he loves might have escaped her death. Rather than seeing his continued life as an opportunity to continue to experience the beauty and goodness of the world, Alessandro instead reads it as a punishment.

Not trusting in a providential future, Alessandro, like Orfeo, determines to take it into his own hands. Rather than admit his own inability to conquer the nature of the finite, Alessandro asserts another cause in its place. Just as Orfeo sees the evils of the future stemming from the typewriter, Alessandro determines that it is Orfeo who is the cause of all of his loss. Without any knowledge that Orfeo has arranged for him to be stationed with the River Guard, Alessandro describes him as the "font of all chaos."[98] Moreover, after his execution has been stayed, and Alessandro is given another chance at life, he takes a brief opportunity he has in Rome, not to see his sister, but rather to attempt to kill Orfeo.[99] Although Alessandro does not follow through, he is nonetheless obsessed with Orfeo, and when there is the chance that his own son might seek to enlist in a war that is still many years away, Alessandro senselessly resumes his hunt for Orfeo, believing that he might still have his sights set on destroying Alessandro. Finally, going through considerable pains, Alessandro brings together the circumstances of Orfeo's death, even if his plan does not proceed according to his will. Notably, at the moment that Alessandro begins his confession regarding Orfeo's death, Nicolò describes him having eyes "like a wolf."[100] Hunting Orfeo is Alessandro's last act of betrayal.

Early in the novel, Alessandro tells Luciana that Orfeo is not evil; he is merely doing what he thinks he must for the sake of the holy sap.[101] However, as Alessandro confesses his story to Nicolò, he has changed his mind. For now Alessandro remarks that Orfeo's insanity is willful: "'He gave up his sanity so his obsessions could flow within him without any resistance and elevate him to a plane of tremendous power, power that, only because he was comical, appeared accidental. It wasn't.'"[102] Orfeo is insane because he tries to achieve eternity within and by the means of finitude. The impossibility of doing so drives him mad. In all of his vice, Alessandro mimics this same descent.

The novel begins, as we have noted, with the elderly Alessandro racing to catch his bus, ignoring the presence of the angels who light his path. He correspondingly explains to Nicolò that the moon is sometimes preferable to the sun. The moon reminds Alessandro of his wife's beauty, which would have been perfect "had her eyes not been so full of love."[103] In some way corresponding to his love for his wife, is Alessandro's love for the city of Rome, for as the moon rises, so the city of Rome lights up and the two sources of nighttime light are rivals for his attention.[104] Neither the moon nor the distant city can be seen when the sun rises. Its light obscures theirs. Alessandro notes that, unlike the sun, which "is always holding forth, and butting you like a ram," the moon, "without saying anything . . . says so much."[105] The particular things that Alessandro loves are never complete, but always limited and finite. Their beauty is thus more endearing insofar as he knows it to be fragile and transitory. Alessandro describes an eagle descending on a flock of small birds: "The eagle was in command of forces that can put you in thrall enough for you to forget and relinquish life; the birds were the life that, despite its weakness and vulnerability, or perhaps because of it, rose above the perfections arrayed against it."[106]

While Alessandro notes that the rising of the sun results in the disappearance of both the moon and the city, he does not acknowledge that, in setting, the sun also allows for their appearance. Overarching, and at the root of all of Alessandro's vice, is a disordering of his loves, such that the finite and particular world takes precedence over and against the universal and infinite. Alessandro fears that the particular people he loves will be lost and does not believe that they might be saved in and by the absolute.

To love the finite order more than the infinite, is to place what is impermanent and necessarily subject to change and therefore loss, over what is permanent. Seeking love and beauty in the realm of the particular, Alessandro chooses as his end something that will inevitably change, leading him to despair. Hence, once Alessandro believes that Ariane has died, he comes to the conclusion that he is being punished and that his punishment is that while everyone else dies, he must remain alive: "His punishment was that nothing in the world could touch him. His punishment was that God had put him into battle and preserved him from its dangers."[107] Although Alessandro does again find love, even at the end of his life there is a sense that he has not overcome this deficiency. Ariane has been found, loved, and by now has died. Alessandro's son Fabio enlists in the Second World War and dies as well. Alessandro now spends so much of his time alone that the animals think he is one of them. Whatever joys he has taken from human companionship, he no longer risks the possibilities that might still lie ahead.

FINALLY ASCENDING

Dante does not travel through Inferno alone. While he is motivated to make the descent by Beatrice, it is Virgil who walks with him. Left alone in Inferno, Dante would doubtlessly get lost in any one of the ditches in which he stops. In comparison, Alessandro does not make the descent into his soul by himself, but tells his tale to Nicolò. Through the awakening of Alessandro's sense of justice and then love for another, specifically this young boy, he recollects the rest of the loves of his life and is able to escape Inferno.

At first glance, Nicolò seems to be an inferior and comic substitute for Virgil. Virgil, although a pagan, achieved a life of stoic virtue; Nicolò, who is just a young man, has not even begun to think about the nature of ethics, and Alessandro has to explain to him the value of a life of austerity.[108] Virgil is a philosopher and a poet; Nicolò cannot read and thinks that aesthetics are "stupid."[109] Most notably, Virgil is dead and eternally a resident in limbo, while Nicolò is just at the beginning of his adult life.

From this last point that one can begin to see where, and, perhaps one reason why, Helprin diverges from Dante on his choice of companions. For many readers of the *Divine Comedy*, the apparent treatment of Virgil is troubling.[110] Virgil guides Dante through Inferno to the upper reaches of Mount Purgatory. He is described as Dante's master, parent, and beloved.[111] As invested as the reader is in the outcome of Dante's travels, so too are we taken up in Virgil's story. It is with great poignancy that Virgil disappears, without even a goodbye, as Dante enters the Garden of Eden and is reunited with Beatrice. Virgil does not accompany Dante through Paradiso and, while it is not explicitly stated where he ultimately goes, he describes his own state as without hope, suggesting that whatever the will of God or the reader might be, he himself wills nothing more than a return to limbo.[112] While Dante provides occasional cause for the reader to question whether or not Virgil's position in the afterlife might be challenged and changed, including the placement of pagans in Paradiso, there is no conclusive answer to this difficulty. (When asked his view about Virgil's fate, Helprin indicates that Virgil may very well have ended up in New Jersey. Whether New Jersey compares more to Heaven or Hell, he leaves to our imagination.)[113]

There is been much scholarly debate as to whether Virgil should even be considered as anything other than an allegorical figure in the *Comedy*, with many scholars reducing Virgil to an image of human reason. Even if we recognize that such a view is overly simplistic and denies Dante's poetic powers much of their flesh and blood intensity, a difficulty remains. While there is undeniable depth of character to Virgil (he is not one of Bunyan's two dimensional virtues), his role nonetheless is primarily as a representative of antiquity—its virtue, intellect, and culture.

The character of Nicolò may also have representational meaning, but he is clearly and primarily a real person, for whom the stakes are high in terms of his own understanding and moral progress. At the end of *Soldier*, Nicolò is not present when Alessandro dies and we do not know if Nicolò ever reaches his destination, geographical or otherwise, although he is cautioned by Alessandro not to lose his way.[114] Yet, one has grounds for greater hope for a good end for Nicolò than one has for Virgil. In some part this hope is merely situational. Nicolò is still alive and a young man, with many opportunities to choose and re-choose the right path. In other ways, this hope is grounded in the education that Alessandro provides during their time together. While Dante occasionally offers Virgil advice on the way forward, more often than not he depends on Virgil to show him the true path. For instance, in Canto XXI of *Inferno*, Dante is more aware of the danger that the demons of the Malbowges pose to them, but, when his warnings prove true, Virgil rescues him, carrying him on his back the way a parent would carry a child.[115] The *Comedy*, after all, is not about the moral development or salvation of Virgil.

The situation in *Soldier* is quite different. While Nicolò is the unintentional cause of Alessandro's journey by foot and his questions have the effect of prompting elements of Alessandro's reflections, it seems that this is where his guidance ends. Instead, it is Alessandro who guides Nicolò and by these means Alessandro is saved. While Virgil is sent to Dante because of Dante's great need, Alessandro first attempts to assist Nicolò and then joins him because Nicolò has been treated unjustly. Moreover, when Alessandro first clearly sees Nicolò, he is struck by the degree to which Nicolò reminds him of a son.[116] Literally and figuratively, Alessandro teaches Nicolò both how to see and how to walk.[117] Thus, Affleck notes that, "Alessandro is at once Dante, guided by the unseen but ever-present love of Ariane, and Virgil, guiding Nicolò through the night."[118]

In *Soldier*, the account of love is more obviously reciprocal than it appears to be in the *Divine Comedy*. Virgil is moved by the beauty of Beatrice to respond to Dante's need. He wills Dante's deliverance. However, his own plight is much more static. While he is able to will the good for others, there is no obvious way that another might reciprocate in turn. The sadness that Dante feels at Virgil's passing is in part because of what Dante has thereby lost, but this sadness is compounded when we consider that the loss of Dante's companion is eternal. Unless Dante returns to Inferno, he will not be reunited with Virgil, regardless of the love he has felt for him or the good that Virgil has done him. In this it seems that Dante's love and our love for

Virgil goes unfulfilled. While we benefit from his tutelage, Virgil himself is gone.

By contrast, Alessandro's remembrance of his life is not merely for the sake of his own soul, but for the sake of Nicolò. The effects of his efforts are almost immediate, for having begun the evening's walk asserting that aesthetics is stupid, with the help of Alessandro's glasses, Nicolò finally sees the moon, and, in the beauty of its detail, "for the first time in his life . . . was lifted entirely outside of himself and separated from his wants."[119] By means of Alessandro's glasses, Nicolò is given a sense of a whole that surpasses anything he might have previously imagined. Alessandro is both pilgrim and guide. In this he more properly reflects the full role of Dante who exists as both the character of the *Divine Comedy* and its author. As a character, Dante's work seems primarily for his own sake, and although he promises to pray for the souls he meets in Purgatory we do not have an image of his active love in this regard. This is presumably the work of Dante the author, who in telling us the story of his particular journey, seeks not only his own redemption, but that of those who read his poetry.

Inferno ends with Dante having made his way to the bottom of Hell seeking now to rediscover the light of the stars. He has recollected his corruption, knows it for what it is, and is prepared to hope for a better end. Showing Nicolò the path up the mountain requires that Alessandro become like Virgil and even Beatrice. In the *Comedy* Beatrice confronts Dante at the top of Purgatory, requiring him to finally, in light of the good he remembers and now knows, realize and confess his greatest faults. In *Soldier*, for the sake of himself and Nicolò, Alessandro does the same.

Almost immediately before leaving Nicolò and making his way to his death, Alessandro is brought to a final reflection again on *La Tempesta*. He advises Nicolò to go some day to Venice and view Giorgione's painting. In telling Nicolò why he should do this, Alessandro identifies red as the color of mortality. It is therefore connected to loss. However, Alessandro's main point is that red is "a most precious sign," representing both life and love.[120] It is on this point, that all of the passion and worth of life is somehow inseparable from mortality and loss, that Alessandro has been troubled, throughout his life.

> I think had Giorgione painted a sequel to *La Tempesta* . . . he would have reddened them and made parts of the landscape reverberate in crimson. All the gold and green, the lightning, the reflected sunlight, and the cool colors of the storm, make for a dream-like air. It's like . . . the separation of the body from its sensations prior to the separation of the senses from the soul before the soul's ascension. . . . In Dante, too, the colors are refined . . . until . . . one has risen through lighter and lighter blues, silvers, and golds, and what is left is merely white with a silver glare, far too bright to see or comprehend.[121]

This reference to Dante surely cannot be offhand. It is precisely at the climax of the *Comedy*, that all color is transmuted into the whiteness of the beatific vision that is Dante's true end and, thus, the end towards which all of our hopes are directed. Rather than suggesting that he is ready for this end, Alessandro instead reflects, "'What if you *didn't* want to go in that direction?'" What if, he asks, you wanted to descend?[122]

At this moment, Alessandro has dichotomized creation. The Neoplatonic idea of procession and return is replaced with a dualist vision, whereby either nature or the divine can be grasped, but neither can be held without the loss of the other. This is not Dante's view of course. In the conclusion of the *Comedy*, the pilgrim is confronted with two mysteries, one connected to the other. In the vision of the Trinity, there is a reconciliation of unity and division, the one and the many. Somehow, Dante sees the three persons as separate. This vision, granted by grace, defies both reason and words, as Dante confesses.

This is connected to the other mysterious revelation that Dante receives. In the simple light of the divine, every particular thing is present. Dante sees "Bound up with love together in one volume, what through the universe in leaves is scattered."[123] The diversity of human particularity, and all of nature, existing in its individual integrity, is here, by love, preserved and understood as part of the whole. Nothing has been lost, nor have individuals been dissolved in their return to their divine origin. Unity, without dissolution, is the form of the *reditus* in the *Divine Comedy*. Alessandro, even here, in referring to Dante, does not acknowledge the possibility of what the *Comedy* proclaims at its end. There remains another step before Alessandro can begin his return.

Alessandro's final recollection is of his beloved son Paolo. We learn, with Nicolò, that Paolo was killed in the Second World War, in Libya, in 1942. We learn that Alessandro and Ariane lived in denial of his death, until years after the war when they visited the battlefield where Paolo died. In recounting this final tragic story to Nicolò, Alessandro is brought to recognize the order and beauty in the world in which he has lived, and finally to express his love, hoping, rather than despairing, that he might be reunited with the ones he loves. He both comes to a new understanding and confesses it to Nicolo. He reflects, "'I'm awakening to the fact that I may not have chosen well. Perhaps my judgment is too much clouded by fear and too little enlivened by faith and trust.'"[124] He has feared his own death, believing that only his memory preserved those whom he loved, as if in pictures on a museum wall. The possibility of faith is enough to free Alessandro from his fear—the fear of losing forever those have died.

The last few pages of the novel depict Alessandro alone. His assumption was that the singing that he had heard periodically throughout his life "had come purely from memory."[125] Now, in the light of this newfound faith in even the possibility of the redemption of nature, he considers the possibility that this "aria" might be coming from the other side of the "gate." He is, in an instant, "washed clean of the petty shame and embarrassments of a lifetime."[126] He now understands that those emotions "are tests of grace and forgiveness." He has now, evidently, received both gifts. He has doubted the power of the universe, or of some agent in it, to bring about restoration. This has been joined to a similar doubt that any power exists great enough to forgive his failings. If there is the possibility of universal restoration, why might there not similarly be universal forgiveness?

Watching a flock of swallows being shot down by a hunter, Alessandro himself prepares to die, praying, now without fear that his death means the loss of those he has loved, "'Dear God, I beg of you only one thing. Let me join the ones I love. Carry me to them, unite me with them, let me see them, let me touch them.' And then it all ran together, like a song." It remains to other Helprin novels to more fully explore the nature of the restoration only pointed at here in the conclusion of *Soldier*.

NOTES

1. Henceforth, *Soldier*.
2. Richard Eder, "Radiance is in the Details," a review of *A Soldier of the Great War* by Mark Helprin, *Los Angeles Times*, 5 May 1995.
3. For a full account of the Augustinian use of memory as well as the Platonic and Neoplatonic roots of such a use, see Paige E. Hochschild, *Memory in Augustine's Theological Anthropology* (Oxford: Oxford University Press, 2012).
4. For the Augustinian foundation of this approach see R.D. Crouse, "*Recurrens in te unum*: The Pattern of St. Augustine's *Confessions*" in E. A. Livingstone, ed. *Studia Patristica*, vol. XIV (Berlin, 1976), 389–92.
5. A clear account of Dante's use of allegory remains Dorothy L. Sayers "Introduction" in *The Divine Comedy: Hell* (London: Penguin, 1949). Dante himself famously explains his allegorical method in his *Epistle to Cangrande*.
6. Dante, *Inferno*, III, 123.
7. Ibid., III, 18.
8. Dante, *Purgatory*, XVII, 105–12.
9. Helprin, *A Soldier of the Great War*, 444. See also Paul Alexander, "Big Books, Tall Tales," *New York Times*, April 28, 1991. On a similar note, see Neil Ferguson, "A Soldier of the Great War," a review of *A Soldier of the Great War* by Mark Helprin, February 2, 2014, last accessed 6 April 2014, http://bookinwithsunny.com/soldier-great-war/; Thomas Keneally, "War and Memory," a review of *A Soldier of the Great War* by Mark Helprin in *the New York Times*, May 5, 1991.
10. This is a theme that Helprin regularly takes up in his political commentary. For example, see Mark Helprin, "Contrivance," *Forbes*, September 4, 1999; and Helprin, "The Lessons of the Century," *American Heritage* 50 (February/March 1999).
11. For instance, see Shirley Granovetter, "Works of Empathy, Hope, Pretension and Sentimentality," a review of *A Soldier of the Great* War by Mark Helprin in *the Jerusalem Post*, December 10, 1992; Anthony Quinn, "Book Review: Memoirs of a Hero Stuck in the Mud," a review of *A Soldier of the Great War* by Mark Helprin in *the Independent*, May 2, 1992; Alan Wade, "A Soldier of the Great War: Book Reviews," a review of *A Soldier of the Great War* by Mark Helprin in *New Leader*, August 12, 1991. Alternatively, Hawley writes that Alessandro's life really doesn't amount to much and wonders why he would be the subject of any story. See

John C. Hawley, "A Roadside View of Life," a review of *A Soldier of the Great War* by Mark Helprin in *San Francisco Chronicle*, May 5, 1991.

12. *Nel mezzo del cammin di nostra vita.* Dante, *Inferno*, I, 1.

13. Helprin, *A Soldier of the Great War*, 20.

14. See Shirley Granovetter, "Works of Empathy and Hope, Pretension and Sentimentality."

15. Ibid., 2.

16. Ibid., 6.

17. Ibid., 9

18. Ibid., 47.

19. See McMahon, *The Medieval Meditative Ascent*, p. 70 ff. See also Hochschild, *Memory in Augustine's Theological Anthropology*, Chapter 7, and, R.D. Crouse, "Recurrens in te unum," 390–92.

20. Helprin, *A Soldier of the Great War*, 369.

21. Dante, *Paradiso*, XX, 43–48.

22. Ibid, XX, 67–72.

23. Dante, *Inferno*, III, 18.

24. Mark Helprin, e-mail to authors, May 22, 2013, and May 23, 2013.

25. Helprin, e-mail to authors, May 23, 2013.

26. L.S. Klepp, "A Soldier of the Great War," a review of *A Soldier of the Great War* by Mark Helprin. Other reviewers who recognize the allegorical nature of Orfeo include T.J. Binyon, "Walking Back to Happiness," a review of *A Soldier of the Great War* by Mark Helprin in *Times of London*, May 3, 1992.

27. Helprin, *A Soldier of the Great War*, 518.

28. Ibid., 124.

29. Ibid., 171.

30. Ibid., 418.

31. Ibid., 420.

32. Augustine, *Confessions*, VII.

33. Dante, *Inferno*, I, 82, 86–7.

34. See Stephen Amidon, "Beauty and the Beasts of War," *Financial Times*, April 18, 1992.

35. Book VII of Aristotle's *Nicomachean Ethics* (1145a–1152a) distinguishes between the various forms of moral defects, in accordance to the degree of deliberation involved in the act. In Canto XI of *Inferno*, Virgil and Dante pause while Virgil explains the structure, telling Dante that it is ordered according to the same logical principle. This principle is then explicitly assigned to the *Ethics*. See Dante, *Inferno*, XI, 79–84.

36. Dante, *Inferno*, V, 127–41.

37. Ibid., XX, 28–30.

38. Helprin, *A Soldier of the Great War*, 245.

39. Ibid.

40. Ibid., 90.

41. Ibid.

42. Genesis 29 tells the story of Jacob and the two daughters of Laban, Leah and Rachel. Jacob is conned by Laban into working for him for seven years to earn beautiful Rachel, only to have "weak-eyed" Leah substituted in the end. This necessitated another seven years of labor in order to win Rachel. The medievals turned this story into an allegory about the relationship between the active and the contemplative lives. This interpretive tradition has its roots in Augustine. See *Contra Faustum*, XXII, 52.

43. Dante, *Purgatory*, XXVII, 97–108.

44. Helprin, *A Soldier of the Great War*, 142–43.

45. Ibid., 200.

46. Ibid., 210,

47. Ibid., 296.

48. Ibid., 287–88.

49. Ibid., 288.

50. Ibid., 262.

51. Dante, *Inferno*, VIII–IX.

52. Helprin, *A Soldier of the Great War*, 310.
53. Ibid., 308.
54. Ibid., 722.
55. Ibid., 767.
56. Dante, *Purgatorio*, XXXI, 127–32.
57. Ibid.
58. Helprin, *A Soldier of the Great War*, 313.
59. Ibid., 345.
60. Ibid., 373.
61. Ibid., 391.
62. Ibid., 396.
63. Ibid., 443.
64. Ibid., 436,
65. Dante, *Inferno*, XXXII–XXXIII.
66. Helprin, *A Soldier of the Great War*, 444.
67. Ibid., 427.
68. Ibid., 400.
69. Ibid., 426.
70. Ibid., 411.
71. Ibid., 486.
72. Dante, *La Vita Nuova*, translated by A.S. Kline, 2001, II, last accessed 6 April 2014, http://www.poetryintranslation.com/PITBR/Italian/TheNewLifeI.htm#_Toc88709640.
73. Dante, *Inferno*, II, 52–75.
74. Dante, *Paradiso*, XXXI, 73–78.
75. Helprin, *A Soldier of the Great War*, 146.
76. Ibid., 158.
77. See Hankey, "Conversion," where he demonstrates in his treatment of Jane Austen's novels that a similar elevation of the elements of ordinary human life are indicative of a particularly modern (secular) perspective, that nevertheless might be accompanied by a transcendent or contemplative *telos*.
78. Helprin, *A Soldier of the Great War*, 553.
79. Ibid., 777.
80. E-mail, Mark Helprin to Keith Morgan, May 20, 2013.
81. Helprin, *A Soldier of the Great War*, 457.
82. Ibid., 570.
83. Ibid., 722.
84. Ibid., 723.
85. Ibid., 732.
86. Ibid., 750.
87. Ibid., 762.
88. Ibid., 558.
89. Ibid., 558.
90. Ibid., 586.
91. Ibid., 5.
92. On Dante's resemblance to Orpheus, see Robert Hollander, "Tragedy in Dante's 'Comedy,'" 253. That Dante refers to Virgil finally as his father when he discovers that he is no longer with him indicates something essential about Dante's recognition of the temptation of all humans to remain in a state of childhood. See Christopher Ryan, "Free Will in Theory and Practice," 102.
93. Helprin, *A Soldier of the Great War*, 588.
94. Ibid., 97.
95. Eder notes that Alessandro's "Edenic Joy [is] replaced by a joy shaped out of pain." Eder, "Radiance is in the Details."
96. Helprin, *A Soldier of the Great War*, 98.
97. Ibid., 799.
98. Ibid., 301.

99. Ibid., 513.

100. Ibid., 816.

101. Ibid., 421.

102. Ibid., 810.

103. Ibid., 61.

104. Ibid., 62.

105. Ibid., 59.

106. Ibid., 846.

107. Ibid., 578.

108. Ibid., 71.

109. Ibid., 28.

110. For example, see Robert Hollander, "Dante's Virgil: A Light that Failed," *Lectura Dantis* (1989) 4, 3–9; Robert Hollander, "Tragedy in Dante's Comedy," *Sewanee Review*, 91:2 (Spring 1983), 250–60. Alternatively there are those who believe Virgil's ultimate placement is an open question. See Allan Mowbray, "Two Dantes: Christian versus Humanist," *MLN* (January 1992) 107:1, 18–35.

111. For example Dante, *Inferno*, I, 85; XXIII, 51, 148.

112. Dante, *Inferno*, I, 42.

113. Helprin, e-mail to authors, 8 March 2014.

114. Helprin, *A Soldier of the Great War*, 853.

115. Dante, *Inferno*, XXI, 27; XXIII, 12–17, 37–39.

116. Helprin, *A Soldier of the Great War*, 15.

117. Ibid., 49, 56.

118. John Affleck, "Birds of a Feather: The Ancient Mariner Archetype in Mark Helprin's 'A Dove of the East,' and *A Soldier of the Great War*," M.L.A. Thesis, Auburn University, 1996.

119. Mark Helprin, *A Soldier of the Great War*, 60.

120. Ibid., 831

121. Ibid., 832–33.

122. Ibid., 833.

123. Dante, *Paradiso*, XXXIII, 85–87.

124. Helprin, *A Soldier of the Great War*, 850.

125. Ibid., 853.

126. Ibid., 856.

Chapter Two

The Habit of Love

In terms of their vice, very little distinguishes the souls of Dante's *Purgatorio* from those of *Inferno*. Individuals in both realms committed the same types of crimes during their mortal lives and there is a remarkable similarity in the physical depictions of both groups. While souls in Inferno are blown about by hot winds or endure rain made of fire, those in Purgatory wear cloaks of lead or have their eyelids sewn shut with wire. The only significant difference between the two groups is that those in Purgatory have faith and hope that the divine will overcome their deficiencies such that they might be reconciled to God. That their hope is fulfilled is evident in their placement in Purgatory; all who reside on these terraces will inevitably make their way to Paradiso. The vice represented in Inferno reveals an inherent truth about human nature. All humans, even those who seek and will the good, will fall into temptation and vice. In other words, the finitude of our natures is in itself incapable of being reconciled to the infinite. Recognizing this insufficiency and seeking divine help is how one achieves Purgatory. Grace, Dante argues, is the sole means of human justification. Those in Inferno have despaired of the possibility of grace.

Accepting divine love, however, does not erase the activity of one's life. All individuals, Dante argues, participate to a lesser or fuller degree, in vice. Having lived in the finite world, all people are habituated to it. It is the world in which we live and its rules and methods are ingrained in our natures, for, regardless of our virtue, everyone eventually dies. Our finite lives must be transformed so that reconciliation with the infinite is possible. As in Inferno, this is not the imposition of some external order or judgment on individuals, but rather the recognition of the autonomy and integrity of individual choice. Just as they were granted the freedom to follow their desires while mortal, these individuals must habituate themselves to the new lives they have chosen. The souls in Purgatory are tasked with the work of properly ordering their desires, so that the habits of the natural world might be overcome by the virtues of the infinite.

In Purgatory, the will, in the form of love, is progressively corrected by the acquisition of habit, even as the mind is illuminated. Each of the possible errors in love is treated in order. Love that is directed at the wrong object, love that is lacking in strength, and love that is disordered in terms of primary and secondary objects are all the subjects of purgation. Finally, at the top of Mount Purgatory, Dante's love has been properly reordered and Virgil declares that the pilgrim's desires can now guide him reliably and he is thereby free to follow his own will:

> I have brought you here with intellect and skill
> From now on take your pleasure as your guide.
> You are free of the steep way, free of the narrow.
>
> No longer wait for word or sign from me.
> Your will is free, upright, and sound.
> Not to act as it chooses is unworthy:
> Over yourself I crown and miter you. [1]

All of Helprin's novels have a purgatorial element. Notably, in the world of Helprin's fiction, the activity of purgation takes place in the natural world. Hence, in *Soldier*, the habits of Alessandro's vice are purged by means of the physical climb up the hill and the psychological struggle involved in the confession of his life. Similarly in *Winter's Tale*, Peter Lake, who falls into despair when Beverly dies, is returned to New York and given the opportunity to recollect his love almost 100 years later before he can be reconciled in the infinite. In *Freddy and Fredericka*, the titular characters are given a similar opportunity when they are parachuted into New Jersey, clothed with little more than rabbit fur and snakeskin. In each of these dramas Helprin heightens the significance of an individual's mortal life. In this life and this world, Helprin suggests, divine grace is recognized and it is here that one begins, at least, the hard work of preparing oneself for reconciliation with God. Just as the souls in Dante's *Purgatorio* are assisted and strengthened in their climb by means of grace, Helprin's characters recognize the nature of the divine in the things and, particularly, in the people that they love, and are similarly strengthened. In *Purgatorio*, Dante affirms the integrity of individual souls who have ordered their loves such that they might be made one with God. By translating this work to the earthly realm, Helprin indicates the further degree to which he understands the integrity of the particular as a vehicle to reconciliation with the divine.

Like Dante, who moves from Inferno to Purgatory, the two protagonists in *In Sunlight and in Shadow*, Harry and Catherine, are depicted as having gone through an Inferno, and then choosing love. [2] The work of the novel lies in their habituation to the good as the love that they have for each other directs them towards it. *Sunlight* unites several of the themes present it Helprin's other novels. It concerns a soldier but moves from the context of World War I to a post-World War II setting, with several extended recollections of moments in the war itself. The meditation upon the city of New York, at the heart of *Winter's Tale*, is taken up here as well, except the romantic, generation shifting city of that novel is here presented in a near contemporary reality, stripped of fantastic elements. The nature of Jewish identity, prominent in Helprin's first novel, *Refiner's Fire*, is, in *Sunlight*, both peripheral and essential to the story.

The romantic essence of all of Helprin's novels is again present, this time in the love story of Harry and Catherine. The two epigrams with which Helprin prefaces the novel, one from Dante and one from Lucretius, make clear that love is his theme. Catherine Hale is a classic northeastern blue blood—Episcopalian, wealthy, educated at Bryn Mawr—her life has been seemingly idyllic and shielded from all suffering. However, we come to learn that she has been, since the age of thirteen, the victim of Victor Morrow, several years older and the scion of another prominent family. What we understand to be rape has formed the foundation of a twisted relationship that has brought Catherine to the brink of marriage, which is described even by Catherine as a kind of inevitable outcome.

Harry Copeland is a New York Jew, whose father has made his success in the leather trade. The first page of the novel raises the issue of discrimination and identifies the kind of institutions in the protestant establishment, from Harvard to Pimlico, that were open to those "Jewish . . . tailors, wholesalers, rabbis, and doctors" who were able to assimilate themselves, by means of things so simple as the adoption of a common name. We also learn, within the first three paragraphs, that Harry is a veteran of World War II.

The novel unfolds along two main story lines, each of which is supported by a sub-plot. The romantic story is that of Harry and Catherine and their movement towards reconciling their different backgrounds and aspirations. The dramatic complement to this love story is the threat posed to the family business that Harry has inherited by a vicious gangster. By way of context, we are given insight to Harry's experiences in the War that have shaped his character. Parallel to this is the struggle experienced by Catherine against first the injustice suffered at the hands of Victor and the subsequent injustice suffered as an actress at the hands of vicious newspaper critics bought off by Victor in retribution for Catherine leaving him for Harry.

Unlike Dante's journey, where he progresses but Virgil is left behind, and Beatrice is already perfected, Harry and Catherine travel through Purgatory together. Their journey is reciprocal, as each assists and mediates the progress of the other. Moreover, although it seems, not having met each other, that they are alone during the initial trials of their lives, this is an illusion. Through the course of the novel, they realize that they have always known each other and their love is present even as they journey individually through Hell. In this, both Catherine and Harry act like Beatrice, who, while not present, initiates Dante's movement through Inferno and remains his motivation. However, Catherine and Harry also reciprocally assist in the moral and intellectual progression of each other. In this they are shown as truly equal to one another, a point which highlights the degree to which their freedom with respect to the other is retained. Neither Catherine nor Harry is ever overcome by the other in the way that Beatrice's beauty overcomes Dante throughout *Paradiso*.

In Purgatory, one prepares for reconciliation with the divine in its fullness. Part of this work, Dante suggests, requires one to broaden one's particular position so that the perspective one had in one's mortal life is sublated—taken up insofar as it is true, but additionally reconciled with other positions that together afford a fuller truth. The image of Rachel and Leah in Purgatory suggests the dependency of opposing virtues that marks a city of virtue. It is not merely that the active life is subordinate to the contemplative life, but as the allegorical interpretation of the story suggests, the higher life cannot be engaged without the preparation acquired through the active life.

The religious progression of Harry and Catherine throughout *Sunlight* is instructive as to the account of the universal that Helprin suggests. At the start of the novel, Catherine believes she is Christian and is described in terms that indicate her faith in a transcendent end. She falls in love with Harry, who is a Jew, and discovers that she herself is a Jew as well. She then experiences the weight of the finite order, taking up, it seems, the historical experience of the Jewish people in her own life. Correspondingly, Harry at first understands his end in relation only to the natural world. By means of his relationship with Catherine, however, he is brought to hope for a transcendent end. In the marriage of Harry and Catherine, and the reconciliation shown therein between Judaism and Christianity, Helprin suggests that the divine takes up and incorporates the particularity of all perspectives, insofar as they have their basis in the truth. While Catherine's Jewish heritage becomes important for her progress within the book, on another level it is less significant, not because the Jewish tradition is of less significance, but because by the argument of the book, the Jewish and Christian traditions are reconciled within and as part of the absolute itself. One sees something of this argument in Harry's responses to the interrogation concerning their proposed marriage posed by Billy Hale, Catherine's father. In his questions, Billy indicates theoretical as well as practical difficulties in a marriage of Judaism and Christianity. While acknowledging the truth of what Billy suggests, Harry responds that in these matters God will take care of the details. On the specific limitations of any particular faith, Harry explains, "'[God's] commandments are fundamental and of the heart and soul, even if man has drawn them out into orthodoxies of his own making in a forest of dry reeds. Sometimes a storm rises and flattens the reeds to open the world to the sky.'"[3] Harry's point seems clear—the doctrine and dogmas of any particular faith are only partial views of the whole. Given that, despite all of the obstacles that should have precluded his falling in love with Catherine, including their religious and socioeconomic differences, Harry *has* fallen in love with Catherine. Harry can only trust that it is providential, intended by God, and in God's hands.

Interestingly, in *Soldier*, neither of the relationships in which a Christian and Jew are paired work out. As discussed, Alessandro loses Lia when her brother dies, while Luciana, Alessandro's sister, is left heartbroken when her fiancée, Rafi, is killed in the war. Although both Alessandro and Luciana eventually fall in love with others and have presumably happy marriages, the philosophical perspective of *Soldier* is much narrower, and mirrors the narrowed perspective of all of those in Inferno.

In the course of *Sunlight* Catherine and Harry each traverse the path of the other's faith. In part, this occurs as a way of habituating them to the whole. Importantly, it is not our argument that these religious positions are overturned in Catherine and Harry's marriage. Just as in a marriage, where both partners are separate and autonomous individuals while, at the same time, united as one, each of these religious positions retains its integrity, and recognizes the other as part of the whole. Helprin suggests that nothing is taken away from either perspective. Instead, each is maintained and known as integral to the other.[4] By means of these images, Helprin further indicates that reconciliation with the whole does not destroy or subsume the particular, as feared by Alessandro, but allows the particular, even particular forms of faith, to exist.

One of the recurring images in *Sunlight* is that of a young child on a swing. While she is just a child, Catherine sees a young boy swinging on a rope under the El. Although she does not know it, the boy she sees is Harry. Dante falls in love with Beatrice when he sees her for the first time when they are children and before he even knows her, and so Catherine falls in love with this young boy. The image of a young boy swinging up and then back down—towards her and away—stays with her throughout her life and her love for him remains true. Back from the war, and before he has met Catherine, Harry sees a corresponding image—a young girl being pushed on a swing, ascending towards the sun, and then returning to her mother. Through these images, Helprin indicates something of the end towards which his characters work. In both Catherine's and Harry's visions the child is on the swing by him or herself ascending towards the sun, and descending into the shadows but back towards someone who loves him or her. At the end of the novel Harry dies in a gunfight that he initiates against the mobsters who are driving him out of business, and Catherine must live the rest of her life without him. Whatever Harry and Catherine face, they face it separately. The image of the swinging child, however, suggests the possibility that in their ascent to the divine they need not relinquish their particular loves—the child swings away and returns. Correspondingly, Dante is reunited with Beatrice in Purgatory and we understand that in his return to his earthly life, their love for one another will abide.

Both Dante and Helprin suggest that in being reconciled to the universal and objective good, the particular and subjective are maintained. It is thus not surprising that throughout *Purgatorio* Dante emphasizes human freedom. At the base of the mountain, Virgil and Dante are met by Cato the younger, a Roman republican who kills himself rather than be ruled by Caesar. Seeking to convince Cato that they ought to be admitted to Purgatory, Vigil indicates that Dante seeks liberty.[5] Sordello later explains that, with the exception of those in Ante-Purgatory, the people in Purgatory each individually determine which terraces they are on and how long they spend there.[6] Moreover, the central part of *Purgatorio* is a meditation on the relationship of love to freedom of will. In all of this, Dante indicates that seeking to reconcile oneself to the divine is essentially a quest for freedom.

In *Sunlight*, Helprin presents Catherine and Harry as subjects of external forces initially beyond their control. For Catherine, this is expressed through her rape by Victor and her resulting sense of inevitability as she is marched forward towards marriage to him. For Harry, the vast impersonal forces, plus the simple blind contingency of war that were the difference between life and death, suggest a world in which individual choice is inconsequential. Later, the dilemma facing Copeland Leather as a result of the protection racket seems insolvable. Yet, the entire center of the novel is about the possibility and power of love, which, by definition, requires free choice. Both Catherine and Harry are given explicit moral choices that demonstrate the existence and worth of human freedom. Harry chooses to pursue Catherine, even though he knows she is Christian, wealthy, and already engaged. Catherine pre-empts Harry's plan to disrupt her engagement party by choosing, in a dramatic fashion, to end her relationship with Victor. Harry is presented with several clear alternatives to going to war against the gangster Verderamé, but after weighing all of the moral elements involved, chooses to risk his life instead. Catherine further exercises her free will, insisting that she is unwilling to be passive and will actively stand beside Harry in his struggle. By the end of the novel, both Harry and Catherine have ordered their loves toward true freedom.

As is the case in Helprin's other novels, the existentialist perspective on the universe as an unintelligible and even absurd arena that renders moral systems meaningless is rejected. Instead, Helprin asserts first that eternal principles exist, and second that human beings are called to make consequential moral decisions in relation to those principles. As we will discuss in our concluding chapter, Helprin's *Freddy and Fredericka* extends this theological and ethical position to the political realm, in pursuing the potential for equally affirming human freedom and, at the same time, eternal, transcendent principles.

OUT OF INFERNO

Having travelled with Virgil through Inferno and become conscious of the corrupt nature of his soul, Dante is eager to pass beyond it:

> The Guide and I into that hidden road
> Now entered, to return to the bright world;
> And without care of having any rest
> We mounted up, he first and I the second,
> Till I beheld through a round aperture
> Some of the beauteous things that Heaven doth bear;
> Thence we came forth to rebehold the stars. [7]

Whatever the temptation that has prevented Dante from climbing the mountain, and which would cause him to choose the dark forest, he is now sufficiently conscious of himself and the nature of vice that he readily chooses light. Harry and Catherine take similar journeys through passages wherein they are tempted to acquiesce to vice and corruption but choose love instead.

Harry returns to New York at the end of the war, seeking to rest and resume his life. While at war, Harry witnesses the finitude of the natural order in its full actualization:

> This pointless and tragical fugue had rolled through history to the beginning. The pace may have varied, but the harvest was steady over time, its momentum increasing and undiminished. It moved evenly, treated all passions equally, and was as cold and splendid as the waves in winter. What force, he wondered, could paint such a canvas . . . while never failing to, again and again, to take sons from mothers, husbands from wives, and fathers from children? [8]

In witnessing the destruction and death caused by war, Harry sees the nature of mortality in its sharpest depiction. While all elements of the material order necessarily succumb to change and dissolution, in war the frailty of the human condition is writ large. Recognizing that this is the condition of one's life, one might be tempted to concede that this is all there is, and fall into despair or seek to use this knowledge to the better fulfillment of one's temporal desires. Helprin provides us with an image of the latter in character of Pearly Soames in *Winter's Tale*. Soames is certain that all goods are scarce and finite, including love. [9] As a result, he believes that all that exists might be used to serve his temporal desires, even the lives of others. If there is nothing of absolute value and thus no way to measure the particular worth of individual goods, one's own perceived good takes precedence.

While only a small part of *Sunlight* describes Harry's wartime experience, we are given sufficient detail to know that, like Alessandro in *Soldier*, Harry's experience might have easily led him to despair. The death of Townsend Coombs, Harry's own near death, and then finally the description of Harry holding his dying friend Hemphill are all potential moments when Harry could succumb to Inferno.[10] Despite his experiences of pain and loss, Harry chooses love. Dante is convinced by Virgil to descend into Inferno for the sake of Beatrice.[11] Harry describes his efforts in the war as having their purpose and end in Catherine: "The war effort was for you. We were fighting for you."[12] That Harry did not know Catherine during the war is, in some way, irrelevant. He recognizes temptation, vice, and finitude, and fights against them for the sake of beauty and the consummation of all Harry loves and will love. By means of his faith and hope in beauty, Harry makes his way through Inferno to ascend Purgatory.

Helprin's point is threefold. First and most broadly, he indicates that beauty is the source of one's desire and activity, for beauty is "both what creates love and what love creates."[13] In all of Helprin's novels, the beautiful is a mediating force that has the capacity to draw characters to their redemption. In *Soldier*, Alessandro is moved by the artwork he sees, and, in *Winter's Tale*, Peter Lake is moved by the beauty of a portrait of his beloved, Beverly. In this, Helprin suggests, as Plato and Dante have before him, that the beautiful and the good are intrinsically linked, and that the good might be the most beautiful thing of all. Even Pearly Soames from *Winter's Tale* is motivated to action because of the beauty of color and Peter Lake recognizes this desire as a desire for the light of heaven. Throughout *Purgatorio*, works of art precipitate the proper activity of souls. For example, on the terrace of the proud, individuals are moved by sculpted images of pride and humility, so artfully carved that, "Nature's self, had there been put to shame."[14]

Second, it is not merely a love of abstract beauty that Helprin suggests properly motivates our activity. More specifically, it is the recognition of beauty in another person and the hope that one's love will be reciprocated that is the most effective motivator. When, during the war, Harry believes he is dying, Helprin tell us that "the only regret that stayed . . . was that he had yet to love or be loved as he had always hoped. All the magical lights, airy and bright, the floating orbs, the effulgent stars, were lonely things and would not suffice."[15] Harry maintains hope throughout the war that his love for beauty will be reciprocated and consummated. At the start of the novel, and before his love and understanding of the good are mediated by his love for Catherine, Harry is not certain as to how this might occur.

Finally, Harry's love of beauty and his more particular love and desire for Catherine, reflect his further desire and hope for the continuation of these goods into the future. Harry indicates that his love of the beauty of women is, in part, caused by his recognition that women are the proximate source of life. In defense of the courtly love tradition, wherein women are venerated and honored, Harry, echoing Alessandro from *Soldier*, tells Catherine: "'the more I suffered, and the more I saw . . . the more I knew that women are the embodiment of love and the hope of all time. . . . This is what I learned and managed to bring with me out of hell. . . . Love of God, love of a woman, love of a child—what else is there?'" [16] The beauty that is represented by women for Harry is a beauty that speaks to all future existence and activity; it represents the possibility of eternal life. Helprin underlines this point dramatically in the novel when, at the end, even though Harry has died, Catherine is pregnant with his child. Harry indicates that the cause of his action and the means by which he escapes Inferno is beauty generally and the beauty of women more specifically.

Even further, however, we understand that it is his love for a particular woman that compels him. While Harry may not yet have met Catherine, from *Winter's Tale*, we discover that a linear understanding of time is not the only option, and Harry tells us that regardless of when he met Catherine, he has always loved her. [17] To ensure that we do not miss this point, Catherine recognizes at the end of the novel, after Harry's death, that he was the boy swinging from the El who she fell in love with when she was a young girl. Moreover, at the very beginning of their relationship we are told of a similar memory that Harry has, one that he now believes is about Catherine, although he is not sure how or why. [18] Harry and Catherine's love exists before they are aware of it and extends into the future even after Harry has died. As such, we are given a sense of love as eternal, restricted by neither place nor time. Moreover, insofar as one reflects on and understands the infinite nature of the love that is born for others, these particular loves then mediate a fuller understanding and love of the universal. Hence, although Harry is most particularly motivated by Catherine, at the very end of the novel, having been mediated by Catherine's love, he risks his life and the continuation of their earthly love for the sake of justice and presumably the good itself. While the efficient cause of Dante's movement is his love for Beatrice, we know that Beatrice was summoned and sent by Mary, and ultimately, the divine itself. Dante follows Beatrice through Paradiso, but, at a certain point, he is aware that his love of God surpasses his love for her, and that this is the proper ordering of things. [19] By means of his continued love of beauty and his hope that his desire will be satisfied, Harry leaves Inferno and enters into the light of Purgatorio.

In contrast to the explicit narrative of the *Divine Comedy*, Catherine makes a similar journey. While Beatrice is already perfected by the time

Dante reaches her, and serves as the object for his adoration, Catherine and Harry make their journeys together. Indeed, in many ways, Catherine is still very much travelling through Inferno as the novel begins and requires Harry's explicit presence to ascend to Purgatory. When Harry first meets Catherine, she is already in a relationship and on the verge of announcing her engagement to Victor. Almost twenty years junior to Victor, Catherine reveals to Harry that he raped her when she was thirteen. Despite the abusive nature of their relationship, she has persisted in it and is uncertain as to whether she should or could break it off. On the day that she and Harry meet, Catherine is supposed to be meeting Victor, who is going to pick her up on his yacht. He does not show up and, on the ferry ride home, Catherine takes the opportunity to meet Harry. Reminded of the yacht later, Catherine "could not banish [it] . . . from her mind. . . . Haunting, seductive, easy, it called for many kinds of surrender, each comfortable and tragic. Were she to have rowed out, she would have been lost to this. She would have regretted and grieved for the rest of her life. She had come that close, and would have disappeared had it not been for the winds and tides."[20] Catherine is tempted to remain in her relationship with Victor—it is expected of her, and her marriage would ensure a life of luxury and ease. Nonetheless, it would be a marriage without love, born of violence, and would end in resentment and hatred. To choose Victor over Harry means choosing finite comfort and ease over and against the infinite nature of love.

Dante is brought out of his dark woods by means of Beatrice; and Catherine rejects Victor because of Harry. Resigned to marry Victor, Catherine attends what is supposed to be her engagement party, and is surprised to see Harry, who has snuck in, planning somehow to convince her to be with him. Harry, however, needs to do nothing for the mere sight of him forces Catherine to reconsider her choice, and she realizes that with only one life, choosing love over hatred is all important.[21] However much Harry is motivated by a love of the beauty represented in women, in the movement of Catherine, Helprin suggests that this is particular to Harry and that others, like Catherine, will be moved by love for that which is particularly beautiful to them.

Like the pilgrim Dante, Harry and Catherine ascend from Inferno to Purgatory by means of their love. While Catherine has perhaps lacked courage, that she chooses Harry is not surprising, for, as Harry discovers, her motives have always been similar to his. Although Catherine chooses a career in the theatre because she believes that the idealized world represented there is better than reality, she nonetheless recognizes that in the context of eternity, there is a production greater than any: "What she saw was not random . . . for the threads of beauty and meaning that ran through it shone brightly in the dark, the whole a work greater than art. . . . This she knew because she had seen it and felt it since infancy, and would not be turned away from her faith and trust even by all the war and suffering in the world, even were the suffering her own."[22] By means of the beauty that she perceives in the world, Catherine maintains faith that she will find redemption.

As a result, Catherine is able to evoke in the song she sings at the start of the play she is in the very nature of the end that she seeks. In her singing, Harry recognizes a force that "embrace[s] seemingly all things. Her voice summoned and fused images in their thousands: memories, colors, views, other songs, fading light, blooming trees swaying in the wind. It united past, present and future, limning and lighting faces and souls, their expressions carried forth over time, holding them as long as it could."[23] Catherine's faith, like that of Harry's, is made evident in her life and love.

Like all people, neither Catherine nor Harry is a paradigm of virtue. During the war, Harry participates in the fallenness of the earthly order, deceiving and killing his enemies. When he comes home, he lacks any immediate will to participate fully in his father's business even though it is the last remnant, excluding Harry himself, of his father's life. Catherine lacks self-consciousness and goes along with a relationship rooted in violence, because it is expected of her and holds the promise of the continuation of material wealth. Despite their failings, neither Harry nor Catherine is lost to Inferno because both are motivated by hope and love. Their tale is thus one of Purgatory rather than Hell.

WORKING THROUGH PURGATORY

Harry's father dies while Harry is still at war, and when Harry comes home he discovers that his father had arranged to have most of his possessions already disposed of: "Even the curtains had been removed, and the walls were painted freshly white. . . . His father had had warning and enough time to dispose of his clothes, the contents of drawers, and the things that would be difficult for his son to either throw away or keep. The message was clear: start over and anew."[24] The image is suggestive of the "clean slate" that individuals arriving in Purgatory achieve. Whatever the crimes of their past, the penalties have been absorbed by the divine, and they are granted a kind of freedom in the face of their future joy. However, in neither instance is this image simple or complete, for Harry still has his father's business and the heritage of his family to consider, while the souls in Purgatory have the habits they accrued in their lifetime to perfect or correct.

By working to properly order their loves, the souls of Purgatory achieve actual freedom. Freedom requires that the ends that are sought be truly recognized and consciously chosen. In other words, individuals cannot truly *choose* if they do not understand the nature of the options presented to them. Moreover, even if the nature of a choice is understood, but one's will is somehow forced, the action is not fully free. As we know, Dante was familiar with Aristotle's *Nicomachean Ethics*.[25] In that text, Aristotle explains that both knowledge and autonomy are required for an act to be a true moral choice.[26] We are to understand that the individuals on Mount Purgatory have recognized at least something of the divine nature and they have freely chosen that end as their own. The work of Purgatory has the effect of furthering their understanding of the good, so that the end that they are directing themselves to is clear. Secondly, they work to align their desires so that their ultimate choice is not impeded by habits of a former life wherein lesser desires were allowed to overtake the desire for the good itself.

In *Sunlight*, Helprin highlights the role that particularity has in the movement to the good. Dante argues that freedom requires the proper ordering of one's love. Helprin agrees, but emphasizes a further point. One does not relinquish one's particular beliefs or loves in the movement up Purgatory, but instead sees how they are part of the universal whole. Hence, the particular choices we make in our finite lives are seen as redeemed and our freedom, while made complete only by the infinite, is shown as incorporating the choices made while our freedom was only partially realized.

Discovering and choosing love, both Catherine and Harry enter a kind of Purgatory. They each must climb the mountain, habituating themselves to the fullness of divine love so that, when it is fully manifest to them, they are able to understand and will it. Harry and Catherine mediate one another's journey, both practically and theoretically. Practically, they are the objects of each other's affections and are the efficient cause of each other's activity. Theoretically, however, both Catherine and Harry must reconcile their limited understanding of the finite and the infinite with that of the other, thereby broadening their understanding of the whole.[27]

In the terms of the novel, Catherine, a Christian, must also realize that she is a Jew, while Harry, a Jew, is brought to understand how divine grace overcomes the limits of the natural world. He is brought to what appears, at least, as a Christian position. In this movement, neither Catherine nor Harry forsakes their earlier understanding. Instead, their original position is maintained, and more fully realized and understood by the mediating influence of the other. By these images, Helprin indicates something of the nature of love, both in its particular and universal manifestations. Harry and Catherine come from particular faith traditions, and at first it seems that this will result in divisiveness and even loss. However, as we shall see, in reconciling themselves to one another, neither faith is lost, but both are maintained and strengthened. Helprin thereby suggests that the nature of love is such that it incorporates the full integrity of the other into a coherent unity. We will consider Catherine and Harry's progressions separately and then in relation to each other.

Catherine's Ascent

Catherine has been largely untouched by the Second World War. During the war, as a student at Bryn Mawr, her war efforts were confined to giving blood and rolling bandages. No one in her immediate family, it seems, was engaged in the war, and so they suffered no immediate losses. As a result, at the start of the novel, Catherine lacks any awareness of why world events of the most recent past could have any bearing on her. Perhaps, most important-ly, although Catherine is aware of the horrendous suffering of the Jews before and during the war, she considers theirs to be a plight of a different people, in a different place. While undoubtedly she is moved by the terrible pictures she saw and the accounts of injustice she heard about, Catherine's own life has been so different that her response is fundamentally distant. Catherine has not recognized the essence her imperfect human nature and does not see in the suffering of others her own nature and death. Catherine's ascent requires that she be made self-conscious of her finitude and the inevi-table pain associated with it, and, nonetheless, endure in the hope of its eventual sublation.

Prior to meeting Harry, Catherine easily perceives the nature of God's grace and does not doubt the possibility of her ultimate reconciliation with the divine. Aside from her relationship with Victor, which she has never fully considered and lacks any real consciousness of, her life is relatively easy and luxurious. Her experience of the world has been one of beauty and love, and, as a result, she believes that "all souls . . . blinded and blown into the air like dust and tumbling without gravity, can nonetheless find their bearings and rise as intended into the light."[28] Not having really experienced suffering and real loss, Catherine cannot imagine that a person might be moved to despair such that she no longer seeks the good. Catherine is troubled that, despite her great talent, she does not get the lead in the play, nor, in the course of its plot, does she get the man.[29] That such an injustice could occur, particularly within the idealized world of a play, seems absurd to Catherine.

Catherine's life offers a vision of Christianity allegorically and broadly represented. In the Christian account, one has faith in an infinite goodness and that faith is rewarded. One need merely ask, and the challenges of the finite world are, ultimately, overcome. This, however, is only a partial per-spective, for the end that Catherine wills is of an infinite nature and transcends the finite comforts that she currently enjoys. Moreover, her recon-ciliation with the divine requires, first, the sacrifice of the finite, so that it might be regained in a perfected form. Achieving the eternal life offered in Christianity requires one's death in and to the finite world. Readers of the *Divine Comedy*, might, like Catherine, be tempted to overlook that Dante's affirmation of faith does not override the strife and suffering that he has and will experience as part of his natural life. Having passed through the suffering in Inferno, readers might think that the cheerful movement of Purgatory or the joyous singing of Paradiso represents, for Dante, the daily lives of the faithful. As such, readers might dismiss Dante as either smug or naïve, for he would not seem to recognize the real sorrow and struggle most individuals face daily, faithful or not.

Dante, however, was not naïve about the challenges individuals face. To be so, he would have to be willfully blind to the circumstances of his own life. The *Divine Comedy* was written while he was in exile from his beloved Florence and he continued in exile for the rest of his life. Importantly, the temptation to vice that the souls of Inferno lose themselves to has been fully experienced by most if not all the people in the other parts of the *Comedy*. Although the people in Purgatory happily submit to the habituation of virtue, the events they endure on Mount Purgatory are real. That these individuals experience the movement of time is an indication that the physical and psychological states they experience correspond, at least roughly, with these same pressures in the natural order. Moreover, everyone we meet in the *Divine Comedy*, aside from Dante, has died. They have known the inevitable pain that all experience when the limitations of their physical existences are made manifest. In his final moments, Christ reveals his full humanity, asking, "My God, my God. Why hast thou forsaken me?"[30]

The redemption of the finite world requires that it be fully known and only subsequently overcome. Most of the souls in the *Divine Comedy* do not focus on the experience of their deaths. Those in Inferno are too caught up in the nature of their vice, while in Purgatory and Paradiso they are focused on their infinite end. We need only remember Ugolino's terrible description of his and his children's starvation, however, to realize that the physical plight of all these characters has been such that they have known the real limits of nature. Although a recognition and incorporation of the constraints of the finite world are part of the Christian argument, Catherine does not reflect on the limitations of her natural existence until she discovers that she is Jewish.

In Catherine's transformation from Christianity to Judaism, Helprin suggests that the emphasis of the Jewish religion on justice and redemption within the finite order highlights an essential truth about which Catherine has been oblivious. From the time of the prophets forward, the hope of the people of Israel has been for the coming of the Messiah that would bring restoration to the kingdom. From the destruction of the second temple to the persecutions and pogroms of medieval Europe (and beyond), to the Holocaust and the struggles of the state of Israel, the history of the Jews has entailed ceaseless aspiration and struggle for justice on earth. As a faith tradition that historically understands its redemption as promised in the finite and earthly world, the Biblical and indeed subsequent political history of the Jews is one wherein these hopes are consistently thwarted by the nature of finitude and the resultant fallen nature of human beings. The mutation, dissolution, and death that mark nature, prevent the stability and peace of any earthly order, but this seems most markedly to be the case for the Jews. In part, this can be understood insofar as the Jewish people historically understood their end as an earthly rather than a heavenly kingdom. Expecting the nature of the finite realm in and of itself to be redeemed, the Jewish people are witnesses to its degradation. Their faith manifests itself in their continued endurance, hoping for an end that the world they experience indicates is impossible. While the rabbinic tradition has had, since ancient time, elements of transcendent eschatology, suggesting resurrection and even post-temporal redemption, Helprin's novels seem to weave Jewish and Christian theologies together creating a new and unique teleological account for human life.

Catherine's sheltered existence is indicated in the novel by her and her family's complete ignorance to even the possibility that the man she loves is Jewish. Amusingly, they ask him to say grace and are constantly feeding him lobster.[31] Further, when Harry is visiting, they invite Rufus, one of Billy's boyhood friends, to dinner, even though they are aware of his anti-Semitic attitudes. Catherine's mother, who we only later discover is herself Jewish, explains that this is a fault that they recognize and forgive, for "souls are complicated things."[32] Catherine, who does not yet know of her own heritage, goes so far as to assure Rufus, who is dismayed to find out she is in the theatre, a profession filled with Jews, that he need not worry because she will never marry one.[33] Having lived a life of ease, Catherine's purgatorial ascent requires that she, albeit in a much lesser form, experience the plight of millions of Jewish people, and thereby discover the means by which she might persevere, even when all external forces seem to be directed arbitrarily against her.

Importantly, Harry is undaunted by what he takes to be Catherine's Christian heritage. Unlike Catherine, Harry has experienced the suffering precipitated by the natural order. Harry lost his mother at a young age and spent four years in combat, watching as his friends and comrades were killed, only to come home having lost his father. In addition, he has endured the fate of even a relatively affluent Jewish person in twentieth century America, having to battle his way through Harvard, always aware that he would have to work extra hard to achieve what others received easily. Having experienced the limitations of the natural world, Harry also knows they can be endured. In response to Billy Hale's question, "'Don't you know . . . that this is how life is? The world is made up of insoluble problems, of things that are beyond the influence of heroic action—of bitter loss, and no recoupment,'" Harry answers, "'I did know that. . . . I thought you were the ones who didn't.'"[34] Harry's life and his resulting character serve as a form of mediation that broadens Catherine's comprehension of the infinite. Catherine is habituated to this new understanding, first theoretically and then practically. First, she learns that she is a Jew and, second, she experiences the injustice that the finite world offers first hand. In all of this she is guided by her reciprocated love for Harry.

Catherine's understanding of herself is instantly transformed when her parents reveal to her that she is a Jew. Describing her new identity, Catherine says, "'They're me—rabbis in caftans and fur hats, their wives, the children dressed in black, with sparkling, tragic eyes. . . . And, Harry I'm them. . . . Today I became as rooted as a tree, with no voice of its own except the wind that moves through it. . . . Those skeletons in the newsreels, the children stacked dead at the side of ditches like firewood. . . . They're me.'"[35] In learning that she is a Jew, Catherine knows she shares in the identity and fate of all descendants of that race. While Catherine indicates that the transformation in her identity does not require her to believe anything differently, nonetheless, her perspective on the world is transformed. In describing herself as a tree whose only voice is caused by an external and natural force, Catherine suggests something of what she takes to be the plight and perspective of the Jewish people.

Theoretically knowing herself as a Jew, Catherine is then given the opportunity to experience the arbitrary nature of the finite in her practical existence, first in her career and then, finally, in Harry's death. Despite the audience's positive response to her performances, Catherine is shocked, hurt, and angered by the response of the critics. Opening for a short run in Boston prior to its Broadway debut, the Boston critics praise everything and everyone involved in the show, with the exception of Catherine. When the show opens in New York, Catherine no longer receives negative reviews. Instead, it is as if she is not in the show at all. Like many Jews before her, Catherine "had been erased."[36] Catherine knows that the critics are wrong and that what they have written or not written is not true of her ability or performances. Quickly she suspects, and it is later confirmed, that the response of the critics has been the result of Victor's work. However, she has no proof and, even if she did, there is no viable way, at least at first, to overcome the problem. For the first time, without any potential recourse, and, "like a tree without any voice of its own," Catherine must withstand an arbitrary and unwarranted attack against herself.

Harry counsels Catherine on his own experience from the war. Thinking that institutions like churches and hospitals are safe havens, the allied forces quickly realized that they were not: "'Germans. They would shoot from these places. They wanted us not to be sure. They wanted us to die because we were not sure, and because we were good. . . . We discovered that we were not good.'"[37] In attacking places of restoration and peace, the Germans tried to instill a distrust in that which was assumed to be good, leading them to despair of the good itself. Harry suggests that in being so attacked, the allies recognize their own lack of goodness. His point, presumably, is that in fighting back, the allies were required to use similar methods of dissembling. In this, at least, even if they never lost sight of the good in and of itself, or the just end for which they fought, they were not able to find a higher ground upon which to fight and yet win, and so their own deficiencies are revealed.

Victor similarly seeks to dissuade Catherine of any faith she has in her own goodness, first by raping her, and then by means of his control of the theatre reviews.[38] In this, we see something by means of contrast of Dante's recollection of himself. Dante's inward turn reveals his nature and his ultimate desire for the good. Victor seeks to destroy Catherine's perception of the good as mediated by her understanding of herself. Harry suggests that to fight back is somehow to her detriment, a point that will be examined again from the position of Harry's development in the course of the novel. Rather than fighting Victor, Catherine perseveres, such that the good that she seeks and embodies shines forth. In the face of the inevitable strife of the finite order, within and by means of that order, Catherine maintains faith and hope.

For the first time, Catherine recognizes that the things of this world that she has enjoyed all come to some end, for "no matter what she did, she had only a limited time."[39] What has always been true of the material order is now made manifest to Catherine. However, rather than despair about the nature of the world, she is turned into one of the workers in grey, who, despite their seemingly unremarkable place in the world, are still convinced of their own integrity.[40] Catherine realizes the importance of each finite thing, herself included: "In the few hours when flowers catch the sun, she realized, all are equal, then all are done."[41] Whatever might happen to her, Catherine, like Job, self-consciously realizes that she is good and that this knowledge might have to be enough.

Catherine no longer holds any sense that she will eventually be rewarded for her efforts. Instead,

> She could take her cues only from the music. All she could have, and ever have, was this, and if it took her up, and lifted her as she sang, that would have to be enough. Suffering throughout the day and after her performances, she held through with determination so that when the orchestra was struck her singing would be cut loose from the things of the world, and the song itself, fragile and evanescent, could spar with the background of silence.[42]

Motivated by nothing other than the goodness she understands as present in her own song and with no hope other than to sing in this small way and for the short time that her song lasts, Catherine nonetheless asserts her being against the non-being that threatens to encompass everything in the natural realm. When first confronted with Catherine's trial, Harry "was comforted by the fact that God had given her a shield not only in beauty and talent inborn, but in qualities that far exceeded them and would last beyond them."[43] By means of the reviews of her play, Catherine comes to know the nature of the finite world as deficient and that even her own nature has at least a partial root in non-being. Just as she is erased from the show, so her particular existence on earth will someday end. In the face of all of this, Catherine understands not merely the importance of her end in God, but the importance of her particular and finite life, seeking now to live it such that it might be judged as well lived, regardless of its outcome.[44] It is not that she forgets her Christian end, but that she knows it as more fully complete when reconciled with this other understanding.

Catherine thus insists on helping Harry in his fight against Verderamé. At this point Harry believes the eternity he seeks is a continuance of the family in the earthly realm. To risk Catherine's life is to risk the future of his bloodline. If he fails, losing both the shop and her, Harry surrenders his hold on the past and his view into the future. In response to Catherine's insistence that she help, Harry answers, "'if *you* die, everything stops dead.'"[45] Now understanding fully the risks of her finitude, Catherine insists on helping regardless. Just as she must battle against the silence of the theatre, so she must join him in his battle against non-being, saying "'You're not one who dictates. If I don't share in the risk I become nothing, just as you would. We're going to die anyway.'"[46] When informing her parents of her and Harry's plans, Catherine further clarifies her new understanding, "'I'm not immortal. Just like you, I won't last forever, and anyone who won't last forever has to live courageously and well, or she's left with, and leaves behind, nothing.'"[47] Realizing that her natural life is limited, Catherine nonetheless realizes that inasmuch as she has a life, she has a responsibility to strive for goodness, even if that means risking her particular existence.

Harry's Ascent

Catherine comes to recognize the limits of the natural world and the inevitable pain and suffering that this order bears. Experiencing her finitude, Catherine nonetheless perseveres, recognizing that, even in this suffering, there is the possibility of integrity and love. Harry, alternatively, is brought to understand the possibility of an infinite life, even if attaining it requires death.

After having fallen in love with Catherine, and with his father's business under attack, Harry clarifies his initial understanding of immortality—an unbroken chain of ancestors in the past and the generation of the familial line into the future. Importantly, this position is not fully manifest in Harry until after he has fallen in love with Catherine. With the hopes of marrying her and having children, Harry directs himself towards his heritage and overcomes his previous detachment from the fate of his father's business. By ensuring the success of his father's business, Harry seeks to maintain a continued life for his now deceased father while simultaneously trying to extend his family into the future. Understanding time as unified by love, Harry believes he has a responsibility to both the past and the future.[48] In explaining to Billy why he cannot let Copeland Leather go, Harry says, "'I have a family . . . and its fortune, not in money, has a call on me. . . . When I was born, my soul took shape in the promises I would keep. They were there by the score waiting for me, and this was one of them. Catherine will be safe. That's another.'"[49] In this account, Harry recognizes the codependence of all people, or at least those related by blood, even those who are dead and those not yet born. He thereby begins to conceive something of the depiction of universality and interconnectedness that Helprin presents as a central theme in *Winter's Tale*.

What Harry does not recognize is the way by which the finite might be fully redeemed in and by means of the infinite. The continuation of life that Harry seeks for his family is earthly in nature. Hence, when thinking about the inevitable decline of his father's business, Harry believes that "its end was some form of death . . . the last remnant of his father's life."[50] When Harry hears Catherine sing for the first time, he is struck by the way in which her song transcends the limits of time and gathers all people into a unity. However, he also notes its limits, for the song would hold "them for as long as it could until they would vanish except for a remnant of exhausted air."[51] This point is further clarified in the weight that he gives to the ownership of property in the novel. In preserving his father's business, Harry, in part, seeks to serve the matter that will continue his family's material existence. Harry quotes Shylock from the *Merchant of Venice* twice, indicating that his life is intimately bound up in the matter that sustains it.[52] At this point in the novel, Harry perceives his end as dependent upon the material world, his father's memory, and the temporal line of his descendants. This familial piety is in direct contrast to passages in the New Testament as, for example, when Christ famously declares that to follow him, one must hate one's father and mother.[53] By the end, both Harry and the novel posit a transcendent end that goes beyond the finite continuity or restoration of family.

As the novel begins, Harry is depicted as wishing he had a choice, "between the great heaviness of the city looming behind him, and the gravityless air above the water." For "if there were a way to come from darkness into light, and stay there as long as life would allow, he wanted to know it . . . [H]e wanted to leave even the shadows that he himself had made. . . . But he could not imagine how."[54] Even prior to Harry's development in the course of the novel, the possibility of more complete life after death is present to Harry. On three occasions he is shown in train stations and, on each occasion, Harry is drawn to think about the dead and the responsibility the living have towards them. In Penn Station, Harry is reminded of the last time he saw his father, whereas in Grand Central Station, by means of the mural of the heavens painted on the ceiling, Harry imagines all of the dead, and then specifically those who have died in the war:

And now for the sake of those who hadn't come home, Harry lived the dream they had dreamed. . . . Here were the dead in the hearts of the living, to whom the living spoke without speaking, saying: here is the bustling restaurant and its whitened sound; here are the lights of the theatre; the halls of the Metropolitan; the afternoon sun deepening the fall colors of the park; the wind rising on the avenues, blowing dust in your eye; and here is a woman, her touch warm, her breathing deep and delicate, her skin fragrant, her patience loving. [55]

At this point, Harry imagines that the dead remain alive in the hearts of those who loved them.

Harry does not question why he is drawn to such contemplations while in train stations. For the reader, the image is sufficiently clear. All of the individuals Harry sees in the train stations are passing through. For most, the train station is merely a means to the end of the journey they envision. Even if they are drawn to Grand Central Station for the Oyster Bar, no one imagines that this is their final destination. There is the amusing incident of Harry's friend, Johnson, who, amazed by Grand Central Station, is mesmerized by the sight of a woman seemingly striding toward him. He is expecting and hoping that she will speak to him, but instead she blows past, her passage having the effect of a kiss. [56] The train stations of New York, as places of passage, although filled with the living, remind Harry of the dead. Helprin thereby suggests that one's finite life might properly be thought of as a passage, not one's final destination or end. One is reminded of Alessandro's dalliances in *Soldier*, real or imagined, first with a travel agent and then as a tourist guide. These women assist those travelling; they are not the ends in themselves. While Harry imagines the dead as carried in the hearts of the living, Helprin suggests that a more complete life might be available.

Appropriately, Catherine's stage character arrives in the city from Penn Station, for Catherine, like Beatrice, mediates the fuller vision of the infinite that Harry requires. In Harry's first impressions of Catherine, she is depicted as though she is God. Harry's hope that by means of love he might be reconciled to her suggests the further hope he must attain—that he might similarly be reconciled to the divine. Hence, wishing that he might find a way to stay in the sunlight, the next thing Harry sees is Catherine. His description of Catherine's song is similarly telling. Although she does not play the lead, she nonetheless supplies the "transcendent moment" of the production, and when she sings her part for the first time in rehearsal, her breath "was like God breathing into Adam." [57] Catherine is not the lead, nor does she give life to Adam, but as the particular woman who Harry loves, her presence indicates to him that there might be a transcendent life wherein love is fully redeemed. Catherine herself eventually understands the way by which she might help complete Harry's account of the good. At the end of the novel, while she waits for him on the Esplanade, she thinks about comforting him for all that he regrets. Catherine imagines herself, "reaching out to heal a man wounded by war, elevating him, as if in the embrace of an angel . . . and to love him, and carry him up."[58]

Harry arrives at this wider account by acknowledging the natural and inevitable defects of his own will and the possibility that God's nature might be a love such that defects of this sort are fully and finally overcome. When Harry comes home from four years at war, he is not immediately compelled to action. He determines that he needs a year to "absorb" if not "understand" everything that he has seen. Similarly, when Dante first climbs out of Inferno he rests, rather than beginning the difficult trek up Mount Purgatory, and, seeking to ease his soul from what he has just witnessed, he listens to a song about love.[59] Both Dante and Harry, having escaped Inferno, are content to rest in a median state, which, if not Paradiso at least speaks of the beauty and peace that they hope to find.

However understandable this is, in both instances these characters must be spurred on to act. Dante, content to listen to a song about love, is not sufficiently desirous of his fulfillment in and by means of love, and, hence, he is reminded by Cato that he has a greater end awaiting him.[60] In the same way, Harry is content to just exist, without any ambition to act, even though his father's business is slowly being eroded.[61]

While Cato's chastisement spurs Dante into action, Cornell, Harry's friend and the manager of Copeland Leather, is unable to have the same effect. Cornell, looking for direction, asks Harry what he plans to do about the slow erosion of his father's business. Harry's response is telling: "Today, I'm going to meet a girl."[62] It is only by falling in love with Catherine that Harry is reminded of the nature of love and his responsibility to those he loves, even though some of these people are now dead.

However, having met Catherine, but, uncertain as how to proceed, Harry turns to Cornell for guidance. Cornell, a Christian, is shocked when Harry explains he might have a better sense of how Harry should approach Catherine and her parents. It seems absurd to Cornell that a black man in 1945 would have more in common with a wealthy white family, just because they are both Christian.[63] Harry's sense of alienation at this point is such that he either lacks empathy for Cornell's lot in life or genuinely believes that the difference in religion is greater than that of skin color. Nonetheless, Cornell devises a plan. Harry is to "raid" the engagement party—show up unannounced and win Catherine for himself.

Cornell says that it is the shock of Harry's assertion that he might be better poised to know what to do that reveals to Cornell how Harry might succeed. It seems, however, that Helprin is suggesting something more here about the nature of Christianity. Cornell has been asked how, having fallen in love, one should act. In other words, what are the activities proper to love? Cornell's response is that one should act on the basis of one's love, hoping that this love will be reciprocated. In this a theme and suggestion in other of

Helprin's books is repeated. In *Winter's Tale*, facing the seemingly inevitable death of his daughter, the character Hardesty leaves the hospital, hoping that by means of a variety of unconnected and impossible acts her death might be overcome. Hardesty seeks the impossible, saving his child from death. His wife, Virginia, wonders if such a hope might be an indication of vanity, but Hardesty denies that this is the case. For, "it was an act of defiance, danger-ous . . . because it was a rebellion against omnipotence. But love moved him, and he trusted that he would do well."[64] Divine grace and love may always be available, but the consummation of desires also depends on the activity of one's will. By means of actions, the things that are loved are made evident and one's true choices are clarified. Further, to the extent that one is moti-vated by love, whatever might be asked may well be granted. In *Winter's Tale*, Sarah Gamely thus chastises Virginia for not similarly seeking a solu-tion, saying "You've failed a bit. But you're still alive. You may not find a way to save your child. But you have to try. You owe it to her, and you owe it in general." [65]

Harry, through his experiences during the war, already has the *habitus* of acting in the face of fear for a great end. He must now, however, turn the activity of his will towards the fulfillment of his love, and Cornell counsels, "So do it. But be careful, be gentle, because it's all about a woman."[66] Risking rejection and humiliation, Harry seeks love. While Catherine's recip-rocation of his love might not seem as miraculous as the resurrection of Abby in *Winter's Tale*, insofar as all of Harry's happiness depends on it, the stakes are just as high. In the image of Harry seeking the reciprocated love of Catherine, Helprin further imagines the path that all individuals take who, in loving God, hopes, seemingly against all odds, that this love might be re-turned. At their first dinner together, Evelyn, wanting presumably to make a good impression, asks Harry to say grace. Harry, of course, is unprepared. As it turns out, so is everyone else at the table, for the Hales themselves are not in the habit of saying grace before their meals. At the suggestion that they just forgo the formality, Evelyn responds, "'No . . . Grace is hanging over us.'"[67] Harry's task, it seems, is to recognize and accept the grace that ever awaits him.

Further, although Harry does "raid" the engagement party, in the end he need do nothing but simply show up. Although she has resolved to marry Victor, the mere sight of Harry is enough to change Catherine's mind, and without even speaking to Harry, Catherine breaks her engagement and offers Harry a ride home. In *Winter's Tale*, although Hardesty dares a number of impossible acts, in the end all he has to do is dig up Abby's body and what he had hoped for is granted. Helprin thereby suggests that although the individu-al must actively and fully turn her will to the end that she seeks, God's response is ever present.

As noted, a central, and perhaps necessary, element of the peculiar theology that guides Harry, and perhaps underlies Helprin's own position, is revealed in Harry's discussion of religion with Billy. Harry says, "'My tradition, Billy, if I may, considers intermediation secondary. And so, I believe, does yours.' 'But the more you depart from intermediation,' Billy said, 'the more you risk madness, pride, and error.'"[68] The "traditions" referred to here are presumably Judaism and, specifically, protestant Christianity. The amalgamation of Judaism and Christianity that Harry appears to be advocating is only made possible because he places intermediaries, the external forms and institutions of religion, in a secondary role to the immediate apprehension of God in the heart of the believer. This view is not compatible with Catholicism surely, or with many expressions of Judaism. However, throughout Helprin's novels, God is mediated through human relationships, art, and beauty, and not through conventional religious forms or institutions. When asked his opinion about beauty, Harry responds that it is a "holy" and "saintly" thing to be able to see beauty in that which others disregard.[69] By comparison, the vision Dante has of the Empyrean in *Paradiso* is not mediated by images of the church, but, rather, a river of light reveals the celestial city to him. Dante, like the characters we meet in Helprin's novels, is mediated by images of humanity, art and nature, and Helprin, like Dante, mediates using the same. For Dante, the traditional institutions of the medieval world are replaced by images that are more universally available. In this, Dante, like Helprin, reveals something of a "democratic" nature. Billy warns against the religious zealot who would claim a private and direct communication with God, such that all intervention by others is unnecessary and, moreover, that the individual is sufficient unto himself. This, Harry succinctly rejects, as "God's grace" will protect him. At this, ironically an assertion of protestant orthodoxy by a Jew against an Episcopalian, Billy concedes Harry's point.

LOVE CLARIFIED

Catherine and Harry fall in love with each other and are then moved to perceive the nature of their end and the good in light of each other. While in the course of the novel this is achieved by means of circumstances primarily outside of their control, metaphorically, Helprin suggests that this is a component of the nature of love. In willing the good for the other, individuals come to recognize the nature of the good as it is particularly understood by, and manifest in, the beloved. We will take this point up in the concluding discussion about *Freddy and Fredericka*. Having been moved to these new perspectives, Catherine and Harry then reconcile them into a more coherent view of the whole. Practically, Catherine and Harry get married and conspire to bring Verderamé down. By these means Helprin suggests a view of the eternal that incorporates and takes up the fullness of particularity as part of itself. During their brief marriage ceremony, Harry forgets to say his final vow at the prescribed moment, and so he joins Catherine, saying it together: "Her voice, of course, was beautiful and distinctive, and, with his, normally deep but now even deeper, in the background, the sentence became a kind of music."[70] Having entered into the life and understanding of the other, Catherine and Harry now formally join these two positions. The result has the "beauty of song."[71] In this movement, Harry and Catherine recognize that God's love incorporates everything so that nothing need be lost, and all is recognized as part of the good itself.

Helprin, however, argues that a further movement is also required. To love properly, he suggests, Harry and Catherine must live as though this particular life might be all that they have. In other words, Helprin suggests that to love means loving another regardless of whether this love will ever be fully reciprocated and realized. Understood as such, love is selfless; one loves regardless of whether one's love will ever be consummated. Nonetheless and further, in accepting the risk that one's love might not be reciprocated, one continues to have faith in the goodness of the beloved and hope that this goodness will one day be one's own. One is not without hope, but rather is content even should this hope go unfulfilled.

Moreover, and finally, Harry and Catherine understand that as good as their particular love is for one another, its goodness is dependent on an even higher love, for and of the eternal. As is generally the case in Helprin's novels, God is seldom referenced directly or at length. Instead, the divine is represented via eternal attributes: beauty, love, justice, and so on. Accordingly, Harry and Catherine signal their recognition of universal principles by becoming willing to give up their particular experience of each other in the finite order, recognizing that it is not the end that they seek for either themselves or each other. In so doing, they nonetheless hope that their particular love will be reinstated, albeit in a perfected form. We will see a similar position at the end of *Winter's Tale*, where, having remembered his love for Beverly, Peter Lake willingly goes to his death, hoping that he might be reconciled to her, but should that not be the case, he is nonetheless satisfied, saying "'The world is a perfect place, so perfect that even if there is nothing afterwards, all this will have been enough.'"[72]

This point is drawn in sharp relief at the end of the novel. Now married, Catherine and Harry are given a full picture of the future life that they might have together, for in his efforts to assemble his old team of pathfinders for his new mission, Harry and Catherine travel to California to see if his former friend Rice is willing to help them. In Rice, his wife Catherine, and their new baby son, Harry and Catherine are given a full sense of what their life could be, if they would only give up on Copeland Leather. In the end both Catherine and Harry understand that this life and the love that it represents must be risked if their love is going to be of any real worth.

During the drive to the town where Rice is living, Harry has what he believes is a vision that he and Catherine might move to California and start anew. Harry says he knows it will not work, that the idea is just a dream, but his resolve is tested when they are presented with the life he imagined existing in the flesh of Rice and his wife Catherine. After meeting Rice and his wife, Catherine now envisions that this life could be her's and Harry's, saying, "'We could move here. . . . They're wonderful people. They would be our friends. . . . After a war you have the right to start fresh. You can leave everything behind and make a new life.'"[73] Even the stars seem to conspire to tempt them to this choice: "more like gentle lamps than stars, their blinking was not cold and quick like the disinterested stars of winter, but slow and seductive, as if they were speaking in a code that all mankind understood, even if they did not know that such a language existed, much less that it was following its benevolent commands." The life they imagine in California offers Harry and Catherine the kind of earthly peace and satisfaction that they have lost sight of in light of their recent trials. Resolving to persevere against the injustice of the theatre critics and to seek to end the injustice of Verderamé, Catherine and Harry see the possibility of an easy out. They might, as Catherine suggests, move to California and start fresh.

At the end of *Purgatorio*, Dante is similarly tempted. He has struggled through the pits of Inferno and then made the arduous journey up Mount Purgatory for the sake of Beatrice. However, at the top of the mountain and before Beatrice arrives, he is presented with another option—the natural paradise complete with a lovely gardener, Matilda. Dante tells Matilda, "'Thou makest me remember where and what Proserpina that moment was when lost her mother her, and she herself the Spring.'"[74] In alluding to Hades' illicit *amor* and kidnapping of Persephone, Dante suggests that Matilda puts him in a similar mindset. Dante reads Matilda's response as receptive to his strange advance, describing her eyes, saying, "I do not think there shone so great a light under the lids of Venus, when transfixed by her own son, beyond his usual custom!"[75] Dante's address to and description of Matilda leave little doubt that he is tempted by what the Garden of Eden presents. However, the love that Dante seeks is not what Matilda or this Garden offers. The Garden of Eden is empty indicating that the earthly satisfaction it represents and the finite love of Matilda are not proper ends. As indicated in the previous chapter, the fallen character of nature, including human nature, is epitomized in death. The end of the natural order is its eventual decay and destruction. Understanding this, one is brought to have faith and hope for a higher end of infinite life. Fortunately, Dante is not left to his own devices for Beatrice arrives, reminding him of his higher end.

In a similar fashion, both Catherine and Harry are the means by which the other is directed beyond an earthly satisfaction to a heavenly one. Thus, while it is Catherine and not Harry who is most fully tempted by the seeming paradise they see represented in Rice and his family, it takes only slight prompting from Harry for her to concede what she already knows. The Garden of Eden, particularly as described by Dante, is both good and beautiful. Nonetheless, it is not the highest good, nor the true end. As a result, the temptations of the Garden of Eden must be sacrificed. However peaceful the life would be that Catherine imagines in California with Harry and their children, it would eventually end as all lives eventually end. Acknowledging this, they must have courage to risk their present, if temporary peace, in the hope of a fuller satisfaction.

Importantly, although both Dante and Helprin indicate that the finite order must be forsaken, as it is not the good in and of itself, it is the love of a particular other upon which they focus. While the earth is not a proper end, it is nonetheless a sufficient means for indicating the nature of this end and mediating one's desire for it. Dante thus has Beatrice replace the sacrament in the *Corpus Christi* pageant that processes through the Garden of Eden. Beatrice, a particular, if perfected woman, is depicted as a substitute in this moment for Christ's sacrifice and God's grace. Helprin takes this image further for neither Harry nor Catherine has ascended to Paradiso. Instead they become sufficient mediators of divine grace in their particular and still finite lives.[76] This, Helprin suggests, has a further effect on one's finite life. One might imagine that, knowing that the goodness of the finite world is insufficient, one should then distance oneself from the good that it offers, so as to avoid temptation and focus oneself on the true end. Instead, as Dante suggests and Helprin makes clear, the goodness that is present in the natural order is not something to be dismissed because of its limitations, for the mutable natural order is the means to our understanding of the infinite and universal. This is indicative of the goodness that is present within it. Seeing the natural order as good, but also as limited, demands that it be responded to such that its goodness is properly attended to while it still exists.

Catherine indicates that the impermanence of the natural order "clarifies love."[77] While driving to California, Harry is struck by the fragility of human life. He has no other family now besides Catherine, and she is also the only family left for her parents. However, when Harry suggests that he might drive more slowly, Catherine's response is instructive, for instead of slowly, she tells him to drive well.[78] Catherine's point is that in recognizing death, one should seek to ensure that one's life is worthwhile; just as one should drive well, one should live well. That our loved ones and we will eventually die should not be a cause for either caution or despair; instead, we should seek to use whatever time is available to make ourselves worthy recipients of their love. However much Catherine and Harry might want to forget the particular injustices each of them faces, giving up would satisfy neither, even if continuing means risking their ongoing love. Their ongoing love requires that they take up the good in their own lives so as to be in some way worthy of the love of the other. They continue the work of Purgatory, habituating themselves to the virtue required for Paradiso.

Cornell tells Harry to raid the engagement party, committing something of an act of war. We know that in this instance Harry's appeal is on the side of justice, as were his activities in the war that just ended and as they will be in the war that he will wage on Verderamé. Nonetheless, to wage these new battles, Harry must disrupt the peace to which he has only recently returned. In so doing, Harry risks everything he has sought and, up to this point, had understood as his end.[79] Having fought for and won Catherine, Harry is reluctant to engage in a war against the gangsters. He understands that there is no just way to win a war against Verderamé, and he is unwilling to condone a Hobbesian world wherein, for the sake of their own self-interest, all individuals and nations turn to violence.[80]

In her frustration with his inactivity, Catherine further clarifies what is at issue for Harry:

> "If everyone just killed whoever persecuted him, the world would be constant-ly at war." "The world *is* constantly at war." "Not on account of me." "So, you'll surrender?" "Not surrender." "No, just lose, because he's willing to do what you're not. You're ethical, and he's not. So you'll disappear and he'll stay."[81]

Harry seeks a life of peace and believes that the means by which he might attain this is through the righteousness of his own soul. Harry has not recog-nized that his righteousness is not dependent on his own activity or inactivity, but only attained via God's grace. James Vanderlyn draws this to his atten-tion. Vanderlyn wants to help Harry and devises a plan by which Harry might kill Verderamé, save his business, and continue his life with Catherine. Harry has killed many men while at war and is reluctant to do so again, even if his cause is justified. Recognizing that many of the men Harry has killed were as innocent as he was, Vanderlyn notes that, as a result, Harry is "'forever morally impure.'"[82] Vanderlyn argues that acting on the grounds that his own cause is justified is a chance one takes "'as a consequence of [one's] imper-fection.'"[83] The nature of the material world lies in its change and strife. As a result, any sense of peace that one attains here is illusory and ought to point to a realm wherein true peace might be possible. In convincing Harry to act, Vanderlyn highlights how human nature follows the natural world in its fallenness. The impurity and imperfection that Vanderlyn notes as true of Harry's particular nature, is true of all human beings.

Nonetheless, Vanderlyn's response to this imperfection is not to further withdraw from the particular world in which he finds himself. Instead, he discerns, as best he is able, the proper course of things, and seeks this end as his own. When Harry questions what Vanderlyn means by properly, he responds, "'Strongly. Justly. And perhaps tragically, but always beautifully.'"[84] He further clarifies, "'You were plucked from the war. When you came back, didn't all this strike you as a magnificent surplus, as if you had come back from the dead, and here was your second chance?'"[85] Vanderlyn indicates that even if one's cause is hopeless, one should act for the sake of justice and beauty, for in so doing, one might be brought back from the dead, and given a second chance. In other words, recognizing the finite nature of the world in which one lives and one's own corrupt nature, one need not despair, but hoping for an infinite end that overcomes one's deficiency and thus overcomes death, one must act. In case this Christian position should have eluded the reader, we later discover that James Vanderlyn is Jesus' brother.[86] Dante, the character, understands that, when he returns to his natural life, he will live the life of an exile. Having seen the peace of Paradiso, Dante will be thrust back into the strife of the finite world. In exile he will not have the luxury of retreating from the world of strife to focus only on the supernatural vision he has been granted. Instead, he will have to struggle in the world to survive. This, however, does not deter him from good action, as is evidenced by his poetry. Elsewhere, Helprin similarly comments on the mutability of the world and the appropriate response, saying,

> the people you love die, and you don't take it lightly or think it is ironic . . . the absence of terror, or of safety, comfort, or abundance . . . far from being the state to which the unabused universe automatically reverts, are merely illusions waiting to be shattered by suffering and mortality. And because of this, or at least in conjunction with it, visions are intense, love is deep, life overflows.[87]

Vanderlyn clarifies this point. Vanderlyn's son died in the war while estranged from him; Vanderlyn's wife is distant. Vanderlyn has no particular beloved to whom he might demonstrate his worth. Nonetheless, he says, "'What I want to do, second by second, is that which is worthy in itself, that which I would do even if no one in the world were living, that which I would do at the cost of my life, in return for nothing, and against terrible odds.'"[88] In his actions, Vanderlyn suggests that what he loves is the good in and of itself, and regardless of whether his love might be reciprocated in any other way, creating within himself a virtue that approximates this good is sufficient. Vanderlyn indicates that the ultimate object of one's love is the good itself. However, as we see in Catherine and Harry, at the same time, one loves particular individuals. The nature of these loves mirrors each other, for in both cases, in order to be worthy of one's beloved, one must love as though one's love might never be reciprocated and be satisfied solely in the virtue of loving.

Describing her time as a nurse during the war, Catherine Rice further complicates the argument:

> Every time a soldier died, we were taken . . . on the very same wave. In Australia, before it all started, I used to swim in the surf. Sometimes it was so powerful, the waves so fierce, that you couldn't move your arms or legs or try to guide yourself. That's what it was like at each death. Defeat, . . . You see what we are, your heart breaks, and it shows you that the only thing we have, though we imagine otherwise, is love.[89]

Regardless of her courage and skill, the patients that Catherine Rice cared for eventually died. The courage that soldiers have and the justice of their position do not protect them or give them any mechanism of defense against death. In the moment of death, they are completely without power, trapped as if in some uncontrollable wave. Death establishes the limits of finite nature. No matter how much one has loved the good and attempted to replicate it in one's life, in the moment of death all of that is taken away. Earlier in the novel, Evelyn Hale notes that, "'grace is hanging over us,'" Harry later contrastingly says that "'this terrible thing is hanging over us.'"[90] In an essential way, these two positions are the same. Grace hangs over Catherine and Harry, making their reconciliation with each other and the divine possible, but achieving this end requires that a terrible thing also hang over them, for in order to attain their ultimate end, their finite lives must be fully experienced, meaning that they must participate in death. In other words, Helprin suggests that for the infinite nature of the divine to fully manifest itself, in order for the finite world to be truly sublated, finitude must be experienced in its fullness. Otherwise, the full power of the infinite is itself not actualized. This understanding is illustrated in Dante's *Divine Comedy* when Dante is repeatedly made aware of his impending exile from Florence. Just as Dante must experience exile from his beloved city, so he will be exiled from his natural life. Moreover, at the top of Mount Purgatory, Dante is brought face to face with Beatrice and must recognize and confess his crimes. Dante's pain at this moment is such that he is brought to tears. This image suggests that having habituated themselves to the good such that they now know it and love it, all of the souls of Purgatory also realize the corruption and limits of their former lives and must confess their willing participation in a life of non-being.

Catherine Rice indicates further that the moment of death highlights the essential nature of love, for in the moment of death, when everything one is and has seems to be forsaken, one is able to then love with an essential purity. In other words, at that moment when everything is lost and there is nothing to be gained, that one still loves indicates that love, at least, is real and eternal. In a corresponding image, prior to her realization that Harry is dead, Catherine Copeland sees the statue of an angel holding a dead soldier. While the soldier has clearly died, he is nonetheless held in the arms of an angel, who is "winged and strong . . . [looking] upward, undisturbed, about to rise."[91] What Catherine Rice understood in the face of her dying soldiers, Catherine Copeland is reminded of as she prepares for Harry's death.

Harry's death highlights a final movement for Catherine and a further possibility for the nature of love. As discussed, early in the novel Harry witnesses a child being pushed on a swing by her mother: "Away from her mother, and back, but always rising, always returning . . . [A]nd as she rose it seemed she easily apprehended something for which he had to strain and sacrifice to remember even as a trace."[92] In the image of this child, we see something of the end that Harry must see as his own. In swinging, the child ascends away from her mother towards the divine, but at the same time, she returns to her mother. Like Alessandro from *Soldier*, Harry is asked how a reconciliation with the divine that maintains one's more particular loves might be achieved.

On at least an initial level, the nature of romantic love is such that, while uniting two people, it divides others. For Harry's love to be fulfilled, Catherine must be separated from Victor, a parting that then causes the other practical difficulties that the couple encounters. In reciprocating Harry's love, Catherine is divided from her mother and father and the life that they have shared up to this moment. At the beginning of their relationship, while watching Catherine on the beach, Harry hopes that from amidst these people ". . . Catherine would rise in the present daylight as if from the irretrievable past and come to the place where he was standing. He had no desire to separate her from her mother and father or from the world she knew, but the separation was already under way, and he could see it in the picture before his eyes both breaking and still."[93] This division, while unintentional and regrettable, is necessary to the nature of romantic and familial loves. Parents are the source of their childrens' existence and share in their experiences, successes, and losses, as if they were their own. However, no parent wishes, or ought to wish, for these circumstances to continue unchanged. In loving one's children, one hopes that they will emerge as adults, capable of independent and autonomous lives that will someday share with families of their own. In the movement of children away from parents, there is thus both sadness and joy. Having shared all of Catherine's life since her birth, and while sharing in her affection for Harry, their love for Harry is necessarily different than Catherine's and in this they are divided.

Harry further highlights the nature of this division when he notes, "I love Catherine more than anyone in my life, more than my father, more than my mother. In a way that breaks my heart, but it's true, and I have to admit the truth."[94] In this image, we are asked to think about the nature of how one's particular loves both compete with and might be reconciled with the divine itself. Harry's heart breaks because he believes he loves Catherine more than he loves his parents. One wonders if his love for her might compete with his love for God and the good. Certainly, the suggestion that they might give up the fight and live easy lives in California implies that there is in love a temptation to see it as necessarily divisive in nature, separating one from the divine itself.

Catherine and Harry, however, do not stay in California. Moreover, on the eve of his death, Harry writes a note that encourages Catherine to love another and remarry, should he die. Catherine honors his request. While Beatrice chastises Dante for having turned his attention away from her after her death, Harry suggests that this is exactly what Catherine should do. She should, he tells her, allow his memory even to be supplanted, "except in symbols and traces."[95] Catherine acquiesces, but only partially, and in this she perhaps shows greater wisdom than either Beatrice or Harry. For while she does remarry, her love for Harry is not lessened, nor is the love she has for her new family diminished. Instead, Catherine experiences the infinite nature of love. In her memory of Harry swinging as a young boy, Catherine is similarly shown what she must hope for, both his and her ascent to God, wherein her love for Harry is infinitely returned and fulfilled. In the final moments of the novel, after Harry has died, he nonetheless returns to Catherine, if only for a moment in what "the practical might call hallucination and the faithful might call love."[96] Catherine's love for Harry, their child, her parents, and her new family, do not compete with each other, nor do they compete with her love of the divine. Instead, as Dante indicates in *Purgatorio*, unlike finite resources, the nature of love is such that when particularly directed and claimed, it is increased:

> So much it gives itself as it finds ardour,
> So that as far as charity extends,
> O'er it increases the eternal valour.
> And the more people thitherward aspire,
> More are there to love well, and more they love there,
> And, as a mirror, one reflects the other.[97]

The nature and experience of love is such that in being both given and taken it is multiplied rather than reduced. Insofar as one loves, one's love is not depleted, but ongoing.

In Inferno we see individuals joined by means of their vice, with the most striking pairs being Francesca and Paolo and, later, Ugolino and Roger, each couple locked in an eternal and horrifying embrace. These images, however, speak to a perversion of love and community and not its fulfillment. Hence, Paolo does not speak and Francesca does not even give the "lad with the lovely body," a name, while Ugolino is gnawing on the head of a silent Roger. In each instance, although depicted as part of a pair, one understands that the individuals in Inferno suffer their choices alone. In Purgatory, this autonomy is also respected, but these individuals, having chosen love, are assisted in their assent to the divine by the good will of others. Hence, while the actions of the individuals on each terrace may be unified, each person ascends from terrace to terrace on the basis of her or his individual progress. Nonetheless, one also knows that they are not solitary in their efforts, but are constantly aided by the presence and their knowledge of divine love.

While Helprin recognizes the importance of an individual's choice to accept or reject divine grace, in *Sunlight*, he also highlights the role of an individual's relationship with others as part of this journey. In so doing he highlights the specificity of love. Catherine and Harry make their way through Purgatory, at least partially, together and, while they recognize the presence of divine grace, it is their love for each other that is most prominent. Even in the moment of his ascent, Harry is not depicted as alone. In the *Comedy*, as souls in Purgatory ascend the mountain it quakes and all of the souls rejoice in the ascent of another.[98] So, Harry engages Verderamé, is shot, and dies at the precise moment that Catherine sings. While on other nights, Catherine refuses to stay for the curtain call and has not performed an encore, on this night she stays, and, "they made her sing . . . three times . . . although Catherine could not know it, her song was the accompaniment to the battle from beginning to end. But in a way she did know it, and in a way Harry could hear it, in memory and at the present as the two combined, as in great and stressful moments they often do."[99] While death is something individually experienced, by means of love one is not alone.

The souls of Purgatory rejoice as their colleagues ascend, happy for the fate of another. Catherine responds to the audience's desire to hear her sing, rejoicing in a performance well done; at the same time she is imaged as rejoicing in a life well lived and, although she has lost Harry, she realizes that she loved him most while he was swinging away from her.[100] Catherine grieves Harry's death as anyone who has truly loved will, but she knows that their love endures regardless. As Harry lies dying, he wishes that he devoted himself to portraying the things he had loved, the city, his own life, Catherine, "so as to make an echo, fix them in the light, [and] halt them for a moment in their rush to God knows where."[101] Only hours later, while waiting for Harry to arrive, Catherine completes his thought and his wish, for

> She knew that all the busyness of the world, its infinite mechanical actions in city, in surf, in molecules rising in light, in machines and speech and clouds of sparkling dust, and trains and sounds, and crowds, and blades of grass that dance in the sun, all pass into silence, leaving only the soul, which cannot be proved and cannot be seen. And she knew that the brightness of the day and that the passions that flare within it are just a flash of light to fix the soul into an afterimage that will last forever.[102]

While dying, Harry hopes that the things that he loves might last forever, and calls Catherine's name. Similarly, Catherine knows the soul is eternal and that all the things that one loves are preserved forever.

In *Sunlight*, Helprin gives an account of the divine such that it encompasses and incorporates the particular and the finite. The book ends with the death of Harry and the hope that he has achieved his infinite reconciliation with the divine. One might thus argue that the text offers a Christian perspective. However much faith Harry has at the end of the novel for a transcendent *telos*, his attention is still drawn to the continuity of his and Catherine's familial lines, which suggests his ongoing hope for the continuity of his family and something of an earthly end. He thus requests that Catherine remarry and have a family of her own. Helprin indicates that this is not just a lack of understanding on Harry's part, but instead a real concern, for, at Harry's death, the reader and Catherine know that she is already pregnant with his child. The purgatorial movement of the book is one wherein the finite nature of the world is fully understood. Catherine experiences the seemingly arbitrary strife and struggle of the world and Harry's death completes this part of her education. As a result of her new awareness of the limits of time and space, Catherine now sees the importance of the beauty present in this world, and learns how to love it properly. While not the end in and of itself, the finite order is nonetheless shown as redeemed, for it is the means by which one knows of and loves the good. Both Catherine and Harry are brought to see how Christian and Jewish perspectives might be reconciled into a whole that does not affect the integrity of the other.

In addition to reawakening and relearning the nature of love, Harry and Catherine's purgatorial ascent also requires that they direct their wills towards justice as it might be finitely known and experienced. As we shall see more fully in the following chapter, Helprin argues that love and justice are interrelated with the full nature of justice only made possible within and by means of love. That love is the foundation for justice is suggested by the chronology of events in the book, for immediately after Harry discovers that his love for Catherine is reciprocated, he must face the mob that has determined to put his father's shop out of business. Taken more abstractly, in love one directs one's attention to the good of another. One is thereby directed beyond and out of one's immediate self-interest. Love mimics the necessary movement of justice and provides an intermediary ground. When in love, one seeks the good of the particular person to whom one is connected; when acting justly one seeks the good of a larger, more universal whole. By means of love one might be trained in the habits required for justice.

Helprin's argument is not merely that justice has its foundation in love, but, in addition, Helprin suggests that the nature of justice lies in love and thus what is finitely known in the political order is understood as having an infinite end in the divine. This position, however, is not initially evident, for it seems instead that in the course of the novel achieving justice means sacrificing what one loves. This is perhaps most poignantly suggested in the novel's conclusion, for in seeking to end Verderamé's unjust exploitation of himself and of others, Harry dies, leaving Catherine and her unborn child alone. This position however is only partial, and overcoming it is part of the work required for both Catherine, and particularly Harry in their purgatorial ascent. Doing so requires coming to perceive the nature of the divine as it is manifest in a finite and temporal sphere. More specifically, it requires achieving a fuller account of time such that one is able to see the continuity of past to future and recognize the interconnectedness of all individuals— including those who have already died and those who are yet to be born. In recognizing the interconnectedness of all things and all people, one realizes both one's particular dependence on, and responsibility to, each of these parts. The relationship is not a cold or abstract one, but intimate and necessary. Thus it becomes possible to envision a justice that has at its core love. The fullest expression of this argument is manifest in *Winter's Tale*, but, as is perhaps appropriate for Purgatory, in *Sunlight* Harry approaches this position by means of his particular relationships, particularly his relationships to his now deceased father, to Catherine, and to the children he imagines that they will have.

The final clear connection between the *Divine Comedy* and *Sunlight* pertains to the tradition of courtly love. Like Dante before him Helprin embraces that tradition and then re-casts it. For Helprin, the relationship between lover and beloved is now based on a kind of equality. Early in the novel, Helprin passionately defends the courtly love tradition against the modernist critiques of Catherine's Bryn Mawr professors, who declared it "twisted."[103] Harry replies, "'I don't know who told you, but I do know that whoever said this was a fucking idiot who must never have seen anything, or risked anything. . . . This is what I learned and managed to bring out with me from hell. How shall I treat it? Love of God, love of a woman, love of a child—what else is there?'"[104] He goes on to distinguish his account of courtly love from that of "Lancelot," because "it's different now." While Harry does not describe what is different, the rest of the novel demonstrates that there is now a reciprocity and recognition of mutual virtue, one that allows the veneration of the beloved to go in both directions. Catherine and Harry can be partners in the war against Verderamé, even if it places both of them in danger. The revision to courtly love does not reduce the opportunity for devotion or sacrifice in the least in Harry's view.

Purgatory is distinct among the three realms in Dante's *Divine Comedy* as it is the only place that experiences both day and night. Inferno is enclosed in perpetual gloom, shut off from the sun, the moon, and the stars. Paradiso is bathed eternally in the light of he who moves the sun and other stars. Thus, alone among all those whom we encounter in the *Comedy*, the souls in

Purgatory experience time, thereby exhibiting the possibility of moral growth and meaningful human choice. However, as Dante learns from Beatrice at the top of the mountain, even with redemption in sight, it is still possible in Purgatory to feel pain.[105] *In Sunlight and in Shadow*'s very title suggests the same comprehension of the fullness of human experience. No doubt, its end is unsatisfying in some respects in that Harry dies and does not return to Catherine. We are given to understand by the merest of signs, however, that this reunion is only postponed, not denied.

In some ways the end of *Sunlight* is the same as *Soldier*. The possibility of transcendence and redemption is only pointed to. Yet, this is enough for Alessandro in *Soldier*, and Harry and Catherine in *Sunlight* to find peace and move forward. Both of these novels are essentially realist. *Winter's Tale* allows for a wider metaphysics, and thus portrayal of the nature of the transcendent.

NOTES

1. Dante, *Purgatorio*, XXVII, 130–42.
2. Henceforth, *Sunlight*.
3. Mark Helprin, *In Sunlight and in Shadow*, 295.
4. Mark Helprin, e-mail to authors, March 3, 2014.
5. Dante, *Purgatorio*, I, 71.
6. Ibid., VII, 42.
7. Dante, *Inferno*, XXXIV, 133–39.
8. Helprin, *In Sunlight and in Shadow*, 246.
9. Helprin, *Winter's Tale*, 739.
10. See for instance Helprin, *In Sunlight and in Shadow*, 505.
11. Dante, *Inferno*, II, 69.
12. Helprin, *In Sunlight and in Shadow*, 69.
13. Ibid., 10.
14. Dante, *Purgatorio*, X, 32–33.
15. Helprin, *In Sunlight and in Shadow*, 452.
16. Ibid., 126. See also 48, 63
17. Ibid., 22 and 94.
18. Ibid., 702, 107.
19. See, Dante, *Paradiso*, XXXI, 112–20.
20. Helprin, *In Sunlight and in Shadow*, 83. See also 85.
21. Ibid., 122.
22. Ibid., 45. See also 91, 129.
23. Ibid., 63.
24. Ibid., 39.
25. See *Inferno*, XI, where while pausing in their descent, Virgil explains to Dante that Aristotle's *Ethics* provides the philosophic explication of the structure of Inferno.
26. See Aristotle, *Nicomachean Ethics*, III, 3.
27. Helprin indicates that he wrote a story (that went unpublished), entitled "Reconciliation," with a similar theme in 1969. In that story, he says, a Jewish husband and a Christian wife, ultimately find "confirmation of their beliefs and of the other's, and, thus, reconciliation." Helprin, e-mail to authors, March 3, 2014.
28. Ibid., 46.
29. Ibid., 50.

30. Matthew 27:46.
31. Helprin, *In Sunlight and in Shadow*, 165.
32. Ibid., 198.
33. Ibid., 208.
34. Ibid., 334.
35. Ibid., 306.
36. Ibid., 383.
37. Ibid., 322.
38. See also, *Winter's Tale*, 383.
39. Helprin, *In Sunlight and in Shadow*, 512.
40. Ibid., 322.
41. Ibid., 513.
42. Ibid., 513.
43. Ibid., 310.
44. Ibid., 519.
45. Ibid., 519.
46. Ibid.
47. Ibid., 540.
48. Mazzeo argues that Dante understood that at the moment of their creation, individual souls experience, if only momentarily, oneness with God that they have intimations of in life, but which they cannot fully remember, but yearn to experience again. See Mazzeo, "Dante's Conception of Love," *Journal of History of Ideas* (April 1957) 18:2, 147–60.
49. Helprin, *In Sunlight and in Shadow*, 539.
50. Ibid., 142. See also, 294 and 375.
51. Ibid., 63.
52. Ibid., 367.
53. Luke 14: 26.
54. Ibid., 9.
55. Ibid., 507. See also 150 and 324.
56. Ibid., 607.
57. Ibid., 48.
58. Ibid., 701.
59. Dante, *Purgatorio*, II, 106–11.
60. Ibid., II, 121–23.
61. Helprin, *In Sunlight and in Shadow*, 59–60.
62. Ibid., 61.
63. Ibid., 97.
64. Helprin, *Winter's Tale*, 628–29. See also 615.
65. Ibid., 665.
66. Helprin, *In Sunlight and in Shadow*, 98
67. Ibid., 164.
68. Ibid., 296.
69. Ibid., 26.
70. Ibid., 392.
71. Ibid., 392.
72. Helprin, *Winter's Tale*, 742.
73. Helprin, *In Sunlight and in Shadow*, 604.
74. Dante, *Purgatorio*, XXVIII, 49–51.
75. Helprin, *In Sunlight and in Shadow*, 64–66.
76. We see a similar moment of temptation for Freddy and a moment of mediation by Fredericka when they meet Lucia in *Freddy and Fredericka*. See *Freddy and Fredericka*, 414.
77. Helprin, *In Sunlight and in Shadow*, 594.
78. Ibid. See also 519, where Catherine says to Harry: "If you hold as tightly to life as you propose, you'll smother it."
79. Ibid., 369.
80. Ibid., 368, 374–75, and 528.

81. Ibid., 368.

82. Ibid., 530.

83. Ibid., 530.

84. Ibid., 374.

85. Ibid.

86. In one of the many jokes and allusions that Helprin delights in, the legendary OSS agent and later infamous CIA figure, James Jesus Angleton, is here surely also referenced.

87. Helprin, "The Canon Under Siege," *New Criterion* (September 1988), 39.

88. Helprin, *In Sunlight and in Shadow*, 557.

89. Ibid., 602–3.

90. Ibid., 165 and 557.

91. Ibid., 699.

92. Ibid., 33.

93. Ibid., 183.

94. Ibid., 297.

95. Ibid., 704.

96. Ibid., 701.

97. Dante, *Purgatory*, XV, 71–77.

98. Ibid., XX, 127–38.

99. Helprin, *In Sunlight and in Shadow*, 674.

100. Ibid., 702.

101. Ibid., 691.

102. Ibid., 698. See also Helprin, "Bumping into Characters," *New York Times*, October 3, 2012.

103. Helprin, *In Sunlight and in Shadow*, 125.

104. Ibid.

105. Dante, *Purgatorio*, XXXI, 13–69.

Chapter Three

The City of Justice

Mark Helprin's *Winter's Tale* revolves around the theme of justice, a city of perfect justice, to be precise. The most narratively complex of Helprin's novels, it involves several story lines and moves characters across time and place in ways that defy conventional limitations. By the end of the novel, the diverse stories have been reconciled into a unity, and, if only momentarily, a city of justice is realized. The reconciliation of love and justice is at the heart of the novel, and, in this, *Winter's Tale* takes up the theme of Dante's *Paradiso*, where, in the heavenly city, we see justice perfected by divine love. As suggested at the end of the preceding chapter, *Winter's Tale* is the most explicit of Helprin's novels in addressing transcendence. Arguably also the most poetic of his novels, *Winter's Tale* employs elements of fantasy to speak of redemption beyond the limits of the finite order. Thus, temporal love and the quest for temporal justice are explicitly linked to the absolute.

Winter's Tale begins, like all great epics, *in medias res*. A white horse, Athansor, possessing self-consciousness, escapes from its stable in Williamsburg and travels to lower Manhattan just in time to rescue Peter Lake from the criminal gang, the Short Tails and the villainous Pearly Soames. While the novel is comprised of several plots and covers over a century of time, the stories of Peter Lake and Athansor remain central throughout. The first part of the novel treats the love story of Peter Lake, who has made his living as a burglar and thief, and Beverly Penn, daughter of a New York publishing magnate. The love affair is short and tragic, as Beverly dies of a consumption-like disease from which she has suffered for some time soon after they are married. Less than a third of the way through this novel, this tragedy is completed. Pearly Soames pursues Peter and the white horse throughout the ages and throughout the novel.

The next story line begins several decades later with a young woman named Virginia Gamely, who lives with her mother and her baby in a mystical place in upstate New York, the Lake of the Coheeries. Like Peter Lake, she is drawn to New York City, where she too comes in contact with the Penn family, becoming a columnist for their paper.

Virginia will eventually meet Hardesty Marratta, son of a wealthy San Francisco father, who is given the choice between inheriting his father's money or receiving instead a silver salver, finally choosing the latter. On the salver are written four virtues: honesty, courage, sacrifice, and patience. In the middle is the inscription: "For what can be imagined more beautiful than the sight of a perfectly just city rejoicing in justice alone."[1] Hardesty understands this as an invitation to set out on a quest for the perfectly just city and he too makes a pilgrimage to New York, where he falls in love with Virginia Gamely. These later stories are clearly rooted in the contemporary world, as we are given the exact date of his father's will, September 1, 1995. Alongside Hardesty and Virginia's romance is a relationship between Christina, who once saved Athansor from drowning when she was a child, and Asbury, who is the pilot of *The Sun*'s ship.

We also meet the mysterious figure of Jackson Mead, a bridge builder who eventually is revealed to have ambitions on a metaphysical scale. Connected to him is the comic character of Cecil Mature, who journeys through time parallel with Peter, at times an ally, at other times an impediment. Other characters of note include the Baymen, a mysterious tribe of people who live on the outer marshes of Manhattan's shoreline, and a sentient Cloud Wall that provides a passageway to some form of the absolute.[2]

The theme of justice runs throughout *Winter's Tale*. Not only does Hardesty understand that his father's dying wish is for him to seek the most just city, but the novel's protagonist, Peter Lake, while a baby, washes onto the shores of New York in a model ship bearing *City of Justice* as its name. Several other characters, including the Baymen, Sarah Gamely, Jackson Mead, and the Cloud Wall, indicate that this city is also their end.

In Dante's *Paradiso* we are given just such a city. The Empyrean is an assembly of citizens, each in their particularity contributing to the whole. The dream of Rome, as told in Virgil's *Aeneid*, is to establish the *Pax Romana*, an empire of peace wherein all individuals and cultures are united under its good governance.[3] Dante, following Virgil, is caught up in the political turmoil of Italy and his *De Monarchia* suggests that he too imagines the possibility of a world empire that will bring an end to strife, achieving something of a heaven on earth. *Paradiso*, however, suggests that Dante has come to recognize the limitations of his earlier position. The city of the celestial rose surpasses any possible earthly city as imagined by ether Virgil or Dante. Dante compares the state of a Florentine seeing the heavenly city to the Barbarians who first saw Rome:

> If the barbarians, coming from some region
> That every day by Helice is covered,
> Revolving with her son whom she delights in,
>
> Beholding Rome and all her noble works,
> Were wonder-struck, what time the Lateran
> Above all mortal things was eminent,
>
> I who to the divine had from the human,
> From time unto eternity, had come,
> From Florence to a people just and sane,
>
> With what amazement must I have been filled! [4]

Dante suggests that part of his and Virgil's error lies in investing their hope in the earthly political sphere when their true end can only be achieved metaphysically.

One of the most significant elements of Dante's *Paradiso* is its unity. When Dante encounters Piccarda on the heaven of the moon, he asks if she is dissatisfied with her placement, seemingly on the outer edges of heaven. Piccarda explains that

> Brother, our will is quieted by virtue
> Of charity, that makes us wish alone
> For what we have, nor gives us thirst for more.
>
> If to be more exalted we aspired,
> Discordant would our aspirations be
> Unto the will of Him who here secludes us. [5]

Piccarda, like the other souls in Paradiso, loves and wills only the good. All of the citizens of the Empyrean are fully in accord with the divine will. As a result, and in contrast to the images of Inferno, there is neither strife nor discord amongst the individuals in Paradiso. Inasmuch as these souls each love the good, in willing and achieving it, they are internally satisfied as well.

Piccarda indicates that Dante's perception of her as being on the outer rim of Paradiso is caused by his finite and limited capacity to comprehend the absolute. [6] The limitations of Dante's perspective suggest the difficulties of achieving an earthly peace similar to that described in *Paradiso*. Dante arrives here after travelling through Inferno and Purgatory, and has been "transhumanized," ascending into Paradiso. Despite the education of this pilgrimage, he still imagines that Piccarda might imagine and prefer something more satisfying than the fulfillment of divine will. Presumably, this understanding stems from the finite world, where scarce resources mean that the more one person has, less must be available for others, causing inevitable competition and strife. Alternatively, the goods that are available to Piccarda and all the souls of Paradiso are infinite in nature, meaning that all wills can be equally and fully satisfied. Despite the journey he has just taken, Dante still imagines that the laws of the finite world govern the infinite.

Although all of the individuals in *Paradiso* are unified, they nonetheless retain their particular natures. Hence, as we have seen, in the heaven of the doctors, for example, various philosophers are all present, each representing the particularities of their own thought, even while acknowledging the virtues of their intellectual rivals.[7] This is the rule for all of the inhabitants of Paradiso. So, Cunizza and Rahab, "harlots" in this life, retain their air of sensuality, even if their desires have been ordered anew.[8] The justice of heaven is not achieved by overcoming or erasing the diversity of the particular world. Instead, the particular natures of these souls are reconciled to the universal, while still retaining those characteristics that make them individuals, including the choices they made while mortal, both just and unjust. Although all the souls in Paradiso have been justified, as the penalties of their vices have been assumed in Christ's death, the particular choices that they made while alive are respected and incorporated into the divine city. Even though Piccarda resides in the heaven of the celestial rose, she and the other dwellers in Paradise "have sweet life in different degrees, by feeling more or less the eternal breath."[9] Alessandro's fear in *Soldier*, that the particular people he loved would be lost in the universal, is addressed directly in *Paradiso*, and is represented as being unwarranted. Dante's vision is not of assimilation, but of each individual being brought to the distinct and perfect form of her or himself.

While we do not see the heavenly city in any extended form in *Winter's Tale*, we are given glimpses of it, and Helprin's story indicates how it might be approached while still in the finite world. Throughout *Winter's Tale*, the characters and the reader are asked to imagine the nature of eternity, the transcendence of time and space, and the perfection of justice and love. In each of these, we are asked to imagine Paradiso. The end of the novel involves all of the characters involved in a similar pursuit, saving the city, which, it turns out, is parallel and inextricably linked to saving an individual child.

Near the end of the novel, while the city of New York burns, Abby, the daughter of Hardesty and Virginia, dies. Her death, however, is not final and she is resurrected. At that same moment, the city is momentarily bathed in a golden light. Abby lives and the city will be rebuilt. Helprin suggests that the particular, imagined here in the form of a very young girl, is commensurate with the universal, the city. Willing the good for one is equivalent to willing the good for the whole.

Abby's final reawakening and the rebirth of the city are both consequent to Peter Lake's recognition of the eternal nature of love and his faith that such love survives even death. Peter Lake willingly accepts the death of his finite nature, in the hope of an eternal reconciliation in and by love. In

Christian theology, the corruption of human nature that ends in death is understood as being overcome by the infinite love and sacrifice of God. In Helprin's novel, Peter Lake, a good man, a just man, but not a saint, is a Christ-like figure. Just as Beatrice can replace the image of the sacrament in the *Corpus Christi* pageant in *Purgatorio*, and is the end towards which Dante directs his hope and love, so Peter Lake is sufficient to act as an image of God in *Winter's Tale*.[10] However, unlike Beatrice, who we discover only in her perfected form, we see Peter Lake as participating in the fullness of nature, including its corruption. Helprin thereby highlights the transformative effect that divine grace has in the material world, such that even in its finitude and even in Peter Lake's corruption, the goodness of the divine is still apparent.

Finally, through these images, Helprin suggests that the nature of divine justice is such that it extends beyond its perfection in eternity to the possibility of a better, if not perfect, earthly world. Although Peter Lake dies and presumably ascends to Paradiso, the characters who remain set to building cities that reflect their new understanding of the good.

PARADISO IN TIME

All of the souls that Dante meets in *Paradiso* have a full account of time, knowing the past, present, and future. Hence, Dante's own future is told to him on several occasions. Most poignantly, Dante meets his great-great-grandfather in Paradiso who then tells him of his future exile from Florence.[11] The vision of all those who are unified by God's love is omniscient. Made eternal, and thus no longer "in time," these souls are able to view all of time in its completeness. Dante, heavily influenced by Boethius, suggests that the nature of the divine, as absolute and eternal, exists outside of time.[12] As such, all of time is comprehended from a singular position; past, present, and future, are eternally perceived as occurring now.

The souls in Purgatory have a corresponding view of time, indicating that they too will inevitably make their way to Paradiso. Nonetheless, these individuals still mark its passage as they themselves seek to change, habituating themselves to the good they have chosen. Even the souls in *Inferno* are given something of this omniscient view. People in Inferno are now outside of time, as their situation is eternally chosen. In habituating themselves to a life of vice, these people are no longer able to recognize the good so that they might choose it; they have "lost the good of the intellect."[13] As a result, they are unable to perceive things in the present. In other words, they have blinded themselves to what should be immediately before them. Nonetheless, their eternal state still allows them some sense of what is past and what is future. Farinata explains,

"We see, like those who have imperfect sight,
the things," he said, "that distant are from us;
so much still shines on us the Sovereign Ruler.

When they draw near, or are, is wholly vain
our intellect, and if none brings it to us,
not anything know we of your human state." [14]

The souls in Inferno are able to judge what is furthest from them with accuracy, but, as those who are caught in vice, they are unable to accurately recognize their current activity, willing it as the "good" even though it is otherwise.

Jackson Mead in *Winter's Tale* describes the idea that, given the proper distance or perspective, one might apprehend the universal. Having died on several occasions only to be "reborn" each time, Mead believes there is no necessary divide between the finite and the infinite, and he sets out to build a bridge connecting the two. He sees no necessary distinction between the nature of time and eternity, describing the relationship between the two using the metaphor of a film: "'Just as in film, there are only stills arranged in an illusion of motion, so in life and time. It is all locked hard within a matrix, and breathtakingly complicated, as if an infinite number of miniaturists had been employed forever in its startling depictions. But I assure you there is no anarchy, everything happened/happens at once, and it does not move.'" [15] Mead suggests that, given sufficient perspective, one can view all of time in the way that one who sees a film (or reads a novel) can hold the whole plot line in mind, perceiving and comprehending the whole. [16] It is an open question whether this appropriation of the divine perspective by Mead is an expression of *hubris* at best, or a suggestion of something more sinister, as we will discuss shortly.

Regardless of one's judgment of Jackson Mead, characters throughout *Winter's Tale*, while seemingly mortal and finite, are, like the character Dante, given opportunities to experience time from an eternal perspective. Some characters travel in time, such as Peter Lake who is born in one age, and then finds himself in another. For others, time operates more slowly, and so the Gamely's and the Baymen age at a much slower rate, enabling them to live much longer lives. Finally, characters, such as Jackson Mead, Revd. Mootfowl, Cecil and Abby, die and then live again, or otherwise evade death.

The extent to which these characters realize their transcendent position is sometimes unclear, but the reader is given to understand that, in the argument of the novel, one's finite experience of time is caused by a limitation in one's perspective. In other words, like Dante who cannot take in the full nature of Paradiso, requiring the souls to array themselves in a way that allows him some understanding, Helprin suggests that our perspective of time is limited. Seeking to escape Pearly Soames and the Short Tails, Peter Lake periodically takes refuge in the ceiling of Grand Central Station. Allegorically, Peter Lake is shown fleeing from the mutability of the finite order in favor of an eternal view of the whole. Hence, he sleeps above the constellation of the stars that line Grand Central Station's ceiling. However, we are told time and again that despite the presence of these stars, few of those who pass by take the time to look up: "No one ever looked up. The ceiling had been dark and cloudy for so long that it had been forgotten . . . for most people the barrel vault was too high to bother with."[17] Too focused on what is close to them, most individuals never think to draw back from their particular interests and desires and look to the whole. *Winter's Tale* explicitly invites us to imagine time from a universal perspective. All of time might be imagined as existing in an eternal now. Jackson Mead explains this by saying that time itself is an illusion.[18] This, however, is not to suggest that what occurs in time has no meaning or value. Instead, as we shall see, the argument of both the *Divine Comedy* and *Winter's Tale* is exactly the opposite. The choices that are made in time have an eternal effect.

If all of time exists in the present, normal limitations no longer hold. As a result, actions and events that are generally thought of as past, and beyond the scope of one's intentions and hopes, need be no longer. Jackson Mead reflects on a painting of St. Stephen's ascension and says, "'most people who have come to venerate St. Stephen, do not think he actually rose. . . . They think to the contrary, that he is rising, that he rises. The act is not complete. Even the painting freezes him in midair. It is, rather, in progress. . . . What I am saying is that, until the canvas is set, actualities are no more than intentions, and intentions are as much as actualities.'"[19] From a divine perspective, all of time happens concurrently and is ever present; as a result the past is not past, but rather is present, just as the future is not an event that will happen, but which happens. Practically speaking this would suggest that events in the past and those in the future are not so distant nor complete that they cannot be affected by an action that occurs now.

While Peter Lake eventually perceives this, even early in his life he senses something of it. Having been exiled from the marshes by the Baymen, a young Peter Lake encounters a dying girl in a tenement building. He is horrified by her condition, but does not think he has any resources with which he might help her: "Peter Lake's instinct told him that there was not much life left for it to live. He wanted to help, but he had no experience or memory to guide him. He could neither leave nor stay. He watched it shake and bob in the near-darkness until, somehow, he fell reeling back into the light."[20] Twenty years later, even though he recognizes that there will be little to nothing he can now do, Peter Lake decides to seek out this young girl and somehow help her.[21] The mortician he meets tells him to give up, after all "'The city is burning and under siege. And we are in a war in which everyone is killed and no one is remembered.'"[22] Despite the mortician's claim, Peter Lake's intention to help the child is fulfilled almost a century later in Abby's resurrection. Sarah Gamely thus explains to Virginia, "'A benevolent act is like a locust: it sleeps until it is called.'"[23]

These points help to explain the account of history given by the narrator midway through the book. Nothing, the narrator explains, is either random or predetermined. All actions are part of a plan and at the same time each action is individually and freely chosen. The seeming paradox of these claims is resolved if we understood the nature of the plan as one that incorporates the free intentions and actions of its participants. If all time is divinely known as present, then, from a providential perspective, all individual choices, even those we think we have yet to make, are already known. The divine incorporates one's full freedom into the completed whole. Jessica Penn, describing how she perceives her role as an actress, makes this argument clear:

> "Only bad actors memorize lines. Good actors
> are perpetually writing them as they act."
> "Even though the playwright has already written them."
> She nodded her head.
> "Isn't that presumption?"
> "The playwright understands.". . .
> "The play has been put down, but it is still new to you.
> When you say the lines, you are saying them for the first
> time. They are as much yours as they are his. How can
> you explain that?"
> "I can't, but I *can* tell you that this is the quality that
> distinguishes the good actors from the bad."[24]

Two things are evident in Jessica's account. The playwright, like the film-maker, and presumably, like God, has an account of the whole; the plot has already been written. Regardless of this, a good actor still fully wills the content of each of her lines. They are not externally given, but internally generated. A good actor writes their lines while they are acting and the nature of the playwright is such that they incorporate this particularity into the universal plan.

Second, Jessica indicates a difference between a good actor or action and a bad one. Good actions stem from the internalization of providence. The good actor says the lines and they are their own. In other words, when a person plays their role properly, they gain the perspective on time that the director has, such that they are aware, at least, of the end to which their actions are to be directed; they direct themselves to "the good of the intellect." In so doing, thier part is made clear and they knowingly and willingly play the role as it was intended.

The bad actor, alternatively, merely apes what the script dictates. Bad actions, it seems, still accord with the plan, for the plan incorporates whatever we might choose, and thus these actions are interwoven into whatever the final act might be. However, the intent of the actor does not agree with the intent of the playwright. While the outer form is made to correspond with presumably some good and just end, the intent of the actor is otherwise. We might think of an actor who says their lines all the while thinking about what they are going to have for dinner once the play is over, or, worse, who says thier lines while resenting the fact that they are in this play at all.

Interestingly, we see something of this in the mortician's cold advice to Peter Lake. The mortician offers no hope to Peter Lake in his search for the young girl who died so many years ago. Instead, he grimly tells him that the city is on fire and at war. His only advice to Peter Lake is to go home to Beverly, the woman he loves, for he is the only one who might remember her.[25] The city at this point is neither on fire, nor at war; however, from the position of the man who takes in its dead, it might very well seem to be. By the end of the novel, we know that what he is says is prophetic. Just as Dante will be sent into exile, so New York will be at war and on fire. Moreover, as we find out, all Peter Lake has to do at this future moment of crisis is remember Beverly and then everything else will fall into place. The mortician seems to have no knowledge of the prophetic and hopeful meaning of his words. If anything, he is a man who has no sense that he has any role to play in a just end, seeking instead to discourage Peter Lake from his quest. Nonetheless, his words, if properly attended to and remembered, would direct Peter Lake to what he has to do to achieve justice for the girl he currently seeks and later knows in Abby.

At first glance, it seems strange that the mortician's position suggests a failure in vision—how, after all, is he supposed to comprehend what will happen a century later? Surely such an expectation is unjust and unfair. Indeed, Peter Lake himself does not understand the mortician's advice as providential, nor does he explicitly recall it when it would be appropriate to do so, requiring instead that Harry Penn remind him of Beverly by bringing him to see her portrait.[26] Nonetheless, like other characters in the novel, Peter Lake is given a number of indications, and thus opportunities, to recognize that he is part of a larger plan. Leaving aside the truly fantastical things that seem to happen to Peter Lake, like the appearances of Athansor at exactly the right moment, he might contemplate the very route his life has taken. Orphaned as a small child, he is rescued by a benevolent race, and, when seemingly orphaned again and again, someone else claims him as his or her own: the Baymen, Little Liza and Jane, Mootfowl, Cecil, Pearly, and then Beverly. If Peter Lake were to stand back from the events of his life, he would have to concede that his continued existence is nothing short of miraculous. Even these things might seem to be too extraordinary, however, to be taken as suggestive of anything most people have access to, for few of us have ever been adopted into a mysterious tribe that lives on the edges of the world. Nonetheless, there are presumably other "fortuitous" events that intervene in our lives when most required. We might read this as the work of chance or, as Helprin suggests, providence.

Isaac Penn tells Peter Lake that everything is working towards the culmination of a plan, a golden age wherein justice will be made manifest: "'by luminous and surprising connections that we have not imagined, by illustrations terrifying and benevolent—a golden age that will show us not what we wish, but some bare awkward truth upon which rests everything that ever was and ever will be.'"[27] Like most of the characters in the book, Isaac Penn awaits the coming of the most just city. Moreover, through the course of the novel the reader is shown that by drawing back far enough from one's immediate experience of the world, one can perceive, if only vaguely, the nature of this plan and one's role in it. Like Jessica Penn, Helprin suggests that a just individual comprehends the nature of the plot before her and then internalizes its essence so she can play her part well. The just city, Helprin argues, is made possible within and by means of just individuals. In this, he indicates that the individual can be made sufficient for universal ends—those of the earthly and even heavenly city.

THE MANY BECOME ONE

While Isaac Penn waits for the perfectly just city to arise, other characters in the novel actively seek it. Hardesty takes the inscription on the platter to be his father's dying wish for him and leaves San Francisco to find the perfectly just city. After a strange series of adventures, Hardesty arrives in New York. He does not think that New York could possibly be the city he seeks, for in a just city "all forces would smoothly align, and all balances would be brought even. That would never occur in this ragged place of too much energy and too many loose ends that lashed about like taut cables that suddenly are parted. New York could never be fully at peace with itself; nor could one vision defeat, compress, and control its crooked and varied time."[28] The city Hardesty searches for is, like Paradiso, unified in its vision and at peace, with all of its parts working together toward a common and known good. New York, alternatively, is discordant in its particularity. There are too many different elements working to what appear to be too many different ends. Hardesty cannot imagine any universal purpose being manifest, desired, or achieved in such a place.

Almost immediately after arriving in New York, Hardesty falls in love with Virginia Gamely. Nonetheless, he decides that he must leave and continue his quest for the just city, choosing what he takes to be his duty to the universal truth of justice over and against the particular fulfillment of his desires.[29] He is moved by a sense of duty to forgo his particular satisfaction for the sake of universal truths. This is not surprising, given that Hardesty has had two tours of military duty. Prepared to sacrifice his life for the sake of justice, we should not be surprised that he is willing to sacrifice his particular satisfaction in love. However admirable Hardesty's sense of duty and his accompanying ascetic lifestyle, Helprin suggests that it is incomplete. Hardesty cannot imagine a justice wherein his own particular desires are fulfilled. Instead, he lives his life with the belief that to seek his satisfaction would be an indication of his corruption and he assumes that insofar as New York is driven by disparate individuals seeking to fulfill disparate and particular desires, it can never be fully just. Hardesty is thus prepared to leave Virginia and her young son, even though he knows they love him, and even though he knows they have been left before. His sense of duty overrides not just his happiness but also the potential happiness of the people who love him.

In almost direct contrast with Alessandro from *Soldier*, Hardesty chooses the universal over the particular, and justice over love. Missing the ship that will take him to Europe, Hardesty goes so far as to jump in the harbor and swim after it. His tenacity is rewarded and Hardesty is pulled aboard. When the Cloud Wall appears in front of the boat, Hardesty is given a taste of the absolute peace that he imagines he is seeking, for "as it touched Hardesty's heel, he felt rapturous pleasure spreading through his entire body, not the kind of sensuality which robs and burns his soul, but something elevated and ecstatic that he knew might take him very far."[30] The Cloud Wall has engulfed Hardesty before; at that time he was asleep and when he awoke he was in the Lake of the Coheeries, a place seemingly outside of time and impossible to get to unless one already knows where it is. Virginia tells Hardesty that the Cloud Wall is a means of transcending the particularities of time.[31] The peace that he feels when it engulfs his leg is suggestive of the sense of the completeness one would feel if removed from the constant change that accompanies a life in time. Hardesty rejects New York, for "[it] was a frustrating, hard, unforgiving, unkind city, strong on suffering, punishment, and murderous weather. Its climate and population were a scythe that swept relentlessly."[32] The particularity of New York, caused and made manifest by the constant change of all of its parts, indicates to Hardesty that these can never be reconciled nor unified. The Cloud Wall suggests another possibility: a place outside of time, wherein change and motion are overcome. Hence, when Peter Lake enters the Cloud Wall, only to emerge a century later, he is unchanged, and is surprised to find out that the rest of the world has.[33]

Nonetheless, when given the opportunity to experience this form of the absolute, Hardesty realizes he is mistaken, for "everything told him that the city was better. . . . And then there was Virginia."[34] In experiencing the Cloud Wall, Hardesty is forced to recognize by contrast the good present in the city as it particularly exists and in the particular people he loves. Hardesty turns back to the city and back to Virginia, and Helprin thereby suggests these things need not be in such stark contrast. Rather he indicates that they might, in a perfectly just city, be reconciled. This is comedy, not tragedy, and Helprin's aim is to demonstrate the overcoming of this apparent opposition. The classical drama illustrating this opposition is Sophocles' *Antigone*. There the justice of the city is set against the love of one's own. Without a form of mediation, Creon, who represents the former, is brought to as much ruin as Antigone, the advocate of the latter. In *Antigone*, Creon and Antigone, the public and the private, respectively, remain in tension until all is lost. In *Winter's Tale*, this tragedy is avoided when Hardesty turns back to Virginia. Helprin's modern perspective, unlike that of Sophocles, is such that there is no necessary division between the universal and the particular.[35]

As in Helprin's other novels, the movement to a universal principle— love, justice, or beauty, depending on the novel—is inextricably tied to the particular. On the one hand, it is through the particular instantiations of these principles that characters learn of the universal forms. On the other hand, particular examples of the principles stand initially in tension with characters' apprehension of the universals. That is, the temptation is to believe that the particular embodies the whole of the universal and to seek nothing more.

As we have discussed, in the *Divine Comedy* the character Dante also faces this challenge. When Dante meets Virgil, readers are given occasion to suspect that Dante's attachment to the Roman poet is partially the cause of his being lost in a dark woods. In those early moments of the poem, Dante calls Virgil not only his teacher, but also his author and refers to Virgil's *Aeneid*, using the Italian word *volume* rather than the more commonplace *libre*, suggesting that Virgil plays the role of a god in Dante's eyes.[36] Having taken Virgil as sufficient, Dante has substituted an individual human in place of the universal. Hence, when having moved through Hell and Purgatory, accompanied by Virgil, Dante then laments the loss of his friend and guide, even as he comes to the greater mediator, Beatrice.[37] Beatrice, however, affects a fuller form of mediation, leading Dante through the lower heavens of Paradiso. As a result, by the time he reaches the celestial rose in Paradise, Dante is better equipped for the moment when Beatrice leaves his side, for he knows that, unlike Virgil, Beatrice is not lost forever.[38]

Although Virgil is able to prepare Dante for Beatrice, his perspective is too limited to move Dante to the absolute. Correspondingly, his fixed place in Inferno means that Dante is unable to enter into a reciprocal relationship with him, assisting in Virgil's progression. In contrast, Helprin's characters, who are diverse in virtue as well as free, are able to mediate the universal for one another. Insofar as each is helped and transformed by another, it is clear that no one character is the good itself. Instead, by means of their transformations, they point to a fuller good as their, and their loved one's, satisfaction.

That Hardesty's end is discovered in his love for Virginia and their daughter, Abby, is fitting, given that Virginia's nature and desires are in great contrast to Hardesty's own. Bringing these two characters together and then uniting them with Christina, Asbury, and finally Peter Lake, Helprin suggests a way by which distinct and particular individuals might be reconciled to achieve a larger whole. The individual need not be abandoned, as Hardesty has thought; the individual is in fact necessary for justice to come to fruition.

During a particularly difficult winter at the Lake of the Coheeries, Virginia decides that she and her infant son will set out for New York, thereby making it more likely that her grandmother will have sufficient supplies to make it through to spring. It might appear that Virginia, like Hardesty, is motivated by a sense of duty. After all, she will have to ski a long portion of the trip in dangerous conditions, and she will arrive in New York without any contacts, not even knowing where she will stay. This, however, is not the full picture, for Virginia decides that she will go to New York only after she has dreamed that the city has become her lover: "She took it without inhibition, grappling with it breathlessly and nude. She sweated, rolled her closed eyes, and sawed back and forth from thigh to thigh, as it overwhelmed her with its surging colors."[39] As an employee of the newspaper, *The Sun*, Virginia then becomes the city's lover, publishing what are essentially love letters to and about New York.[40] Virginia dreams the city will fulfill her desires and she loves it in response. Through the course of the novel, the city becomes an image for the universal itself. In seeking perfect justice, the characters in the novel desire the fulfillment of universal ends. Granted, we discover in the course of the novel that this city, New York, while a very great city, is not the universal itself. Instead, it functions as an intermediary for the divine. In seeing that the city might be the means and source of her particular, even physical satisfaction, Virginia apprehends a truer image of the divine than Hardesty. In the image of Virginia we are asked to think not of an absolute that exists in contrast to our particular satisfaction, but rather one wherein our particularity is taken up and satisfied.

Even prior to boarding the ship that will take him to Europe, Hardesty has an apprehension that he might be leaving the very thing he is searching for: "He could not have loved Virginia Gamely more, and he wondered if what he assumed lay at such a great distance were present in this very city—or even in Virginia herself, if the future were to be fair and imaginative enough to take refuge in a single soul."[41] In this moment, Hardesty imagines the possibility that the universal might reconcile itself to the individual such that the individual is fully retained. Virginia already believes that this is a possibility; she thus waits for her dreams to indicate what she should do, and her dreams tell her.[42] Jackson Mead and Isaac Penn suggest that one must gain a perspective of distance to be able to see the whole. Virginia's future comes to her by means of her dreams. In one's dreams, one is often the bystander,

watching the activity of the dream as if as a third person. Virginia sees the
city become her lover; she gains sufficient perspective on herself that she is
able to thereby recognize what she should do. At first glance gaining this
perspective seems unlikely, given that, unlike Dante and Virginia, we normally are not given the means to ascend to Paradiso, and thereby look down
at all of time, nor do we all have such prophetic dreams. Virginia, we are
told, "had always known that her future was in her," and, unlike Hardesty,
who would search the entire world for the city that is his end, Virginia need
only search herself.[43] Helprin thus provides an image of the universal as
already residing with the individual, suggesting that there is a corollary to the
idea that humans are made in God's image. That is, an image of the divine
exists within humans, a position common to Jewish and Christian theology.

Helprin suggests that we do not have to wait on dreams to recognize the
nature of our true purpose or end. Instead, Hardesty imagines that the perfectly just city might be present in the woman he loves. And we know that
the truth, as Virginia understands it, complements and helps complete Hardesty's understanding. Correspondingly, our narrator says that there are four
gates to the city, each corresponding to a specific motivation: acceptance of
responsibility (east), the desire to explore (south), devotion to beauty (west),
and selfless love (north).[44] Four people then enter the city, each from one of
these directions: Christina (east), Asbury (south), Hardesty (west), and Virginia (north). We also know that in addition to the proclamation of the beauty
of justice, four virtues are inscribed on the platter: honesty, courage, sacrifice, and patience.[45] There is no obvious way to line up specific virtues with
each character; however, by providing four of each, Helprin tempts the reader to find a way to reconcile the individuals to gates and to virtues. The four
individuals then become two couples, united by romantic love, and then the
two couples are reconciled through friendship.

The individual characters of the novel are each particular people, with
particular characteristics and virtues. The absolute, as it is present in each of
them, takes on a particular aspect of the good. While they may be unable to
recognize the divine as it is present within themselves, they come to see
themselves through the eyes of their lovers. Even further, in loving someone
else, they are made aware of the good as it is particularly manifest in another
human being. Their account of the nature of the good is thereby broadened.
Mead and Penn suggest that one needs perspective to see the whole. By
means of Virginia, one recognizes that this whole might be present in each of
us. However, individuals do not often have sufficient distance from themselves to truly see their characters. Helprin directs his readers to another
means by which such perspective might be gained: in and through the people
they love, and, even further, in the nature of love itself.

Virginia, Hardesty, Asbury, and Christina each have a role to play in the
final outcome of the novel, a city of perfect justice. Their reciprocated love

for and thus knowledge of each other is, in part, the means by which the perfect city is achieved. Inasmuch as one loves the good, one would expect to find some element thereof in the people one loves. Attending to this good can be the means by which one gains a view of the larger whole that is the nature of the divine and the end that both Helprin and Dante suggest we seek.

PETER LAKE AND BEVERLY

Virginia and Hardesty, Asbury and Christina, are not themselves sufficient for realizing the city of perfect justice. They need Peter Lake and Peter Lake in turn needs Beverly. Of all the couples in *Winter's Tale*, Peter Lake and Beverly most obviously mirror Dante and Beatrice. Just as Dante explicates divine love by means of the reciprocated love between Beatrice and Dante, so the love between Peter Lake and Beverly mirrors that of the divine and becomes the foundation of justice.

As discussed earlier, the Helprin novels treated in this work do not simply correspond to *Inferno*, *Purgatorio*, and *Paradiso*. Rather, they each explore Dantean themes: spiritual self-destruction, the acquisition of virtue through suffering, redemption and enlightenment through divine grace, to name a few. Each novel has a particular emphasis that mirrors the main thematic thrust of each of Dante's canticles. In the treatment of time that we see in *Winter's Tale*, along with the perspective of eternal justice possessed by several of the characters, which in the *Divine Comedy* belongs only to the divine and is shared among the redeemed, we see the closest relation to *Paradiso* among Helprin's novels.

After having looked into the seemingly infinite eyes of the white horse, Athansor, Peter Lake seeks to transform himself. Not certain as to what to do, he decides to complete some significant heists so that he will be free to leave the city and escape. Instead, Peter Lake meets Beverly, falls in love, and the two are married for a short while. Like Beatrice, Beverly dies at a young age, leaving Peter Lake alone. When Beverly is alive, it is clear to Peter Lake that he "'was not born to be protected, but . . . to protect.'"[46] He understands that his purpose lies in the love revealed to him by means of his relationship with Beverly.

However, when Beverly dies, Peter Lake acts as though the very nature of love has died. With no longer an immediate and proximate end to love, Peter Lake instead seeks strife and even death.[47] In *Purgatorio*, when Beatrice meets Dante, she chastises him, for, in having lost sight of her physical self, he lost his metaphysical way.[48] When Beverly dies, Peter Lake is similarly lost. Just as it is Beatrice's love that awakens Dante in the dark woods, so too is Peter Lake brought back to himself and his true end when he recognizes the continued love that exists between him and Beverly.

Prior to discussing the means and end to which Peter Lake is drawn by Beverly's love, it is important to note an essential difference between the story of these two lovers and that of Dante and Beatrice. The couples described in the previous section share a reciprocated love in which each is strengthened by the virtue or perspective of the other. It is clear how Beverly's perspective of the universal and absolute in the course of the novel is necessary to Peter Lake's good end. We might be tempted to think that Beverly, much like Beatrice, has nothing to learn from her love of Peter Lake. It makes sense that Dante can add nothing to Beatrice's virtue or perspective of the whole when she has already ascended to Paradiso, perfected by divine love. However, unlike Dante, Peter Lake engages in an actual relationship with Beverly while she is still alive. She is thus given the opportunity to gain some further perspective on the absolute by means of the good she sees in him.

In *Soldier*, we do not learn enough about Ariane to discover what she gains from Alessandro. In *Sunlight*, Catherine and Harry mediate each other to a higher end. However, Harry dies and we know that however good Catherine is at the end of the novel, her life will hold further temptations, failures, and growth. *Winter's Tale* offers the most complete vision of the need individuals have of the reciprocated love of others. Beverly is almost in her perfected state and thus most closely resembles Beatrice. However, even she becomes better by means of her relationship with Peter Lake.

A Beatrice in Need of a Dante

Prior to her death, it is clear that Beverly already recognizes and comprehends something of the divine. While the other characters in the novel realize the nature of the absolute via the city and people they love, Beverly, who is close to death, is given an even more universal perspective. Dying from consumption, she spends most of the time on the roof of her home, attempting to regulate the temperature of her body. Beverly spends long nights gazing at the stars, and they in turn become her lovers: "Even astronomers did not take in the sky with such devotion, for they were constantly occupied with charting, measurements . . . Beverly had the whole of it; she could see it all. . . . The abandoned stars were hers for the many rich hours of sparkling winter nights, and, unattended, she took them in like lovers."[49] Looking at the stars, Beverly is given something of a supernatural understanding of the whole. Isaac Penn, Beverly's father, tells Peter Lake that she has seen the golden age, while Beverly herself tells him that she has, at times, already crossed over to whatever lies beyond her finite existence.[50] Even further, when her father tells her that he does not understand the nature of her visions, for the gods that he has understood have always been far away, Beverly responds, "they are here."[51]

Dante tells us that his poetry will necessarily fail to describe the beauty of Paradise, and Beverly is unable to fully communicate what she knows of the divine. Unable to explain to the astronomer what she understands of the heavens, Beverly tells him only that the universe "'growls'" and "'shouts',", while the "'light is silent, but then it clashes like cymbals, and arches out like a fountain, to travel and yet be still. It crosses space without moving.'"[52] When she tries to tell Peter Lake about the immense animals that appear to her in the constellations, he can only believe that what she says is true, but he cannot comprehend it.[53]

Despite her apprehension of the absolute, Beverly's life is not complete. One thing that her life lacks and that Peter Lake brings to her is the possibility of romantic and erotic love. Beverly knows the love of her family and "mines" love from the stars. In neither of these instances does she know if she is loved for herself. Beverly's family loves her, but given that she is a daughter and a sister, their love is unconditional. It appears that the stars return Beverly's love, but they are universal and she knows them abstractly. Peter Lake, however, loves her specifically because of who she is and the good she embodies. Hence, when he first happens upon her playing the piano, he comprehends her greater virtue and loves her because of it: "He didn't know what was happening, and was resentful of the deep emotions that he tried to control and could not. . . . He had unspeakable admiration for the way she had risen from obvious weakness to court with such passion the elusive and demanding notes that he had heard. . . . She had risen above herself, right before his eyes. She had risen, and then fallen back, weakened, vulnerable, alone."[54] Peter Lake then takes great pains to ensure that it truly is Beverly that he loves and not just her money that he is attracted to.[55] In Peter Lake's love, Beverly experiences what it is like to be recognized for exactly who she is, and by means of his knowledge of her, Beverly gains a clearer sense of herself. Peter Lake's experience confirms that this is indeed part of the nature and import of romantic love, albeit somewhat differently. When Beverly first sees him, her response is less than flattering, although it is honest and loving: "'If you're what I got . . . then you're what I'll take.' He might have been offended, but she did not sound in the least sorry for herself. It was as if she knew about him more even than he did. . . . For the first time in his life, he felt exactly what he was and he was not impressed."[56] In Beverly, he sees something to be admired and emulated and his love for her reflects the worth of her short life. In Beverly's love for Peter, all of his shortcomings are revealed to him, and she loves him regardless. He is thereby encouraged to overcome his deficiencies so that he might be made worthy of her love. Through the love of Peter Lake, Beverly gains a fuller appreciation of her nature, just as she reveals Peter Lake to himself.

Second, by means of her physical relationship with Peter Lake, Beverly is finally given an opportunity to experience her body not as something weak and dying, a thing that hampers her experience of life, but rather as a cause of joy and of pleasure, for although "she had imagined with stunning accuracy everything they did in their rush to find one another out, she had not the slightest idea of the power and abandon with which they united."[57] By way of their erotic relationship, Beverly fully understands the goodness present in the finite and physical world that she will soon depart. Again, this is a significant difference between Helprin and Dante. As we have argued previously, the embodiment of the divine in the present is central to Helprin's argument. The sex in his novels is not thrown in for titillation, but is an affirmation of the capacity of the particular world to participate in the eternal. Helprin insists on describing particular exemplars that are not faint and ghostly images of absolute principles, but vibrant and real representatives, through whom others can experience communion with the same. While Dante, who famously uses the same means of mediating the divine through the natural, would not deny this principle, the emphasis is different with Helprin. Dante's characters require moral purification in order to ascend to the divine. Helprin, on the other hand, steadfastly affirms the necessity of the down and dirty, the broken and defective, the mortal clay that keeps his characters continually tied to their natural relationships, even as they are linked to something eternal.

Again, both authors affirm the essentially Platonic principle of a continuous ascent from images to physical things to ideas to the apprehension of the indescribable first principle, and in contrast to, for example, the Kantian denial of the possibility of knowing the metaphysical realm by means of the natural. This is certainly one of the elements that unsettles Helprin's critics, even if they cannot quite put their fingers on the nature of his worldview that appears to be so distasteful. It is at once a radically pre-modern position and yet, one that is expressed in peculiarly modern images. Using a horse as the means to journey to the divine goes back to at least to Plato himself.[58] In Helprin's novel, this image is deepened when that horse is engaged in menial labor and is subject to the violence of terrible men. This is reflective of a position that goes beyond the classical forms of antiquity. A step further is to retain the elements of our "corruption" in our perfected forms. In *Winter's Tale*, the good of the city and of particular individuals requires the redemption of their real natures, not just their translation into some idealized dream. Pearly Soames will exist in the rebuilt New York City, just as Peter will continue to desire Beverly as a flesh and blood person.

A Dante in Need of a Beatrice

Despite the reciprocal nature of their love for each other, it is nonetheless Beverly who takes on the role of Beatrice, guiding Peter Lake to his proper end. In Beverly's love for him, Peter Lake recognizes an essential element of love, the willingness to forgive the faults of the beloved. Yet, however much Peter Lake enjoys Beverly's forgiveness for his previous failings and seeks to redeem himself in her eyes, he is unable to initially "forgive" her for her mortality, and after she dies he despairs of ever loving or being loved again.

When Peter Lake initially comes across the dying child in the tenement building, he is unable to do anything because he has no experience or memory of what might be done.[59] Although the Baymen have taken care of him and the Anarindas have had sex with him, he has not recognized what it means to love or be loved. While given other opportunities for love, specifically with Mootfowl, whom he says he loves, and Cecil Mature, whom we find out loves him, it is not until he meets Beverly that Peter Lake experiences the full nature of love.

Dante describes his first meeting of Beatrice wherein his heart spoke to him, saying "'Behold a god stronger than I that is come to rule over me.'"[60] In this both Dante and Helprin suggest that all love has its proper end in the transcendent, and insofar as one loves finite beings, one does so because one recognizes that which is divine in them. Helprin makes this point even more specifically by means of the character Pearly Soames. Pearly loves pure color, and, with some irony, seeks to fill a room with light reflecting gold, exactly the color that is supposed to illuminate the cloud wall when a city of perfect justice is achieved. Pearly mistakes what he loves as something finite and is moved to injustice and hatred rather than justice and love. Yet, the source of what he desires, however he understands it, is still the divine itself. Even Peter Lake recognizes Pearly's love as a love of the light of heaven and thus an image of transcendence.[61]

Peter Lake is finally moved to consciously seek an external and objective end by Athansor. Looking into Athansor's eyes, Peter Lake sees that they are "infinitely deep, opening like a tunnel to another universe. The horse's silence suggested that the beauty of his gentle black eyes had something of all that ever was or would ever be."[62] Athansor, whose very name suggests eternity, provides Peter Lake with a perspective on the transcendent that he has never before experienced.[63]

Having looked in the horse's eyes and seen the absolute, Peter Lake responds by seeking to transform himself, avoiding what he takes to be an eventual death at the hands of Soames. Metaphorically, having seen the eternal in Athansor, Peter Lake now desires his own immortality. He meditates, "They say that in his devotion St. Stephen changed form before the eyes of those who watched, that he could rise in the air, . . . that he knew the past and future. . . . Now I'm no St. Stephen, but if I can concentrate hard enough on something apart from me, perhaps I can be changed."[64] While Peter Lake does not recognize the full nature of his intent, his desire to be transformed and avoid death speaks to a desire for transcendence nonetheless. However, as he indicates, he must first find an object apart from himself to focus on, and, being "no St. Stephen," it appears that the object of his focus cannot be the divine in and of itself, but rather something or someone who mediates the divine in a more accessible form. Athansor then leads Peter Lake to Beverly, sitting in the snow like a dog in front of the Penn home, until Peter Lake concedes that there might be a "prize" inside that has been left "unattended."[65]

Peter Lake breaks into Beverly's home with the intent of robbing it and is startled by the beauty of her piano playing: "it moved him not as a succession of abstract sounds, but, as if it were, rather, as simple and evident as the great strings of greenish-white pearls that glistened along the bridge catenaries at night . . . the symbol of something he loved very much but did not really know. . . . This music sounded to Peter Lake like the sparkling signal that the lights tapped out in the mist."[66] Like Beatrice who appears as a god come to rule over Dante, Beverly appears as the source of the light that Peter Lake has always loved. In her playing, Peter Lake witnesses her rising above herself, becoming an image of the divine for Peter and the proper object of his love. By means of his love for Beverly, the change that he desired when he saw eternity reflected in Athansor's eyes begins. Telling Isaac Penn that he understands that his duty is to love, to protect, Peter Lake is reminded of his desire to help the child he met so many years ago in the tenement building. Seeking to transcend himself, Peter Lake finds love, suggesting that this might be both the means and end of his transformation.

After Beverly's death, however, Peter Lake's desire to help others, specifically the countless and nameless poor, dissipates, such that he can no longer think of anyone that he might care for: "For Peter Lake, who had never before known loneliness, the city was now empty."[67] Even Athansor, who he at least manages to feed, is neglected, looking more and more like a milk horse, and nothing like a statue.[68] As a reader of the novel, one knows that Peter Lake's response, while understandable, is inadequate. For although Beverly dies, one is given to believe that her death, while the end of her finite life, is not the end in itself. Hence the reader knows that other characters who have died are somehow brought back to life, specifically, Jackson Mead, Mootfowl, and ultimately Abby. There is the hope that Beverly might live.

Prior to Beverly's death, Peter Lake is aware of the possibility of rebirth, for having witnessed Mootfowl's death he meets Cecil, who tells him that Mootfowl is alive. While he does not see Mootfowl and can only trust that Cecil is telling the truth, he nonetheless "was beginning to see a pattern in such things. According to Cecil, Mootfowl was once again alive. Peter Lake wondered what would the fate of the many others who lived mid the city's machinery and hearthlike engines."[69] However, when Beverly herself dies, Peter Lake is thrown into a state of despair. What Cecil has told him was true for Mootfowl, Peter Lake does not hope for Beverly. Instead, he understands her to be gone, and with her death everything else that he might have loved is destroyed and the city is emptied.

Peter Lake accepts that Beverly is sick and will die, and Beverly is surprised to discover in him a capacity for love that is like her own, for she "had the courage of someone who is often confronted by that which is gravely important, [but she] had not expected that someone else would be that way too. Peter Lake . . . loved her in exactly the same way that she loved everything that she knew she would lose."[70] Knowing that she is soon to die, Beverly has a heightened awareness of the good she will thereby lose and this makes her love for it that much stronger. Her recognition of the very finitude and essential limits of the people and things she loves is in part the cause of her love for them.

She senses the same understanding in Peter Lake's love for her and, given the nature of his life, this makes sense. From a very young age, Peter Lake experiences the essential mutability of the finite world. At the age of thirteen he is exiled from life with the Baymen and left alone in New York, a place he does not know and can barely comprehend. He becomes a ward of Overweary's Home for Lunatic Boys and learns to become a mechanic with the help of Reverend Mootfowl. Later implicated in the death of Mootfowl, Peter Lake joins the Short Tails and becomes a thief. In each instance where he might have felt some stability, the world shifts and his entire life changes with it. When he first contemplates Beverly's eventual death, he is unmoved, for he "had no illusions about mortality. He knew that it made everyone perfectly equal, and that the treasures of the earth were movement, courage, laughter, and love."[71] At this moment, Peter Lake turns his attention to the millions of poor that share Beverly's disease, but do not have the comforts that Beverly has to make their illness bearable.[72] He turns his attention away from Beverly to seek out the young child that he had seen in the tenement almost twenty years ago.

There is a sense of justice in Peter Lake's desire to help those he does not love, those no one seems to love (and so he later becomes the registrar of the dead). In loving Beverly, he understands that love is his responsibility more broadly speaking. However, there is also something wrong in his easy acknowledgment that Beverly will die. After all, the mortician tells him, and we know it is true, that in the end it is only by means of remembering Beverly that the injustice of the death of the child in the tenement building is redeemed.

Although Beverly senses in Peter Lake that his love of her incorporates an understanding of his eventual loss of her, his response to the actuality of this loss indicates something has been missing in his appreciation of the finite world and even in his love of her. He knows the world changes and that things found will soon be lost. However, having perceived the transcendent in Beverly, he does not fully attend to her actual mortality. If the absolute good makes itself known by means of and within the created order, then the goodness of this order, as it finitely exists, should be recognized. In other words, if the transcendent finds the natural order sufficient for its manifestation, then to not acknowledge the good as it is finitely presented is an indication of *hubris*. The very fragility that one might be tempted to overlook or dismiss as a sign of weakness should instead be recognized as an essential moment of natural life. We see something of this deficiency in Peter Lake's relationship with Cecil Mature. Having run away from Overweary's, hoping not to be implicated in the death of Mootfowl, Peter Lake is exasperated to discover that Cecil has followed him. Although Cecil loves him "like a brother," Peter Lake thinks he is a mere encumbrance. And while Peter Lake does try to protect him, it is not until the end of the novel, and after he has remembered his love for Beverly that he treats Cecil with any tenderness.[73]

In the Christian tradition that informs Dante's theology, it is only by means of the fall that Christ's sacrifice becomes necessary and God's full love for his creation is made manifest. In eating from the Tree of Knowledge the Garden of Eden is lost, but the full nature of God's love is revealed and Paradiso is made possible. Thus, Dante places the Garden of Eden at the very top of Mount Purgatory and from this Garden one ascends to Paradiso. The Garden, or Woods, as presented by Dante, is without inhabitants. Those Dante meets there do not reside in the Garden but appear there for the sake of his further refinement. Dante thereby suggests that the natural innocence Adam and Eve begin with is neither their proper end, nor the proper end of any human. Instead, humans are designed for a supernatural end. The fall—achieving knowledge of evil, but also of the good—is part of the way by which this end is achieved. Death, in this respect, is not evil, but a means to a greater good.[74] That Beverly will die relatively soon is itself cause for enjoying the moments that she is alive. Further, it is by means of mortality that there can be rebirth. The Beverly that Peter Lake loves is not immortal; she is vulnerable and weak. Peter Lake later views her death as an injustice. However, without death, Beverly cannot be perfected.

The chapter in which Beverly dies is entitled "Aceldama," indicating its movement consists of a betrayal. This is the name of the "potter's field" or a field of blood associated with Judas in the New Testament. Peter Lake imagines that he is the one who has been betrayed. The woman he thought somehow transcendent seems entirely gone and he has been left alone. With Beverly dead, Peter Lake is unable to imagine or hope that her death represents some greater, if different, form of life. Peter Lake rejects the possibility about which Beverly herself was so sure. In this he is a traitor to divine justice as he imagines that an absolute justice would allow someone like Beverly to die without any possibility of redemption. Like Judas, he despairs of redemption and betrays the love that would make it possible.

PETER LAKE'S REDEMPTION

In Purgatory, Beatrice tells Dante that after her death and prior to his descent in to Inferno, she had tried to wake him to her continued, albeit transformed, existence: "'Nor prayer for inspiration me availed, by means of which in dreams and otherwise, I called him back, so little did he heed them. So low he fell, that all appliances for his salvation were already short, save showing him the people of perdition.'"[75] In the same way, Peter Lake is given three opportunities, of heightened significance, to recognize that Beverly's death is not the end of all that is good.

First, mistaking him for a beggar, a young man approaches Peter Lake, giving him money. Rather than graciously responding to a spontaneous act of charity, Peter Lake pockets the money, swearing at the person who gave it to him.[76] Peter Lake next goes to a movie theatre. The film shows the past, present, and, what the reader eventually knows, a providential account of the future. Peter Lake has seen this depiction of the future before in the large and seemingly magical painting housed in the basement of the Penn's home. At the time he sees the painting, Peter Lake knows that Beverly is the key to its miraculous nature and he is torn between looking at the painting and looking at her.[77] The movie moves beyond the miraculous image of the city of the future, and shows that city burning, but the film breaks before the conclusion is revealed. The viewer is left not knowing what happens to the city and, if Peter Lake is right and Beverly is the caretaker of that city, then he is left not knowing what happens to her. Nonetheless he is not moved to think at this moment of Beverly. Instead, tired and worn out, he finds a cellar to spend the night in. Finally, in that same night, Peter Lake dreams of Beverly, who appears as all light, currying Athansor as if some important event is going to take place. Peter Lake tries to capture the bridle she is holding, to keep her with him, but she pulls it out of his hand. The last thing Peter Lake remembers of the dream is "a feeling of unutterable pain and loss, and anger at his sentence of darkness."[78] With Beverly, the source of all light now gone, Peter Lake, like Alessandro from *Soldier*, feels that his very life is a punishment.

Peter Lake is then given a gift, the opportunity to die. Waking, invigorated and surprised to find that his hand has been cut, he discovers that Pearly Soames has assembled his armies to kill him. Peter Lake, however, chooses to fight for his life, telling Pearly, "'It's not over yet.'"[79] Having awakened in the dark woods, Peter Lake, like Dante, looks for a path out, rather than simply surrendering to his despair. Further, when he and Athansor are surrounded on the bridge, facing what seems like an inevitable and bloody death, Peter Lake determines that if he has to die, then he would prefer the "lovely blue of water" below him, a blue that is reminiscent of Beverly's eyes.[80] Believing his death is now inevitable, Peter Lake chooses to die surrounded by beauty, rather than "the bloodstained boards of the Great Bridge."[81] Finally, when Athansor rises rather than falls and speeds through the Cloud Wall, Peter begins to think about the city: "A shelter from the absolute and the lordly, it now seemed like such a loving place, even though it had been so hard . . . he ached for the color, the softness, the sheen of the city."[82] Thus, when Athansor breaks through the Clouds, revealing something of the heavenly city that Beverly had described, although awed, Peter Lake knows that if he stays on Athansor he will die, so he lets go and falls: "He fell, and he fell, and he had no will. His arms and legs flailed. His neck was like the soft neck of a baby."[83] Lost in the Cloud Wall, Peter Lake eventually falls back into the lovely blue of the Hudson and is, in essence, reborn.

No longer able to recognize the goodness and justice of life, Peter Lake seeks to die, but when granted the opportunity his understanding of the beauty and goodness of the world is restored. The city he had thought was empty, he recognizes again as a place of love, and color and beauty. In seeing the clear world that exists outside of time, he understands that to continue towards it means death. It is unclear at this moment if death would mean to ascend to the heavens or not. Regardless, Peter Lake is not prepared for it. He chooses to live and relinquishes his will to whatever kind of life will be restored to him.

In his previous life, except for brief moments, Peter Lake's attention is focused on himself. Prior to meeting Beverly, he realized that in order to change he would have to concentrate on something else. After her death, he believes there is nothing good left in the world and so his attention reverts to his own state of despair. He is then given another chance, and, appropriately, this time he cannot think of himself, for he has no idea who he is. Having returned from the Cloud Wall almost a century later he is without any memory and it is only by concentrating on the things external to himself that he is inexplicably drawn to—certain places, machines, white dogs, and then white horses—that he is able to recollect his now transformed self. Harry Penn later tells Peter Lake that he can show him who he is by showing him what he loves. It seems that this is something that Peter Lake already instinctively knows. In the *Divine Comedy*, souls are found in particular ditches, cornices, or heavens based on the particular things that each soul loved in life. Rather than being punished or rewarded, the individuals of the *Divine Comedy* are simply given what it was that they loved. Their own choices, intentions, and identities are made clear to them and to Dante as he moves through the afterlife. By means of Peter Lake, Helprin suggests that this is true for all people. Peter Lake, like everyone else, will only know himself when he knows the things that he has loved.

Following the pilgrim Dante in the *Divine Comedy*, Peter Lake realizes the deficiency of his understanding and habituates himself to a new account.

After falling from the Cloud Wall and waking in the hospital, he is transformed, for while he is alone, he nonetheless has hope: "If there had once been those whom he had loved, who had loved him, he was now separated from them. Even were they to suddenly appear . . . he might not know them. Though the way he was lost was the most serious way in which a man can be lost, still, he hoped it would pass."[84] Although Peter Lake has no conscious remembrance of the "high clear world" he saw above the Cloud Wall, he hopes that the mists that cloud his memory will clear, so that he might know himself once again

Further, whereas Peter Lake had previously not conceived the possibility of a divine justice able to reconcile all of the moving parts of the natural world, upon seeing the machine room of the *Sun* he is reminded of what Mootfowl taught him and knows he is a mechanic. He knows that all of the machines and all of the parts of the machines must work together as part of an intricate whole, telling the mechanics who work for *The Sun* that "'the whole business is like a giant puzzle. It's sort of an equation. The pieces are interrelated, as if they were the instruments of an orchestra. To be the conductor . . . you have to know every instrument. And you have to know the music.'"[85] Peter Lake is described as often falling into a trance in front of the machines, for there he "thought he could hear the coming of the future. . . . Cockeyed and still, directing his attention to their sermons, he stood before them like a climber who has made some glorious peak."[86] Facing the basic infrastructure that gives power to *The Sun* or the means by which the divine plan is made manifest in the visible world, Peter Lake recognizes it and by means of it knows something of himself. His purpose, it appears, is both to understand that music or end to which all the machinery works and assist in ensuring that it moves towards this goal.

In the *Divine Comedy*, the character Dante is similarly presented with an image of the divine as it makes itself manifest in the structure and ordering of the universe. As readers, it is often easy to lose track of what Dante learns about himself, particularly as one moves beyond *Inferno* and into *Purgatory* and *Paradiso*. Helprin, however, reminds us that Dante's entire journey is a psychological allegory. Whatever Dante learns about the structure of the divine by means of his otherworldly vision is intended to reveal the nature of the human soul as well. For example, the reciprocity in the heaven of the doctors, where Aquinas's thoughts are counterbalanced and completed by those of Bonaventure, is a clear explication of the superiority of such an intellectual vision in place of narrow and partisan thought that precludes the possibility of grasping the whole.

Although Peter Lake understands the end to which all the machines at *The Sun* work and how to assemble them such that this end is achieved, determining the divine plan that, by analogy, these machines point towards is not as readily apparent to Peter Lake. However, rather than give up on his pursuit, as it seemed he did previously, instead he, "pushes on," becoming apparently more and more unhinged. [87] Just as he sought to understand and achieve justice for the child he saw dying in the tenement building, now, not remembering why, he continues to visit the tenements and wanders the streets, seeking clarity, "screaming about order in the world, balance, rewards, justice, and veracity. There was no justice, he said. Oh yes there was. But it was very high and very complex, and to understand it you had to understand beauty, because beauty was justice without equation. 'Tugboat.'" [88] To the other mechanics and perhaps even to readers, it appears that Peter Lake is mad. This recalls the Allegory of the Cave, in which the freed prisoner, having escaped his shackles and finally the cave itself, is eventually able to view the sun. Returning to the cave to share his new wisdom with those still in chains, he is not greeted with reverence. Rather, his experiences, so wholly unknown to his hearers, are taken to be the imaginings of a dangerous lunatic. [89] In the same way, near the end of his poem, having reached the height of heaven, Dante warns his readers that the vision he has had is beyond his ability to either fully comprehend or clearly articulate. The nature of the divine, while rational, supersedes his finite capacities. [90] While what Beverly sees in the stars and what Peter Lake experiences in the Cloud Wall cannot be articulated nor fully comprehended, in seeking to understand what they have been granted they might "by unforgivable stubbornness . . . burst through to worlds of motionless light." [91] This parallels Dante's aspiration to make manifest the vision of the afterlife he has been granted, for in so doing he presumably is able to better understand what he had apprehended and thereby will the good that he desires. Dante does not allow the limitations of language to move him to despair, but tries to further understand and articulate the good that he loves such that he might will it.

We see a version of this with Peter Lake. Drawn further and further into what appears to be a kind of insanity, he roams the city in a quest to recollect himself and find peace. Not knowing why, he is continuously drawn to places that had import in his former life. Finally, succumbing to a painful hysteria over papaya juice, he is granted a vision that brings him a form of peace—he awakes to discover that he is being propelled through all of the earth's graves, accounting for all who are dead in whatever their state of burial: "Some were merely dust, others the ivory bones that children fear spookishly luminescent . . . some were in tattered shrouds and others wrapped in tape. Some had cradles of silk and wood, and many many more lay without any accoutrement in the soft or stony ground." [92] Like Dante, in striving to recollect who he is, Peter Lake is given a vision of the afterlife.

When he registers the dead, Peter Lake continues the work he began for the sake of the young girl in the tenement building. All who have lived and died are here accounted for; no one life, no matter how brief or inconsequential, is left unnoticed: "Something within him refused not to honor each one."

Even Dante is included in Peter Lake's tour, for among those he passes are, "Renaissance servants in red caps."[93] If, previously, Peter Lake failed in that he did not sufficiently account for death as a necessary element of the finite world, he is now asked to acknowledge and register it by means of accounting for all who have died. His earlier fears, although not now conscious to him, had been that, in death, the individual was lost.[94] Peter Lake, however, remembers all of the dead, suggesting that no one is ultimately lost. One curious aspect of this journey is that there is no particular notice given of Beverly, who should be counted among the dead. Perhaps Peter Lake's particular attachment to Beverly would have had the effect of distracting him from his universal mission. Or, alternatively, he is not ready to remember her. In either case, it is not clear whether her absence is a choice made by him or by some other power.

Importantly, at this point Peter Lake's bare acknowledgment of the dead is sufficient. The mortician that he visited earlier spoke of the innumerable dead that he has to deal with each day. As he slices open a young woman's abdomen, describing it as "'inedible meat,'" he explains his lack of love: "'I can't feel for each and every one of them. I'm not God. I don't have that much in me.'"[95] As cold as the mortician is, we see a similar lack of love in Peter Lake as he witnesses the dead. He is described as "without emotion," for "he was unmoved, and he did not feel compassion."[96] At this point in the novel it is important to recognize that he has been alluded to as "the just man," but it is also indicated that he is not a saint nor will he ever be one.[97] Peter Lake, falling in love with Beverly, is moved to seek justice for a young girl who had died twenty years earlier. Now, as a just man, he acknowledges all of the dead, but seemingly does so without compassion or love.

This, however, is not the full account of justice that Peter Lake desires, nor that towards which Helprin points. The child that Peter Lake saw in the tenement building was left unattended and died seemingly "without grace or redemption."[98] The child dies apparently unloved. While some form of justice is achieved in Peter Lake's tour of the dead, it is a justice that exists apart from love. That the dead are not forgotten suggests that they might also be redeemed. The mortician tells Peter Lake that he is not God and thus cannot have compassion for all of the dead.[99] Peter Lake also does not feel compassion or love for the dead that he registers. Instead, they are recognized as having been and honored as such. However, the mortician further counsels that Peter Lake should go home to the woman he loves and remember her. Neither the mortician, nor Peter Lake, is God. After all, neither is even a saint, and as such their capacity for love is limited to particular individuals. The mortician believes that everything ends here. However, Peter Lake is a mechanic and knows that all things are interrelated. In the final images of the book Helprin suggests that the love one bears for a particular individual might be the means by which another finds redemption.

Having seen the cities of the dead, Peter Lake is surprised to find that his face has become kind and he begins to search for love: "I'll buy a white dog, and take him to my room. He'll be a good companion. I've always loved dogs."[100] Eventually realizing that it is horses that he loves, and a particular white horse specifically, Peter Lake meets Christina, who is also searching for Athansor, and, through her Peter Lake comes to know Asbury. Concentrating on something outside of himself, at first he focuses on abstract principles like justice and beauty, and is rewarded with a vision of the city of the dead and a kind of peace. Turning his attention from the infinite to the finite, Peter Lake finds love: "Peter Lake parted from Christina in a daze, because he seemed to have made a friend. A friend implied happiness, and too much happiness might lead him to give up his struggle. But why not fix the Asbury's engine? . . . It did belong to *The Sun*, after all, and, as far as he could tell, taking care of *The Sun's* engines was his reason for being."[101] Peter Lake worries that having a friend, finding love, will make him less attentive in discovering who he is, not yet knowing that it is only by means of love that he will be able to recover himself. This recalls the beginning of the *Divine Comedy*, where in Canto II of *Inferno*, Dante is unwilling to even begin the descent into Hell. In order to move him, Virgil must awaken his *eros* by evoking Beatrice. It is only then that Dante is willing to move forward physically, and thus spiritually. Similarly, in *Purgatorio*, Canto XXVII, Dante hesitates in fear before the last trial, the wall of fire that purifies lust. Again, it is only the name of Beatrice and the love that she represents that is able to overcome Dante's terror.

Peter Lake, however, is not prepared to see Beverly or, as we shall see, even hear her name. Like the souls in Purgatory, he must first be habituated to love. Befriended by Christina and befriending Asbury, Peter Lake encounters the curious character Abysmillard, the last of the Baymen, now alone and dead on the ice. The most "abysmal" of all the Baymen, Abysmillard has lived his entire life without love. He is not, however, without hope, for though "he had come through without ever having been embraced . . . he supposed there were others like him, perhaps whole legions. And he imagined it would not be just for so many people to have lived through such loneliness and not come to a final reward."[102] Abysmillard dies, seemingly unloved, only to be found by Peter Lake, who recognizes him and holds his body in his arms.[103] Abysmillard's hope that love will find him occurs in the finite realm and the reader is left to hope that this love has been infinitely achieved as well.

In Abysmillard, Peter Lake sees an image of himself: "He saw in his memory a shabbily clothed child lost and contented in the world of the marsh, where it seemed to be summer all of the time, and the strength and accuracy of his recollection suggested that although he had left that time behind, it was still replaying itself."[104] When Beverly dies, Peter Lake is thrown into despair, imagining himself now unloved and with no one to care for. His memory reveals to him that, unlike Abysmillard whose life has been truly without love, his own life has always been one of summer—filled with miracles born of love. Peter Lake now remembers what he should have remembered at Beverly's death: he has never been alone. In response to Asbury's suggestion that Abysmillard is the last of the Baymen, Peter Lake responds, "'No . . . I am,'" taking Abysmillard's place and seeking the love he must now hope to find.[105]

By means of Abysmillard, Peter Lake is reminded that when he was a small child, others, specifically those who had no particular reason to, took care of him. He is then confronted with Abby, who is now dead, and is reminded of the girl he had seen in the tenement, and his previous desire and indeed what he had taken to be his responsibility to assist her. He now knows that Abby is the girl that he had previously encountered while in the heights of his seeming madness at Petipas. There, seeing Jessica Penn and being reminded, although unknowingly, of Beverly, Abby slipped through the gate and "flew" up into his arms. Peter Lake realizes that Abby and the girl in the tenement are somehow the same person: "'This is the child that flew to me. And this is the child in the hallway. . . . She was dying and blind, but she remained standing. She didn't know that it was her privilege to lie down.'"[106] As noted, Sarah Gamely previously indicated that good intentions often sleep like locusts until they are required. The suggestion is that the nature of time is such that the past and the future are not indivisibly separated by days and hours, but with sufficient perspective one can see all moments of time as occurring simultaneously. Peter Lake's subsequent capacity to manipulate the physical world when fighting the now returned Short Tails indicates that the spatial order might be more complicated than we generally believe as well. In the metaphysics of the novel, it is thus not surprising that a dead girl from a century ago might indeed be Abby.

If all of this is so, then there is the further possibility that Peter Lake might be able to fulfill the good intentions that he had, when at thirteen, he stumbled unwittingly upon the girl in the tenement. Peter Lake, however, is not ready to act. Hence, although Hardesty thought that Peter Lake was going to bring Abby back to life, "it soon became clear that that he did not even intend to try."[107] Moreover, when Sarah Gamely recognizes and in shock tries to articulate who he is, Peter Lake does not want to know, cutting her off as soon as she mentions Beverly's name, and screaming "'Shut up, old woman. . . . Shut up or I'll throw you halfway around the world.'"[108] On the very cusp of having everything that he desires, in order to enter the Garden of Eden, Dante has to walk through fire, and be willing to sacrifice everything that his physical existence allows him. Upon hearing what is required, Dante becomes "As he is who is put into the grave."[109] And, like Peter Lake, Dante initially balks, and "against . . . [his] will" refuses to go forward.[110]

Both Dante and Peter Lake allow an intermediary desire to overcome the greater end that they also will. This division in their wills implies a characteristic common to human nature, such that we can choose lesser goods even as we desire another end that we know is better and more satisfying. Even further, on the verge of realizing the end he has been seeking and thus his ultimate satisfaction and peace, Peter Lake initially rejects it, choosing instead the life of strife to which he has grown accustomed. The return of the Short Tails and Peter Lake's apparent delight in resuming this fight is indicative of a temptation present in human nature for a state of becoming and ultimately non-being, rather than the willingness to sacrifice whatever partial pleasures are available in the finite realm for the absolute satisfaction of the infinite. The lights in the city go out, signifying the end to which Peter Lake's rejection of Sarah Gamely's recollection would direct him: "The whole city went dark. Even the distant towers, where the lights had never dimmed, now looked like smooth black slabs. . . . Without the lights, the fire seemed many times brighter than it had been. It was strong enough to illuminate the room. Clouds of smoke miles away reflected the firelight, which flashed onto walls and faces as if it were a lighthouse beacon."[111] Refusing the light of recollection and knowledge, Peter Lake is left with the light of the fire that would destroy the city and its struggling inhabitants.

Dante has Virgil to remind him of the end he seeks and Virgil persuades him to walk through the fire. Peter Lake is similarly not left alone. The nature of grace is apparently such that one has to be very stubborn to refuse its constant reminders. When the lights go out, Peter Lake is granted a kind of reprieve; not prepared to face the past, he is instead directed to what he understands as his formal purpose—he has to tend to the machines at *The Sun*. Peter Lake recognizes the interdependence of his machines and his place among them, even if he not able to see a similar harmony as existing in and among humans. Just as Peter Lake's machines are necessarily and even mechanically dependent on each other and on him, a similar necessity is suggested as existing amongst human beings, the mechanics of which are driven by love, sleep even though the participants may not be aware of the parts that they are playing.

Peter Lake restores power to the presses at *The Sun*, thereby restoring Harry Penn's hope that all he has built and hoped for is not lost. Wanting to express his gratitude to the new master mechanic, Penn discovers Peter Lake and restores his identity for him.[112] While Sarah Gamely tries to tell Peter Lake who he is in words, for which she has a formidable and peculiar aptitude, Harry Penn shows him, for he has recovered the two life-size portraits of Peter and Beverly that had been in the Penn's home at the Lake of the Coheeries. While words and reason had failed to restore Peter's memory of himself, seeing the painting provides an immediate apprehension. As with other works of art depicted in the novel, there is a presentation of the whole in the visual image. This is something that is uniquely the faculty of art, as opposed to philosophy, for example. For one who has eyes to see, the entire truth is present to be grasped in an instant.

Like Augustine and Dante, Helprin thereby suggests that one's weight is one's love, or, in other words, one's love moves the soul to the object of its affection, just as the weight of matter determines its place in the natural order.[113] Harry Penn shows Peter Lake who he is by showing him what he loves. Although painted as separated in their portraits, the couple was standing together when the portraits were created, with their hands almost touching. Helprin writes, "Though their hands were not together, one would, if one were to know the circumstances of the sitting, see them on their way."[114] Peter Lake and Beverly are painted as if separate; they are individual paintings just as they are individuals in life. Peter Lake knows in seeing them that this separation is not the full story, for they stood together and are in love. When she died, he assumed that he had lost Beverly; having been separated from her, he assumed that the love they shared had also been lost.[115] These paintings, however, remind him that he and Beverly have always been separate and particular individuals, just as they will always be fully together. They are separate moments acting independently of each other, like moments in time, and, at the same time, their love is always wholly binding and complete. Peter Lake is thus reminded of the end of his love and that love does not die, but is ongoing, for their painted hands are in the state of rising and of coming together and our narrator says that these paintings are alive. In Beverly's eyes, the portrait depicts knowledge of "something excellent and good," for "she had seen everything" and by means of his love for her, Peter Lake's love is directed to a good beyond her.[116] Peter Lake remembers not only his love for a particular woman but also the nature of love, which might be an end in itself.

Dante is moved by Beatrice to look on Paradiso; so Peter Lake is moved by his love for Beverly to bring a similar harmony to the individuals whose lives his has intersected, restoring the ends or purposes that have at least momentarily been lost or forsaken.[117] Hence, he reunites with Cecil for one final robbery and retrieves the salver from its bank vault for Hardesty in exchange for the location of the white horse, whom he thinks he must now send home. Believing that Beverly still lives and knowing that he will be restored to her, he tells Hardesty to dig up Abby.[118] Having recognized that the nature of love is such that does not die, Peter Lake suggests that by means of love, Abby might be restored to life. Walking through the streets and being reminded of his previous life, "Peter Lake knew that these things were nothing in themselves but the means by which to remember those he had loved, and to remind him that the power of the love he had known was repeated a million times a million times over, from one soul to another—all worthy, all holy, none ever lost."[119] This universal account of salvation owes more perhaps to Neoplatonism than to either Jewish or Christian theology, although both traditions have contained champions for such an account. [120]

While Peter Lake believes he could be reunited with Beverly, he does not know how to get to her. [121] He does not realize that the division in his will, indicated in his initial refusal to hear Beverly's name, must be overcome. In other words, Peter Lake does not yet realize that in order to be reunited with Beverly, he too must accept death and in so doing fully will his proper end. Peter Lake therefore imagines that Athansor can return to his home beyond the Clear Wall just by jumping: "The very fact of [Athansor's] motion took hold of him, and he started to gallop, faster and faster, until the ground rumbled beneath him and he was far away from Peter Lake, who was deeply saddened. He would never see the white horse again, but he was confident that the horse would find his right and proper place, where he had started, home." [122] Peter Lake is surprised when he finds out that Soames has killed the horse, and believes, at least momentarily, that everything he thought he understood was wrong. In these minutes, "Peter Lake was broken." [123]

Expecting life, Peter Lake did not realize he would first have to face death. However, as the death of Beverly, Abby, and now Athansor indicate, the reconciliation of the finite to the infinite requires the nature of the finite to be fully actualized. For the nature of the infinite to be reconciled to the finite, its full power must be made manifest. In other words, it is not a true reconciliation if what is understood as true about either the infinite or the finite is overturned. Instead they must both be fully what they are, and even in this state be made commensurable. If the nature of the material world includes its eventual dissolution, it must be allowed to dissolve. The nature of the absolute is all-powerful such that overcomes that which seems undefeatable. In this way, by means of death and then resurrection, the finite and the infinite are each actualized in their completeness.

To this point Peter Lake has not been willing to complete this part of the journey. It is interesting that in the lamentable 2014 film adaptation of *Winter's Tale*, the makers of that movie found this decision unintelligible or, at least, unsellable to their audience. The film, its feet firmly planted in clay, can only resort to a formulaic Hollywood fistfight, won by Peter over Pearly, that causes Pearly's death, spares Peter's life, and allows him to awaken, with a kiss, the child Abby, who is asleep in death on a princess's bed. Clearly, more recent myths, this time from the Disney *oeuvre*, were thought to be of greater value than the older tradition from which Helprin drew his inspiration. In the novel, however, logic dictates that Peter must recognize that perfect justice, and perfect love, transcends the merely finite, even if finite choices are required to actualize these principles. Peter willingly accepts, even initiates, his death at the hands of Pearly Soames, for he recognizes a greater power is at work, but he also knows that his actions will be made commensurate with the will of the divine.

As *Winter's Tale* is the most metaphysical of Helprin's novels in terms of its frequent challenges to the limits of time and space, it is also his most detailed exposition of the themes of Dante's *Paradiso*. It is certainly a romance, complete with a quest. However, its deeper association with Dante's work is in its affirmation of the redemption of the natural and particular elements of creation. What is most remarkable about Dante's account of Paradiso, is the image of the celestial rose and all that that implies. The various cantos of *Paradiso* delineate the scope and particularity of divine redemption by introducing character after character, most known to us as historical figures or figures from literature, sacred and profane. At the end of the work, we are given to understand that all of these figures, distinguished geographically and morally, by their diverse location in the heavens, are nevertheless radically equal, as citizens of the heavenly kingdom, gathered in a circle around Christ at the center of the rose.

As we have mentioned, Dante is at pains to illustrate the reciprocity that allows for this city to exist. There is no emptying out or renunciation of human particularity so that all might be one. Rather, the strengths of one soul are counterbalanced against the virtues of another. Each heaven contains souls who embody aspects of human character that distinguish them from the citizens of the other celestial realms. Even within the particular planetary spheres, the inhabitants embody sub-distinctions that are both particular to the historical person and illustrative of sub-divisions within the abstract virtues that they represent.

Where we believe that Helprin's account differs from Dante's, is in the more complete restoration of nature that Helprin depicts. The sensual, erotic, aspects of human nature, along with those elements of human eccentricity that are not, strictly speaking, emblematic of virtue, are preserved and redeemed. The city that Helprin holds up is no mere earthly city. Yet, it is not a city of ideals, abstracted from human failings. There is a general coolness in Dante's Paradise that is contrasted to the hot-blooded passion that still animates Helprin's city. To be fair, Helprin does not intend a complete portrait of the afterlife, and thus Dante's account is not a direct comparison. However, there is an undeniable reluctance to let go of the natural in Helprin's novels, including *Winter's Tale*, that at the very least represents an emphasis different from that of Dante. Hence the epilogue of *Winter's Tale* speaks not of Peter Lake's final outcome, but rather of the cities that the other characters we have met will now build and inhabit, and, perhaps most importantly, the rebuilding of New York City in which Pearly Soames is still a necessary inhabitant.

As we have discussed earlier, it is not that Helprin would deny much of the central truths of Dante's account. Dante's medieval Catholic Christianity, in several important particulars, might not accord with Helprin's Judaism precisely. However, the general theme of the restoration of nature through grace that animates the *Comedy*, alongside a determined insistence on the human freedom that makes true moral action possible, is at the heart of all of Helprin's novels, none more so than *Winter's Tale*. While Dante was not afraid to challenge the popular orthodoxy of his times (think of the popes that he places in hell and the pagans that he places in heaven), his *Comedy* is, in the end, a representation of medieval thought, albeit in its highest form. The freedom that marks modernity, the emphasis on human subjectivity, that one can perhaps find in nascent form in Dante, receives its full due in Helprin's work. *Winter's Tale* illustrates this and hints at how it might be understood in the city. It remains to *Freddy and Fredericka* to explore the social and political character of this union of free subjectivity and objective truth.

NOTES

1. Mark Helprin, *Winter's Tale*, 240.
2. The structure of the plot of *Winter's Tale* roughly mirrors that of Shakespeare's *A Winter's Tale*. Shakespeare's play begins in a harsh city filled with injustice and the tragic "death" of the queen, moves to the pastoral Bohemia, a mystical place much like the Lake of the Coheeries, and finally returns to the city, but now with a love culminating in justice.
3. See Virgil's *Aeneid*, Book VI. Aeneas is given an account of both his destiny and that of the city he will found by the spirit of his father Anchises, when he visits the underworld.
4. Dante, *Paradiso*, XXXI, 37–40.
5. Ibid., III, 70–81.
6. Ibid., IV, 37–42.
7. Ibid., X–XIII.
8. Ibid., IX.
9. Ibid., IV, 34–36.
10. Dante, *Purgatorio*, XXX, 22–24.
11. Dante, *Paradiso*, XVII, 55–60.
12. On Boethius's influence on Dante, see Angelo Gualtieri, "Lady Philosophy in Boethius and Dante," *Comparative Literature* (Spring 1971) 23: 2, 141–50.
13. Dante, *Inferno*, III, 18.
14. Ibid., X, 100–104.
15. Helprin, *Winter's Tale*, 499–500.
16. Peter Lake is given exactly this opportunity when he watches a film that depicts the past, present, and future of New York. See 204–5.
17. Ibid., 639.
18. Ibid., 499.
19. Ibid., 499.
20. Ibid., 64.
21. Ibid., 179.
22. Ibid., 189.
23. Ibid., 665.
24. Ibid., 643.
25. Ibid., 190.
26. Ibid., 711–12.
27. Ibid., 166.
28. Ibid., 316.
29. Ibid., 358.
30. Ibid., 364.
31. Ibid., 363.

32. Ibid., 333.

33. Ibid., 407–17.

34. Ibid., 364.

35. For a more complete discussion of the ancient tragic end to this conflict as seen in *Antigone*, and the comedic resolution possible, for example, in Shakespeare's *A Midsummer Night's Dream*, see Sara MacDonald, *Finding Freedom, Hegel's Philosophy and the Emancipation of Women* (Montreal: McGill-Queen's University Press, 2008).

36. Dante, *Inferno*, I, 84–85.

37. Dante, *Purgatorio*, XXX, 49–54.

38. Dante, *Paradiso*, XXXI, 64ff.

39. Mark Helprin, *Winter's Tale*, 234.

40. Ibid., 432–33.

41. Ibid., 359.

42. In addition to her dream about New York, Virginia also dreams about her employment at *The Sun*, see 262.

43. Ibid., 234.

44. Ibid., 219–20.

45. Ibid., 274.

46. Ibid., 163.

47. Ibid., 202.

48. Dante, *Purgatory*, XXX, 127–32.

49. Helprin, *Winter's Tale*, 105.

50. Ibid., 166–67 and 195.

51. Ibid., 201.

52. Ibid., 107–8.

53. Ibid., 194–95.

54. Ibid., 127.

55. Ibid., 136–42.

56. Ibid., 129.

57. Ibid., 140.

58. See Plato, *Phaedrus*, 246a–254e.

59. Helprin, *Winter's Tale*, 64.

60. Dante, *La Vita Nuova*, Chapter II.

61. Helprin, *Winter's Tale*, 39.

62. Ibid., 87.

63. From the Greek, a-thanatos, without dying.

64. Helprin, *Winter's Tale*, 87.

65. Ibid., 116.

66. Ibid., 126.

67. Ibid., 202.

68. Ibid., 205.

69. Ibid., 182.

70. Ibid., 140.

71. Ibid., 138.

72. Ibid., 165.

73. Ibid., 535–36, 78, 718.

74. See Robert D. Crouse, *Images of Pilgrimage: Paradise and Wilderness in Christian Spirituality*, Chapter VI, Dante (Prince Edward Island, Canada: St. Peter Publications, 1986).

75. Dante, *Purgatorio*, XXX, 133–37.

76. Helprin, *Winter's Tale*, 203.

77. Ibid., 179.

78. Ibid., 208.

79. Ibid., 211.

80. Ibid., 214, 142.

81. Ibid., 214.

82. Ibid., 214.

83. Ibid., 215.
84. Ibid., 412.
85. Ibid., 466.
86. Ibid., 507.
87. Ibid., 523.
88. Ibid., 524.
89. Plato, *Republic*, XXX
90. Dante, *Paradiso*, XXXIII, 106–8.
91. Helprin, *Winter's Tale*, 523.
92. Ibid., 527.
93. Ibid., 528. Both Vasari and Botticelli, for example, portray Dante thusly.
94. See, for example, 64.
95. Ibid., 187.
96. Ibid., 527–28.
97. Ibid., 506, 523.
98. Ibid., 64.
99. Ibid., 187.
100. Ibid., 584.
101. Ibid., 590.
102. Ibid., 600.
103. Ibid., 604.
104. Ibid., 604.
105. Ibid., 605.
106. Ibid., 686.
107. Ibid.
108. Ibid.
109. Dante, *Purgatory*, XXVII, 14–18.
110. Helprin, *Winter's Tale*, 33.
111. Ibid., 686.
112. Ibid., 703, 707–12.
113. Augustine, *Confessions*, XIII, 9. See also Joseph Anthony Mazzeo, "Dante's Conception of Love," *Journal of the History of Ideas* (April 1957) 18:2, 147–60.
114. Helprin, *Winter's Tale*, 712. As one reviewer notes, the unveiling of these portraits evokes the unveiling of Hermione as a statue in Shakespeare's *A Winter's Tale* and just as Hermione lives for Shakespeare, Helprin has us understand that Beverly lives, just as Peter Lake will live. See Benjamin De Mott, "'Winter's Tale,'" *New York Times*, September 4, 1983.
115. Helprin, *Winter's Tale*, 206.
116. Ibid., 711–12.
117. Mark Helprin, "The True Builders of Cities," 107.
118. Helprin, *Winter's Tale*, 717.
119. Ibid., 719.
120. Origen is often associated with the source of "universalism" in Christian theology. See Christopher Bauckham, "Universalism: A Historical Survey." See also Tom Greggs, "Exclusivist of Universalist: Origen, the 'Wise Steward of the Word,'" in the *International Journal of Systematic Theology* 9, 2007, 315–27. The *exitus-reditus* pattern of creation proceeding from the divine and then being returned in its completeness is a common theme in many Neoplatonic thinkers, such as Plotinus and, later, Eriugena. How this tradition is received and re-worked in later Christian thought is worked out by Wayne Hankey in *God in Himself: Aquinas's Doctrine of God as Expounded in the* "Summa Theologiae" (Oxford: Oxford University Press, 1987), 22–35. For an account of the way in which this Neoplatonic tradition influenced Jewish thought (and vice versa) see Lenn E. Goodman, *Neoplatonism and Jewish Thought* (Albany: SUNY, 1992).
121. Helprin, *Winter's Tale*, 712.
122. Ibid., 730.
123. Ibid., 741.

Chapter Four

A Defense of the Democratic Regime

Mark Helprin's novels, like Dante's *Divine Comedy*, are metaphysical explorations of human life and its relation to the absolute. Although particularly obvious in *Winter's Tale*, in all of his novels Helprin directs the particular actions and lives of characters to metaphysical ends. All of the novels that we treat in this book involve some sort of journey or quest and some form of redemption. Finally, they all connect a human romance to the spiritual movement of the characters. That the author himself acknowledges his own debt to Dante only clarifies the relationship of his novels to that greatest of western poetic spiritual journeys, the *Divine Comedy*.

In Dante's *Divine Comedy* it is easy to lose sight of the fact that Dante is still mortal and that, whatever lessons he takes from his vision of the afterlife, he nonetheless will return to earth and continue to live his particular and finite life. In this Dante is something like Peter Lake or the other characters in *Winter's Tale,* who, by means of the Cloud Wall, are given glimpses of heaven, only to return to earth, where they must attempt to make practical use of the truth that they have been shown. While clearly a theological and anagogical allegory, the *Divine Comedy* is at the same time a political allegory, pointing towards an account of earthly justice.

Through the course of this book we have shown how Helprin's account of the universal is one that incorporates and takes up our particular and subjective preferences. The individual is not overcome by the universal, but rather maintained and perfected. Importantly, Helprin's argument has practical and political consequences as well. For, in his novels, Helprin indicates that just as individuals achieve a full freedom in and with the divine, they should also seek to make this freedom manifest in their private and political lives.

In each of his novels, Helprin emphasizes that justice requires recognizing the integrity of all individuals, regardless of their cultural or socioeconomic circumstances. For example, both Copeland Leather in *Sunlight* and *The Sun* in *Winter's Tale* are structured such that both recognize the particular skills of their employees and reward them in a fair and meaningful way, regardless of accidental characteristics such as race or socioeconomic background. Through the course of his novels, Helprin indicates how institutions so structured might encourage the virtue and happiness of their citizens and the good of the regime of which they are a part. This is manifestly the case at the end of *Winter's Tale*. As the city burns and at great risk to themselves, the employees of *The Sun* continue to do their jobs, reporting on the state of the city and seeking to illuminate its citizens with something of the light of the truth.

The most obviously political of Helprin's novels and thus the fullest depiction of his argument for practical freedom is present in his novel *Freddy and Fredericka*. While the novel recognizes (and celebrates) transcendent principles, its interest lies less in metaphysical ends than in the reality of political regimes. In particular, the American regime is compared and contrasted with the constitutional monarchy of England. At the center of the novel are two characters, often seen as thinly disguised portrayals of Charles and Diana. As a result of their great incompetence, these characters, Freddy and Fredericka, the future King and Queen of Great Britain, are sent on a quest to recapture the colonies. Specifically, they are parachuted into New Jersey, virtually naked, and expected to conquer America. Through the course of the novel, however, both Freddy and Fredericka realize the virtue of each other as well as the virtue of a regime wherein each citizen "is a king, subservient only to [God]."[1]

Already aware of what it means to be rich and privileged, in America Freddy and Fredericka traverse the socio-economic landscape. Starting as thieves, they then recognize the need to perform honest labor and join the working poor in Chicago. By means of their hard work and diligence they are able to save and train to become dentists, experiencing briefly a middle class lifestyle. Finally, they are thrown into politics and, by the end of the novel, Freddy is on the verge of winning the Republican nomination for the presidency, thereby coming close to successfully completing their quest. By participating in a variety of lives experienced by individuals everywhere, Freddy and Fredericka are brought to an awareness of an essential human nature that is not dependent on wealth or rank. All human beings, regardless of their circumstances, are shown as fundamentally free and deserving of the same respect and opportunities as everyone else. At the same time, Freddy and Fredericka learn the virtues of each other and fall in love. In so doing they recognize a good external to themselves for which they would be willing to sacrifice their now realized freedom. By means of their particular love for each other, Freddy and Fredericka discover that the true end and actualization of their freedom lies in their willingness to give up that freedom for the sake of a greater end. Helprin suggests that a just regime must recognize and incorporate the subjective freedom of its citizens, for in so doing its citizens will be brought to seek its good—the good of the whole—as one of their particular ends. In this concluding chapter we will explore how the broad themes we have identified in Helprin's and Dante's arguments, specifically the role of love and freedom, might be understood as related to a practical account of justice.

A LOVE STORY

Each of Helprin's novels, like Dante's *Divine Comedy*, is a love story. The romances that he details become essential to the action of the novel, and, in each case, it is by means of their love that the primary characters are moved to higher ends. In *Sunlight*, Harry and Catherine realize that, for the sake of justice and for the integrity of their love, they must fight against Verderamé, even if doing so comes at a great cost. This corresponds to the central action in *Winter's Tale*, where Peter Lake, having remembered the nature of his love for Beverly, believes that by means of his death he might be eternally reconciled to Beverly and to God, thereby achieving, if only momentarily, the perfectly just city.

A similar movement is depicted in *Freddy and Fredericka*, although in this novel the movement to love is shown as having a practical end in addition to the metaphysical ends that Peter Lake seeks in *Winter's Tale*. As *Freddy and Fredericka* begins, one understands that the marriage between the main characters is purely formal. Fredericka has been chosen because she *appears* to be the perfect match for Freddy. From the appropriate class and with the expected education, Fredericka is even Freddy's physical match.[2] It thus seems that Freddy and Fredericka ought to be perfect for one another.

Instead, each of the royal pair is a disaster. For, although they ought to love each other, and while Fredericka seems to love Freddy, he does not love her. Freddy has mistaken Fredericka's appearance for the state of her soul, and when he realizes that there is an incongruity between what he expects and what she is, he is unable to appreciate the virtues that she does possess. Correspondingly Freddy grows immediately frustrated when America does not immediately recognize his royal authority. When Fredericka expresses desires and preferences of her own, Freddy dismisses her as superficial and narcissistic.[3] He judges the first Americans he meets as "savages," and he similarly dismisses his wife.[4]

In America, however, Fredericka's virtue is brought forward and clarified. Although uneducated and yet undisciplined, Fredericka is intelligent and even wise. She has uncanny abilities with mathematics and has internalized the entire content of Shakespeare, without ever having studied it.[5] Moreover, what Freddy had taken to be a desire for celebrity turns out instead to be a desire to be loved.[6] For, as Fredericka later explains to him, "'I've given myself to you, Freddy. You may have my body, soul, everything. . . . You've made the mistake that men often make . . . you believe that your philosophy is deeper than love.'"[7] In realizing Fredericka's virtue, Freddy is shown a deficiency in his own character. If, instead of dismissing Fredericka, Freddy had paid attention to her and sought to love her, her virtue, although different than Freddy's, would have been revealed. Moreover, had Fredericka imagined that Freddy loved her, she would have been more willing to take up the good that he sought in his own life, instead of seeking to sabotage him. What Freddy had taken to be merely the fault of Fredericka is now revealed to be a flaw of his own character. Even further, by accepting the possibility of Fredericka's virtue, Freddy realizes that his own account of the good is deficient. While he has previously disdained all merely social activity as frivolous and does not recognize compassion as a virtue, Fredericka teaches him to dance and reveals that compassion, rooted in love, is the foundation of their ethical life together, and the foundation of justice itself. Freddy further realizes that the good he now recognizes in Fredericka is present in all and thus should be a source of a wider love. Describing a ray of sunshine that illuminates a sculpture that Freddy previously thought to be dull, Freddy describes how recognition and love can draw out the best in individuals: "'The qualities within left on a beam of light and filled the room with butterscotch and gold. . . . It said to me that even souls of grey are gifted and good, if only they will collide with a glorious and accidental ray. It happens with people, you know, it really does.'"[8] Realizing his unjust treatment of Fredericka, Freddy seeks to change for the sake of the woman he now loves.

The romantic relationship between Freddy and Fredericka illustrates an important political lesson. In not being recognized as a person of equal worth, Fredericka rebels and seeks to undermine her husband and her marriage. Hence, although Freddy sought a wife of virtue, his judgment and dismissal of Fredericka preclude that possibility. Instead, it is only when Freddy recognizes Fredericka as an entity in her own right, whose virtues, while different, are nonetheless important, that Fredericka responds by extending her loyalty to him. In their relationship, the subjective nature of the other is recognized as a good in itself, and the result is that they seek not merely to fulfill their own desires, but rather to strengthen the common good of which they are a part, even if it means sacrificing their particular interests to the wider whole. In this way, Helprin suggests that political communities might inculcate virtue in their citizens, not by insisting on a particular expression of the good, but rather by encouraging individuals to freely seek the good as their own natures demonstrate it to them. By these means the particular virtues of citizens are developed and, at the same time, they desire the good of the wider community that knows and endorses their own.

FREEDOM

Love, Helprin suggests, requires recognizing the worth and autonomy of another. In other words, to properly love another, one must acknowledge and encourage her or his freedom. Even further, Helprin's examples suggest that by means of love, individuals might understand how to best actualize their freedom, desiring not just their own good, but also the good of the whole. Ultimately, Helprin suggests that by means of a love or a justice that incorporates the freedom of the beloved, the beloved might be moved to sacrifice her or his very freedom for the sake of the good itself.

Sometimes criticized as a romantic conservative, Helprin clearly recognizes the follies and defects of modern society. The novel is filled with satirical observations, from the shallow, grasping politicians, to the rapacity and even violence existing occasionally in ordinary citizens. His portrayal of America society, while ultimately of its virtue, is not that of Norman Rockwell. The virtues of the American regime, as depicted in *Freddy and Fredericka*, are set against a significant critique. The education and preparation that create an exceptional character such as Freddy are likely only possible in an aristocratic society. None of the American leaders can hold a candle to Freddy or, for that matter, his mother, the Queen. The continuity of the monarchy, immune to the vagaries of popular opinion and rooted in timeless virtues of self-sacrifice and service, has no American analog. Moreover, the American people have generally lost sight of the great principles set out in the Declaration and the Constitution. They have been lulled into a Hobbesian reductionist society of easy pleasures and the pursuit of limited ends.

Despite this critique, at the core of the novel is the clear recognition that all of Freddy's preparation has left him unprepared to be king. In the novel's beginning, the falcon Craig-Vyvian refuses to fly, signaling Freddy's unfitness for the throne. It is only at the novel's end that we see the transformation of both Freddy's intellect and character, as he has acquired both intellectual and moral virtues during his pilgrimage through America. By means of their experiences of ordinary American life, Freddy and Fredericka understand that the virtue of a democratic regime is the realization of freedom.

In *Sunlight*, observing people being herded onto the Staten Island Ferry, Harry observes that very few are willing in that moment to speak: "They weren't cows. Their silence was their dignity, their protest of being herded through channels of industrial iron, ramps, and chains along which they—living, breathing men and women—were moved like wood or ores."[9] While it might be necessary for humans to be so guided to get onto a public ferry, Harry's point is much more insightful. He has just returned from World War II and, as a Jew, he knows too well what it means when basic human dignity is neither recognized nor affirmed. Harry takes Catherine to an automat and reveals the hidden human who, inside the machine, is actually preparing the food. Harry demands an extra hot dog for his baked beans and, in response to the woman's refusal on the grounds that she is not allowed to do that, Harry informs her of the nature of her discretion: "'[Discretion] means you're not an animal or a dummy. You can think for yourself, you can protect your own interests, you're not a creature of the boss.'"[10] Further, *Sunlight* gives us the example of Catherine, who, oppressed by Victor at a young age, realizes and achieves her freedom through the course of the novel. While, at the beginning of the novel, she is not even used to freely making her own choices as to what to eat from a menu, following instead the lead of Victor and then Harry, by the end of the novel she understands that she too has discretion and is responsible for the choices she makes. Although Freddy and Fredericka's experiences are more comic and thus less pressing, the essential point of the novel is the same—a political community that does not see the essential autonomy and worth of an individual human being, an autonomy that allows each individual to determine her own course of action, is tyrannical and unjust.

Individuals and political communities that recognize human freedom are exposed to a great deal of risk. The practical freedom of individuals means that each is responsible for the choices that she or he makes and the life that she or he lives. Individuals are not able to excuse their actions on the grounds that they had no other choice. As readers we might feel pity for Alessandro when he deserts the seemingly meaningless war to go home, only to be caught and imprisoned. Yet, Alessandro has chosen to join the war effort and then betrays this commitment. Further, he knows the consequences for desertion will lie not only with himself, for someone else will be forced to hunt, imprison, and potentially execute him for his actions. Alessandro accepts that this certain risk for another is acceptable and deserts, betraying his country, his comrades, his friends, and his family. By means of Catherine and Harry, Helprin indicates that one is also radically free to act for the sake of a known good. Prior to meeting Harry, Catherine's freedom, while present, has not been manifest to her. Wealthy and privileged, Catherine has never had to actually choose between options. Choosing one thing at one time has not precluded her having the alternative later. The nature of the choices she has made is thus irrelevant.

In *Sunlight*, Catherine realizes that there are choices that only she can make and these will have necessary consequences in her life. Catherine did not choose her relationship with Victor and she was too young at the time to fully recognize the injustice of the power he exerted over her. At the age of twenty-three, however, Catherine's continued relationship with Victor, if unconscious, is nonetheless one that she allows and to which she tacitly consents. Her love for Harry forces her to recognize the choice that she has made and the possibility of choosing something else. The nature of this choice, one that Catherine understands as limiting all other choices, is such that she recognizes the finite nature of her life and thus the significance of her freedom.[11]

Freddy and Fredericka presents an amusing example of this. Not yet exiled, the royals have the difficult task of deciding what they are going to do one evening. Freddy thinks about all of his options: "a private tour of the Tate, or . . . just wandering alone through the National Gallery; a visit to the prime minister or Stephen Hawking; a helicopter flight over London."[12] All of Freddy's plans are thwarted, however, when he discovers that Fredericka has "disco fever," and thus a royal crisis begins. Although as royals they would seem to have the greatest degree of freedom, limited by neither money, nor queues, nor borders, inasmuch as none of Freddy and Fredericka's choices seem to have consequences, all of their choices become trivial. As a result, the full nature of their freedom is not realized by them or made manifest in their activities. True freedom, Helprin suggests, is not merely being able to do what one wants, but rather lies in recognizing that one's choices are limited and that every choice made is important.

Helprin further suggests that we actualize our nature as free and autonomous beings when we freely choose freedom in the face of impediment or enslavement. Catherine realizes that her choices have consequences and these consequences will be hers to bear. This most obviously becomes evident to both Harry and Catherine when it is clear that Verderamé will be stopped at nothing, including murder, to drive Harry out of business. While the war had made the inevitability of his death evident to Harry, Catherine had only a theoretical understanding of this essential limit on choice and life. Now that she and Harry plot to take another person's life and potentially risk their own, the significance of making the right choice is made manifest. Catherine tells her parents that she has "chosen" Harry because of his courage, and that she seeks a similar courage in her own choices. She insists on participating in the plot against Verderamé, saying "'If I risk nothing, then I become nothing,'" indicating that she realizes that the actualization of her humanity depends on her recognizing that she is only truly free when she acts for the sake of the good in the face of what appears to be the ultimate limit, death.[13]

At the end of *Freddy and Fredericka*, as the Queen of England lies dying, she explains to Freddy that she did not abdicate the throne earlier because, in order for him to be king, he must first know death.[14] His mother's death demonstrates to Freddy the necessary limitation on all human life. No one, not even a monarch, is immortal, and by means of this limitation all people are fundamentally equal in nature.[15] This same limit makes one's autonomy significant, for in the face of death one realizes that one will have only a finite number of opportunities, a reality that places great weight on the choices one makes. By the end of the novel, Freddy and Fredericka are both brought to recognize the nature of their freedom and their responsibility to choose properly. Fredericka, who is now pregnant, steps in when before she would not have to prevent a potential affair between Freddy and Lucia.[16] Correspondingly, discovering that they are going to have a child, Freddy is willing to risk his life and his opportunity to be king to save his child and the woman he loves, saying, "'My only purpose in the world, and the only shining thing, is to have done right.'"[17] However, what Freddy takes to be "the one glory left a king," Lucia demonstrates is a glory open to all.[18] Rather than allow Freddy to sacrifice himself, she saves him, sacrificing herself in the process. Lucia's sacrifice is even more significant than what Freddy intended. For while Freddy is willing to die for the sake of the people he loves, Lucia will die for the sake of people she barely knows and a country that is not even her own.[19] By means of Lucia's example, Freddy realizes that the strength of character and freedom he only recently achieved himself are potentially present in all others. Freddy is thus prepared when he gains absolute control over the substance of Dewey Knott's run for the Republican nomination for the presidency.

Having lived in and among the American people and having experienced their lives as his own, Freddy understands that Dacheekan, Knott's strategist and moneyman, is wrong to assume that all individuals want is their comfort. Instead, Freddy argues, everyone wants to "'to be free, to have dignity, to know honour and sacrifice.'"[20] Unlike Dacheeken who imagines because of his success that his desires differ in substance from those of the many, Freddy, alternatively, is aware that everyone wants to be recognized as a free individual, capable of actualizing freedom in the greatest of ways. Part of the nature of Freddy's nobility by birth is a rejection of the Hobbesian reductionism expressed by Dacheekan.[21] In journeying across America, he has come to democratize his understanding, perceiving that nobility of spirit and aspiration for transcendent goods are virtues to be claimed by all citizens.

Further, Helprin suggests that in granting human beings this kind of freedom, regimes encourage the nobility of their citizens. The characters of Freddy and Fredericka serve as an example of this. Although they have lived a life of privilege, Freddy and Fredericka's knowledge is of little use to them in America where they are essentially asked to begin their lives with nothing. Although they initially seek an easy way out, stealing a piece of modern art, they are shown their error and come to their first appreciation of the democratic spirit while regarding the Lincoln Memorial:

> In the middle of this crazed, materialistic, common country, where the lowest of the low is turned up by the strong currents of progress and rides upon the glittering surface of national life more buoyantly than an aristocrat; in the midst of all this that I thought so unimpressive—Gypsies, Cadillacs, houses with flat roofs—we have been outdone by the visage of a peasant, a soul speaking through marble, in a history not our own.[22]

Lincoln, who Freddy identifies as "'love that is ever awaiting,'" sacrificed himself for the sake of the freedom of others, thereby actualizing his own freedom to the fullest degree.

Freddy and Fredericka recognize what they must do and set to work, seeking to build lives that are choice worthy in and of themselves and worthy of free people. In this moment of transformation, Lincoln represents the epitome of the American regime, a place where countless individuals sacrifice themselves for the sake of the freedom of others. In the objective face of that sacrifice, Freddy and Fredericka realize that they have a responsibility to live their lives in a way that makes their freedom significant. Speaking of Lucia's death, Freddy tells Fredericka, "'You become a king not by making yourself great, but by recognizing the greatness of others.'"[23] By means of their time in the United States, Freddy and Fredericka realize that their freedom need not be limited to choices over which museum or disco to go to on any evening, but that their freedom necessitates choices as to what kind of life one wants to lead. Helprin suggests that given this kind of freedom, most, if not all individuals, would seek to live good and decent lives, and this nobility is not precluded if they also desire comfort or if they occasionally mistake the nature of the good that they seek.

Although Freddy and Fredericka return to Great Britain and ultimately ascend to the throne, the monarchy is now understood very differently. Rather than a position of power, Helprin suggests that it is instead an objective political institution that encourages citizens to recognize their freedom and act accordingly. Very early in the novel Freddy tells Fredericka that if he had his choice he would prefer not to be king. Instead, he would prefer to live the life of a normal man.[24] At that point in the book, however, Freddy's claims ring hollow. Having not yet experienced the "texture" of a regular life, Freddy has a romanticized vision of the kind of life that he might alternatively lead. As a result, granted anonymity and dealing with the texture that most people deal with, Freddy attempts to assert his royal prerogative and grows increasingly frustrated when his demands are not met.[25]

However, after their encounter with the Lincoln Memorial, and their realization that their freedom and integrity depends on their "work," the royals begin the long process of habituating themselves to the life of free people whose merit is dependent on what they make of themselves and not on any institutional or natural hierarchy. Having experienced the lives of regular Americans, Freddy and Fredericka both realize that returning to England will entail a sacrifice, for in going back they seemingly lose the freedom that they have only recently learned to enjoy.[26] It is exactly in this kind of sacrifice that Helprin suggests one's freedom is most fully made manifest. Freddy and Fredericka, like Catherine and Harry in *Sunlight*, are given a choice either to find a quiet corner in which to live relatively peaceful lives, or to freely sacrifice the peace that they have found for the sake of what they understand to be a higher end, without even a guarantee of ever achieving that end. By means of their time in America, Freddy and Fredericka are shown what it means to be truly royal, and their lives become objective symbols of what is possible for all people, regardless of the circumstances in which they are born.

DANTE AND POLITICAL FREEDOM

Helprin's political philosophy sheds light on Dante's, revealing the degree to which Dante himself understood the necessity of a political freedom that recognizes the particularity of citizens. This argument is in some contrast to those who argue that Dante continued to see a world empire as the basis of justice. Instead, it seems that the argument of *De Monarchia* is superseded by the argument revealed in the *Divine Comedy*.

The theological argument of the *Divine Comedy* indicates the partial nature of all human virtue. No individual by her own means is able to lay claim to the whole. Nonetheless, despite this particularity, all may will the good and receive divine grace. The character of Dante is a particularly telling example of this. He wakes in a dark forest having lost his way and without the means to move forward. Dante, it seems, is on the very edge of losing himself entirely. However, while in this state of almost complete corruption, he is still loved. Even further, although it is Beatrice and even God that is the beginning and end of his movement, Dante's particularity is recognized. For, instead of Beatrice, whose virtue so surpasses Dante's that he would not be able to recognize it for what it is, he is given Virgil. Virgil is able to direct Dante to a higher good because Dante is able to recognize in the ancient poet the good that he loves. Even though Virgil resides in Limbo, indicating the degree to which he mistakes the nature of the divine, he is nonetheless good for Dante. Beatrice's choice of Virgil indicates both her willingness and God's willingness to incorporate the particularity of all souls, whatever their state.

Further, by means of Virgil, Dante is led to Purgatory, where he is eventually reunited with Beatrice, who then is able to lead him to the sight of the good in and of itself. By these means Dante indicates that incorporating the individuality of human beings has the effect of leading them to a broader understanding of the good. This image is furthered in the description of the souls Dante meets in *Paradiso*. As discussed previously, the souls of Paradiso are individuals who retain their specific identities but all the while will the universal. Thus, Dante's long interaction with his great-great-grandfather Cacciaguida is filled with particular interest in Dante's own family and real, historic events affecting Florence.[27]

The central part of *Purgatorio* and, hence, the central moment of the *Divine Comedy*, is a discussion of freedom of will and its relationship to love. By nature, all humans desire the good, and, Dante argues, they are radically free to choose the good, impeded by neither internal nor external circumstances. So, Marco instructs Dante:

> Ye who are living every cause refer
> Still upward to the heavens, as if all things
> They of necessity moved with themselves.
>
> If this were so, in you would be destroyed
> Free will, nor any justice would there be
> In having joy for good, or grief for evil.
>
> The heavens your movements do initiate,
> I say not all; but granting that I say it,
> Light has been given you for good and evil,
>
> And free volition; which, if some fatigue
> In the first battles with the heavens it suffers,
> Afterwards conquers all, if well 'tis nurtured.[28]

The movement up Mount Purgatory represents an ordering of one's loves, so that all of the secondary goods that are loved are loved in relationship to one's primary love of the divine. The final challenge of Purgatory for Dante is one of temptation. He must walk through a wall of fire to enter the Garden of Eden and, when he is there, he is confronted with Matilda. With his love properly strengthened, Dante must actualize his freedom—choosing between the natural perfection offered in the garden or the supernatural perfection he has been seeking. Although Dante clearly has some attraction to Matilda, once Beatrice arrives Matilda is hardly given a second thought. Dante has made his choice—risking everything the finite world might offer him in order to be "transhumanized" and ascend into the supernatural sphere. Like Helprin, Dante suggests that a political regime that incorporates the particularity of its citizens will lead them to love the good such that they will be willing to give up all of these particular ends for the sake of a common good.

HELPRIN'S MOVEMENT BEYOND DANTE

While Dante might envision such a regime existing in the Empyrean, one would be hard pressed to demonstrate that he thought it could ever exist on earth. The radical equality that is asserted in the founding documents of the American regime would be quite anachronistic in thirteenth century Florence. While so much of the argument of the *Divine Comedy* is reflected in general, and in some cases specifically, in the novels of Mark Helprin, we are not prepared to argue that their political formulations match up.

Instead, we have argued that Helprin, while firmly rooted in an intellectual and spiritual tradition that considerably pre-dates modernity, combines this Platonic-Augustinian, Judeo-Christian tradition with a democratic and liberal spirit that is, in its essence, peculiarly modern. As we have asserted, Helprin's celebrated conservatism is, in reality, a nuanced and complex thing.

If we take Hegel's account of modernity to be accurate, its characteristic feature is the reconciliation of subjectivity and objectivity. In some sense, the polarized political discourse and the "culture wars" that have emerged as features of American public life in recent decades, are illustrations of the consequences of turning away from this reconciliation towards a superficial and inadequate return to one side or the other of that spirit that formed the American regime. Those who assert abstract authority, either of religion or secular law, act as if the "ideal city" of Plato's *Republic* (which can only exist if *eros* is eliminated or utterly subsumed as a factor in human behavior), could actually be realized in the world. On the other hand, those who subscribe to a radical subjectivity that is abstracted from any relation to an absolute good or objective truth imagine that a just society can simply arrive through universal good intention, the very existence of which they know to be lacking in their contempt for the opinions of their political foes.

In Mark Helprin's novels, we find a consistent insistence on both sides of the commonly presumed dichotomy. As we have seen, his protagonists are moved by a recognition of universal principles. Through the course of their quests they come to align their own desires with those transcendent ideals. As such, they might appear as impossible figures, drawn from romantic fantasies of an imagined golden age. It is clearly Helprin's intention, however, that what his characters learn is somehow also of use to us all.

Even *Winter's Tale*, the most fantastic of his novels, involving characters, places, and situations that are far from our ordinary experiences, aims, as we have argued, to demonstrate certain universal truths about human life. The romantic relationships and the portrayal of both loss and redemption are grounded in real human truths. Similarly, *Soldier*, as a historical novel set primarily in the First World War, is both remote and immediate. It is again the love affairs and the encounters with suffering and death that connect his characters with our own lived experiences. *Sunlight* moves closer to our own reality, not only historically, but because the events of the plot are part of social realities that are very much still part of our own time. That some critics derided the novel as some sepia-tinged romanticism, indicates an unwillingness on their part to move beyond the deliberately theatrical drama to recognize the reality at the heart of the story.

With *Freddy and Fredericka*, Helprin sets a novel in contemporary America. While on one level a political and social satire, again easily dismissed as a curmudgeonly conservatism poking a finger at the usual suspects, the book is actually a celebration of the loose and messy society that is the necessary child of freedom. In saying this, we, like Helprin, do not reduce freedom to self-indulgent license, although that certainly exists in plenty in contemporary America. Rather, what Freddy and Fredericka learn, both in their personal lives and in their political education, is that justice requires love and love requires freedom. That much is already present in the *Divine Comedy*, as we have seen. Further, like Dante, Helprin denies that love is incommensurate with the truth, even if the truth is not always knowable in its fullness by us.

What is different in Helprin's account, and what he shares, for example, with Hegel, is the idea that the unity of objectivity and subjectivity, each established in their completeness, is possible in a political regime. That this union is imperfect in its practical execution is not the point. Alone among all of the societies that have existed in history, is the objective recognition in the modern regime (in America, but also wherever else the principles of liberal democracy have been established) of human freedom as the foundation of political society. That the Constitution and Bill of Rights, for example, recognize more than abstract freedom only further underlines the point. Individuals in their private lives and in the pursuit of their subjective ends are not opposed to the good of the regime, but are central to its very purpose. Helprin's novels further suggest that such regimes require, for their maintenance, citizens that are also prepared to sacrifice their subjective interests either for the good of particular people or for the good of the whole.

Again, Helprin is no more a utopian than was Hegel. There is no "end of history" where caprice, accident, or human selfishness will not unsettle justice in the city. War, violence, and loss are part of the human condition, even in democratic societies. However, human actions, often rooted in ends that are no less noble for being quite particular, can and do contribute to the creation of a more just city or nation.

Both *A Soldier of the Great War*, with which we began, and *Freddy and Fredericka*, with which we conclude, consist of long recollections. They are also stories told by the protagonist to an initially simple and ignorant auditor. Nicolò in *Soldier* and the boy, Craig-Vyvian, in *Freddy and Fredericka*, are initially illiterate and more or less uninterested in either the hero of the story or greatness itself. Both are discovered in a state of nature almost, content with the simplest of pleasures and ignorant of the wider geographical world, let alone the world of ideas. Craig-Vyvian is explicitly brought to literacy and is finally, the narrator of the story. However, Nicolò, whose education is much briefer, lasting only the course of the hike up the mountain on the way to Monte Prato, is similarly enlightened. Alessandro describes both he and Nicolò as having experienced an "awakening" in the course of their journey.[29] The self-absorption with which Nicolò began has been replaced with a desire to do something for all of those people who have been part of Alessandro's story and are now gone. Alessandro tells him that recollecting them can be his gift to them. Like Alessandro, Peter Lake, Harry Copeland, and Freddy, and numerous others in the novels of Mark Helprin, and like Dante in the *Divine Comedy*, redemption come via "*l'amor che move it sole e l'altre stelle.*"[30]

NOTES

1. Ibid., 499. In addition, see MacDonald, "Democratic Royalty."
2. Mark Helprin, *Freddy and Fredericka*, 43–44.
3. Ibid., 109.
4. Ibid., 173.
5. Ibid., 43 and 298–99.
6. Ibid., 109.
7. Ibid., 393.
8. Ibid., 444.
9. Mark Helprin, *In Sunlight and in Shadow*, 8.
10. Ibid., 31.
11. Ibid., 122.
12. Helprin, *Freddy and Fredericka*, 37.
13. Helprin, *In Sunlight and in Shadow*, 519.
14. Helprin, *Freddy and Fredericka*, 533.
15. Ibid., 138 and 164.
16. Ibid., 411.
17. Ibid., 426.
18. Ibid.
19. Ibid., 426.
20. Ibid., 467.
21. See Thomas Hobbes, *Leviathan*, ed. C.B. McPherson (Pelican Classics: 1968), Chapter 15, 215.
22. Helprin, *Freddy and Fredericka*, 255.
23. Ibid., 461.
24. Ibid., 42.
25. For example, see *Freddy and Fredericka*, 194–95.
26. For example, see *Freddy and Fredericka*, 325–29.
27. Dante, *Paradiso*, XV–XVII.
28. Dante, *Purgatorio*, XVI, 67–78.
29. Mark Helprin, *A Soldier of the Great War*, 851.
30. Dante, *Paradiso*, XXXIII, 145.

Bibliography

Affleck, John. "Birds of a Feather: The Ancient Mariner Archetype in Mark Helprin's 'A Dove of the East,' and *A Soldier of the Great War*." http://helprin-library.weebly.com/academic-commentary.html.

Alexander, Paul. "Big Books, Tall Tales." *New York Times*, April 28, 1991.

Amidon, Stephen. "Beauty and the Beasts of War." Review of *A Soldier of the Great War*, by Mark Helprin. *Finacial Times*. April 18, 1992.

Augustine. *Confessions.* Oxford: Oxford World Classics, 2009.

Binyon, T.J. "Walking Back to Happiness." Review of *A Soldier of the Great War*, by Mark Helprin. *London Times*. May 3, 1992.

Bowra, C. M. "Dante and Sordello." *Comparative Literature* (Winter 1953) 5:1, 1–15.

Cantor, Paul. "The Uncanonical Dante: The Divine Comedy and Islamic Philosophy." *Philosophy and Literature* (1996) 20:1, 138–53.

Carter, Barbara Barclay. "Dante's Political Ideas." *Review of Politics*. 5:3 (July 1943), 339–55.

Caso, Adolph, ed. *Dante Studies, Volume I: Dante in the Twentieth Century*. Boston: Dante University of America Press, 1982.

Chadler, S. Bernard and J.A. Molinaro, editors. *The World of Dante: Six Studies in Language and Thought*. Toronto: University of Toronto Press, 1966.

Crouse, Robert D. "Dante as Philosopher: Christian Aristotelianism." *Dionysius* (1998), XIV, 154.

———. "*Paucis Mutatis Verbis*: St. Augustine's Platonism" in *Augustine and His Critics*, edited by Robert Dodaro and George Lawless. London: Routledge, 2000, 37–50.

———. "*Recurrens in te unum*: The Pattern of St. Augustine's *Confessions*." *Studia Patristica*. Edited by E. A. Livingstone. Vol. XIV (Berlin, 1976), 389–92.

Dante, "Epistola X." In *The Latin Works of Dante*. London: Temple Classics,1904.

———. *Inferno*. Translated by Robert Hollander and Jean Hollander. New York: Anchor Books, 2000.

———. *La Vita Nuova*. Translated by A.S. Kline. 2001. Last accessed 6 April 2014. http://www.poetryintranslation.com/PITBR/Italian/TheNewLifeI.htm#_Toc88709640.

———. *Paradiso*. Translated by Robert Hollander and Jean Hollander. New York: Anchor Books, 2007.

———. *Purgatorio*. Translated by Jean Hollander and Robert Hollander. New York: Anchor Books, 2003.

Eder, Richard. "Radiance is in the Details." A review of *A Soldier of the Great War*, by Mark Helprin. *Los Angeles Times*. May 5, 1995.

Ferguson, Neil. "A Soldier of the Great War." A review of *A Soldier of the Great War*, by Mark Helprin. February 2, 2014. Last accessed 6 April 2014. http://bookinwithsunny.com/soldier-great-war/.

Ferrari, L.C. "Young Augustine: Both Catholic and Manichee." *Augustinian Studies* 26 (1995), 108–128.

Foster, O.P., Kenelm. "The Mind in Love: Dante's Philosophy." In *Dante*, John Freccero, editor. Englewood Cliffs, NJ: Prentice-Hall, Inc., 1965, 43–60.

———. *The Two Dantes*. London: Darton, Longman and Todd Ltd., 1977.

Franke, William. "Dante's Deconstruction and Reconstruction of Prophetic Voice and Vision in the Malboge (*Inferno* XVIII–XXII)," *Philosophy and Literature* (2012), 36.

———. "Dante's Inferno as Poetic Revelation of Prophetic Truth." *Philosophy and Literature* (October 2009) 33:2, 252–66.

Friedman, Murray. The *Neoconservative Revolution: Jewish Intellectuals and the Shaping of Public Policy*. Cambridge: Cambridge University Press, 2005.

Granovetter, Shirley. "Works of Empathy, Hope, Pretension and Sentimentality." Review of *A Soldier of the Great War*, by Mark Helprin. *Jerusalem Post*. December 10, 1992

Gualtieri, Angelo. "Lady Philosophy in Boethius and Dante." *Comparative Literature* (Spring 1971) 23: 2, 141–50.

Haller, Robert S., translator. *Literary Criticism of Dante Alighieri*. Lincoln: University of Nebraska Press, 1973.

Hankey, Wayne. "Conversion: Ontological & Secular from Plato to *Tom Jones*." A Guest Lecture sponsored by CREOR, McGill Centre for Research on Religion / Centre de research sur la religion in partnership with 'Early Modern Conversions' Tuesday, February 18, 2014, to be published in *Numero Cinq*.

Harrison, Robert Pogue. "Comedy and Modernity: Dante's Hell." *MLN* (December 1987), 102:5, 1043–61.

Hatzfeld, Helmut. "The Art of Dante's Purgatorio." *Studies in Philology* 49:1 (January 1952), 25–47.

Havely, Nick. *Dante*. London: Blackwell Publishing, 2007.

Hawkins, Peter S. "All Smiles: Poetry and Theology in Dante." *PMLA* (March 2006) 121:2, 371–87.

———. "Divide and Conquer: Augustine in the Divine Comedy." *PMLA* (May 1991), 106:3, 471–83.

Hawley, John C. "A Roadside View of Life." Review of *A Soldier of the Great War*, by Mark Helprin. *San Francisco Chronicle*. May 5, 1991.

Hedley, Douglas. "Neoplatonic Metaphysics and Imagination in Dante's *Commedia*," in *Dante's* Commedia: *Theology as Poetry*, Vittorio Montemaggi and Matthew Treherne, editors (Notre Dame: University of Notre Dame Press, 2010), 245–266.

Helprin, Mark. *A Soldier of the Great War*. NewYork: Harcourt, Inc., 1991.

———. "The author, like Israel, takes risks—and lives in opposition to nebbishy Jewish New Yorkers." Interview with Alexander Aciman. Last Accessed 6 April 2014. http://www.tabletmag.com/jewish-arts-and-culture/books/113658/mark-helprin-tale.

———. "Bumping into Characters." *New York Times*, October 3, 2012.

———. "The Canon Under Siege." *New Criterion* (September 1988), 33–40.

———. "Contrivance." *Forbes*, April 10, 1999.

———. "For the Study of Statesmanship and Political Philosophy. *Claremont Review of Books* (Fall 2005).

———. *Freddy and Fredericka*. New York: Penguin Books, 2006.

———. *In Sunlight and In Shadow*. New York: Mariner Books, 2012.

———. Interview by Grover Gardner. Last accessed April 2, 2014. http://www.downpour.com/authors/spotlight/mark-helprin-interview.

———. Interview by James Linville. "Mark Helprin, The Art of Fiction No. 132." In *Paris Review*. 126 (Spring 1993). Last accessed 6 April 2014. http://www.theparisreview.org/interviews/1962/the-art-of-fiction-no-132-mark-helprin.

———. Interview by Jeff Guinn. "Author Q&A." Last accessed 6 April 2014. www.philly.com/mld/inquirer/entertainment/books/12439767.htm.

————. Interview by WNYC. Last accessed 6 April 2014. http://www.voicebase.com/voice_file/public_detail/160089/refine/protagonist.

————. "The Lessons of the Century." *American Heritage* (February/March 1999), 50:1,

————. *Refiner's Fire*. New York: Alfred A. Knopf, 1977.

————. *Winter's Tale*. New York: Harcourt, Inc., 1983.

Hochschild, Paige E. *Memory in Augustine's Theological Anthropology*. Oxford: Oxford University Press, 2012.

Hollander, Robert. "Dante's *Paradiso* as Philosophical Poetry." *Italica* 86:4 (Winter 2009), 571–82.

————. "Dante 'Theologus-Poeta.'" *Dante Studies* 118 (2000), 261–302.

————. "Dante's Virgil: A Light that Failed." *Lectura Dantis* (1989) 4, 3–9.

————. "Tragedy in Dante's Comedy."*Sewanee Review* 91:2 (Spring 1983), 240–60.

————. "'Vita Nuova': Dante's Perceptions of Beatrice." *Dante Studies* 92 (1974), 1–18.

Keneally, Thomas."War and Memory." A review of *A Soldier of the Great War*, by Mark Helprin. *New York Times*. May 5, 1991.

Klepp, L.S. "A Soldier of the Great War (1991)." Last accessed 24 March 2014. http://www.ew.com/ew/article/0,,314436,00.html.

Lafferty, Roger Theodore. "The Philosophy of Dante." *Annual Reports of the Dante Society* (1911) 30, 1–34.

Lampert, Craig. "Literary Warrior: Mark Helprin's Fictional Marvels and Political Heterodoxies." *Harvard*, May/June, 2005.

Looney, Dennis. *Freedom Readers*. Notre Dame: University of Notre Dame Press, 2011.

MacDonald, Sara. "Democratic Royalty: Mark Helprin's Freddy and Fredericka." *American Political Thought* 1:2 (Fall 2012).

MacDonald, Sara and Barry Craig. *Recovering Hegel from the Critique of Leo Strauss: The Virtues of Modernity*. Lanham, MD: Lexington Books, 2013.

Marchesi, Simone. *Dante and Augustine: Linguistics, Poetics, Hermeneutics*. Toronto: University of Toronto Press, 2011.

Mazzeo, Joseph Anthony. "Dante's Conception of Love." *Journal of the History of Ideas* (April 1957) 18:2, 147–60.

————. "Dante, The Power of Love. Dante and the Phaedrus Tradition of Poetic Inspiration." *Proceedings of the American Philosophical Society* (June 1955) 99:3, 133–145.

————. "Plato's Eros and Dante's Amore." *Traditio* (1956) 12, 316.

McMahon, Robert. *Understanding the Medieval Meditative Ascent*. Washington, D.C.: Catholic University of America Press, 2006.

Miller, Henry Knight. *Henry Fielding's* Tom Jones *and the Romance Tradition*. Victoria: English Literary Studies, 1976.

Mowbray, Allan. "Two Dantes: Christian versus Humanist." *MLN* (January 1992) 107:1, 18–35.

Omer-Sherman, Ramen. "Mark Helprin's Politics Don't Get Way of Prose," *Jewish Daily*, October 23, 2012.

O'Rourke Boyle, Marjorie. "Closure in Paradise: Dante Outsings Aquinas." *MLN* 115:1 (January 2000).

Patch, H.R. "The Last Line of the Commedia." *Speculum* (January 1939) 41:1, 56–65.

Petrie, Jennifer. "Dante's Virgil: Purgatorio XXX," in *Dante Soundings.* Edited by David Nolan. (Totowa, NJ: Rowman and Littlefield, 1981), 130–45.

Plato. *Republic*, translated by G. M. Grube. Indianapolis: Hackett Publishing Inc., 1992.

Quinn, Anthony. "Book Review: Memoirs of a Hero Stuck in the Mud." Review of *A Soldier of the Great War*, by Mark Helprin. *Independent*. May 2, 1992

Reynolds, Barbara. *Dante: The Poet, The Political Thinker, The Man*. Emeryville, CA: Shoemaker and Hoard, 2006.

Ryan, Christopher. "Free Will in Theory and Practice: Purgatorio XVIII and two characters in the Inferno." In *Dante Soundings: Eight Literary and Historical Essays*, edited by David Nolan. Totowa, NJ: Rowman and Littlefield, 1981, 100–112.

Sayers, Dorothy L. "Introduction." In *The Divine Comedy: Hell*, by Dante. London: Penguin, 1949.

Schillinger, Liesl. "Halcyon Years." Review of *In Sunlight and in Shadow*, by Mark Helprin. *New York Times*. October 5, 2012.

Scott, John A. *Dante's Political Purgatory*. Philadelphia: University of Pennsylvania Press, 1996.

Shatzky, Joel and Michael Taub. *Contemporary Jewish-American Novelists: A Bio-Critical Sourcebook*. Westport, CT: Greenwood Press: 1996.

Singleton, Charles S. *Journey to Beatrice*. Baltimore: Johns Hopkins University Press, 1977.

Thompson, David. "Dante's Virtuous Romans." *Dante Studies* 96 (1978), 145–62.

Vachon, John. "Book Notes." Review of *A Soldier of the Great War* by Mark Helprin. *Daily Yomiuri*. September 8, 1991.

Wade, Alan. "A Soldier of the Great War: Book Reviews." Review of *A Soldier of the Great War*, by Mark Helprin. *New Leader*. August 12, 1991.

Williams, Charles. *The Figure of Beatrice: A Study in Dante*. London: Faber and Faber Limited, 1943.

Index

About the Authors

Sara MacDonald is a professor and the director of the Great Books Program at St. Thomas University, a liberal arts college in Fredericton NB, Canada. She obtained her B.A. from St. Thomas University and her M.A. and Ph.D. from Fordham University. She is the author of *Finding Freedom: Hegel's Philosophy and the Emancipation of Women* (2008); and, with Barry Craig, *Recovering Hegel from the Critique of Leo Strauss: The Virtues of Modernity* (2013).

Barry Craig is a professor and vice-president (Academic) at St. Thomas University, a liberal arts college in Fredericton NB, Canada. He obtained his B.A. from the University of King's College, his M.A. from Dalhousie University, and his Ph.D. from the University of Wales. He is the author of *Apostle to the Wilderness: Bishop John Medley and the Evolution of the Anglican Church*; and, with Sara MacDonald, *Recovering Hegel from the Critique of Leo Strauss: The Virtues of Modernity* (2013).